Robert E. Lee's Reluctant Warrior

The Life of Cavalry Commander and Railroad Businessman

Brig. Gen. Williams Carter Wickham

Also by Sheridan R. Barringer:

Unhonored Service: The Life of Lee's Senior Cavalry Commander, Colonel Thomas Taylor Munford, CSA

Custer's Gray Rival: The Life of Confederate Major General Thomas Lafayette Rosser

Fighting for General Lee: Confederate General Rufus Barringer and the North Carolina Cavalry Brigade

Robert E. Lee's Reluctant Warrior

The Life of Cavalry Commander and Railroad Businessman

Brig. Gen. Williams Carter Wickham

Sheridan R. Barringer

FOX RUN
PUBLISHING
QUALITY PUBLISHING ONE BOOK AT A TIME

Publisher's Cataloging-in-Publication Data
provided by Five Rainbows Cataloging Services

Names: Barringer, Sheridan Reid, 1943- author.
Title: Robert E. Lee's reluctant warrior : the life of cavalry commander and railroad businessman Brigadier General Williams Carter Wickham / Sheridan R. Barringer.
Description: Winston-Salem, NC : Fox Run Publishing, 2024. | Includes bibliographical references and index.
Identifiers: LCCN 2024942273 (print) | ISBN 978-1-945602-25-2 (hardcover) | ISBN 978-1-945602-26-9 (paperback)
Subjects: LCSH: United States--History--Civil War, 1861-1865. | Confederate States of America. Army. Virginia Cavalry Regiment, 4th. | Virginia--History--Civil War, 1861-1865. | Confederate States of America. Congress--Biography. | Chesapeake and Ohio Railroad Company--History. | BISAC: HISTORY / United States / State & Local / South (AL, AR, FL, GA, KY, LA, MS, NC, SC, TN, VA, WV) | HISTORY / United States / Civil War Period (1850-1877) | BIOGRAPHY & AUTOBIOGRAPHY / Military. | TRANSPORTATION / Railroads / History.
Classification: LCC E581.6 4Th .B37 2024 (print) | DDC 973.7/455--dc23.

Cover design by Sandra Miller

Cover images:

Williams Carter Wickham, Courtesy: U.S. Army Heritage and Education Center, Carlisle, PA

Hickory Hill plantation house, Courtesy: Shannon Pritchard.

Library of Congress Control Number (LCCN): 2024942273

Published by
Fox Run Publishing LLC
4711 Forest Drive, Suite 3, Box 302
Columbia, SC 29206
http://www.foxrunpub.com/

Dedication

The Cavalry Horse

My old friend Clark B. "Bud" Hall, one of the founders of the Civil War preservation movement, was one of the speakers at the dedication of the faithful cavalry horse in Middleburg, Virginia. Bud has a home in Middleburg, and he is one of the leading authorities on Civil War cavalry operations, so it was entirely appropriate for him to speak at the dedication of the monument ten years ago.

IN MEMORY OF
THE ONE AND ONE HALF MILLION HORSES AND MULES
OF THE CONFEDERATE AND UNION ARMIES WHO WERE KILLED
WERE WOUNDED, OR DIED FROM DISEASE IN THE CIVIL WAR
MANY PERISHED WITHIN TWENTY MILES OF MIDDLEBURG
IN THE BATTLES OF ALDIE, MIDDLEBURG AND UPPERVILLE
IN JUNE OF 1863

Here it is, an appropriate tribute to the cavalry horses who sacrificed so much during the Civil War.

Bud Hall on the Cavalry Horse:

The Horses

"Here lies the steed with his nostrils all wide,
But through it there rolls not the breath of its pride.
The foam of his gasping lies white on the turf,
And as cold as the spray of the rock-beaten surf."

Ah! The horses—the blacks and bays, the roans and grays, the sorrels and chestnuts that pulled Lee's army from the Rappahannock to Gettysburg and back, and all the other horses that pulled and tugged at the wagons, at the batteries of artillery; the horses that carried the men, the unstabled horses and the half-fed horses.

Let my right hand forget its cunning if I forget to pay proper tribute to those noble animals that suffered so much for their masters. How often my mind goes back to that horse my mind's eye saw coming across the field from the front at Bull Run with his sides all dripping with blood. He was a hero and coming back home to die.

The cavalryman and his horse got very close to each other, not only physically, but also heart to heart. They ate together, slept together, marched, fought and often died together. While the rider slept, the horse cropped the grass around him and got as close up to his rider's body as he could get. The loyal steed pushed the trooper's head gently aside with his nose to get at the grass beneath it. By the thousands, men reposed in fields fast asleep from arduous campaigns with their horses quietly grazing beside them, and nary a cavalier was trod upon or injured by his steed.

They were so faithful and unfaltering. When the bugle sounded, they were always ready to respond, for they knew all the bugle calls. If it were saddle up, or the feed, or the water call, they were as ready to answer one as the other. And they were so noble and so brave in battle. They seemed to love the sound of the guns. The cavalryman might lie low on the neck of his horse as the missiles of death hissed about him. But the horse never flinched, except when struck.

Lo! As we should, we build monuments for our dead soldiers, for those we know, and for the unknown dead. So, with the ultimate sacrifice of our lamented fallen honored upon their noble deaths, is it not also just that we recall their valiant steeds? What would you think of a monument someday, somewhere in Virginia, in honor of Lee's noble horses?

What could General Lee have done had all his horses balked in unison? Nothing! Then all honor to Lee's horses, which pulled and hauled and fought and died that this might be a very great nation.

> "The good black horse came riderless home,
> Flecked with blood drops as well as foam;
> See yonder hillock where dead leaves fall;
> The good black horse dropped dead—
> That is all.
> 'All? O, God! It is all I can speak.
> Question me not; I am old and weak;
> His saber and his saddle hang on the wall,
> And his horse is dead—
> I have told you all."

With eternal thanks (and apologies) to Trooper George Baylor, his poignant lines have been somewhat revised.

CLARK B. HALL
MIDDLEBURG, VIRGINIA

Table of Contents

List of Images

List of Maps

Preface

I have authored three biographies of southern cavalry commanders in Robert E. Lee's Army of Northern Virginia: Brigadier General Rufus Barringer; Major General Thomas Lafayette Rosser; and Colonel Thomas Taylor Munford. I do not intend to write biographies of all the Cavalry commanders in Lee's army, but I did discover another that I believe deserves a biography: Brigadier General Williams Carter Wickham of Virginia. Wickham descended from a prominate Virginia family, was a natural leader of men, served in the Virginia Legislature and Secession Convention. He was a brave fighter, but he also believed secession was an illegal act and was against it. He rose in rank from captain to brigadier general. He then tried to resign, in order to join the peace movement to try to stop the bloodshed at any honorable price.

After the war ended, Wickham joined the Republican Party, urging compliance with Reconstruction. He became an organizer of railroad improvements and expansion, becoming leader of the Chesapeake and Ohio Railroad. He served again in Virginia's State Senate as a Republican.

Wickham left a rich legacy of documentation for historians to ponder and study. He is deserving of a full biography, and I hope my efforts provide readers of this volume a valuable look into the makeup of this man.

Sheridan R. Barringer
Newport News, VA

Acknowledgements

I wish to express my sincere thanks to the following individuals and institutions for their contributions in the creation of this book:

To Eric J. Wittenberg for his suggestions and for writing the Introduction to this book. To Clark B. Hall and Bryce Suderow for their contributions. Special thanks to Reggie Harris for providing a copy of the rare Hewlett Family Reunion document, which included lots of information of the slaves of Hickory Hill. Thanks to Shannon Pritchard for furnishing nice photos of Hickory Hill and the Wickhams. Thanks to all others who answered my questions or reviewed parts of chapters. Thanks to Fran Walsh Ward, Phd, for her editing of the manuscript prior to my submission to the publisher. To cartographer Hal Jespersen for the fine maps.

Thanks to the staffs at the following institutions: Albert and Shirley Small Special Collections Library at the University of Virginia; Virginia Museum of History and Culture; Valentine Museum; Library of Virginia; Southern Historical Collection at the University of North Carolina; National Archives; Library of Congress; United States Army History Center at Carlisle, Pennsylvania; National Park Service; and Virginia Tech Special Collections.

Thanks to my publisher, Fox Run Publishing, and Keith Jones in particular for his valuable comments and for managing the process of getting this book released.

Sheridan R. Barringer

Abbreviations

NCDAH – State Archives, North Carolina Division of Archives and History, Raleigh, North Carolina.

SHC – Southern Historical Collection, Wilson Library, University of North Carolina at Chapel Hill.

DU – Rare Book, Manuscript, and Special Collections, Rubenstein Library, Duke University, Durham, North Carolina.

SHSP – Southern Historical Society Papers, 52 vols., Jones, J. William, et al, editors, Richmond, Virginia, Southern Historical Society, 1876-1959.

LC – Library of Congress, Washington, D.C.
NARA – National Archives and Records Administration, Washington, D.C.

OR – The War of Rebellion: A Compilation of the Official Records of the Union and Confederate Armies, 70 vols., 128 parts, Washington, D.C., 1880-1901. All reference are to Series I, unless otherwise indicated.

VMHC – Virginia Museum of History and Culture, Richmond, Virginia.

LVA – Library of Virginia, Richmond, Virginia

UVA – Albert and Shirley Small Special Collections Library, University of Virginia, Charlottesville, Virginia.

CHAPTER 1

Family Heritage:
Grandfather John Wickham, Jr. (1763-1839)
Virginia Loyalist and Prominent Attorney
defended Aaron Burr in 1807—Trial for Treason

Williams Carter Wickham descended from a prominent "First Families of Virginia" family. He was born on September 21, 1820, in a small house on Broad Street north of the Monumental Church in Richmond, Virginia. His grandfather John Wickham, Jr. originally owned the 1812 Federal mansion on East Clay Street that became a central historic feature of Mann S. Valentine II's property, which in turn became part of the Valentine History Center. In 1812 John and Elizabeth Wickham, one of Richmond's wealthiest couples, built the elegant "Wickham House," with its magnificent freestanding stairway, rare neoclassical wall paintings, and carved ornamentation, all of which typified late Federal architecture.[1]

The ancestral home, a plantation called "Hickory Hill," was located twenty miles north of Richmond and five miles east of the town of Ashland in Hanover County. John Wickham, Jr. (1763-1839) was Williams's grandfather; William Fanning Wickham (1793-1880), his father. Grandfather John Wickham, Jr., an eminent attorney, married twice, has two lines of descent. His first wife, Mary Smith Fanning (1775-1799) bore his two sons-William Fanning Wickham (1820-1888) of "Hickory Hill," who married Anne Butler Carter (1797-1868)-and Edmund Fanning Wickham of "Rocky Mount" (1796-1843), who married Anne's sister, Lucy Carter (1799-1835).[2]

Williams Wickham's great-grandfather, General Thomas Nelson, Jr., was one of the signatories of the Declaration of Independence and a governor of Virginia during the American Revolutionary War. Other ancestors include Thomas "Scotch Tom" Nelson, one of the founders of Yorktown in the 17th century. He also descended from Robert "King" Carter (1663-1732), who served as an acting royal governor of Virginia and was one of the wealthiest landowners in the late 17th and early 18th centuries. Williams's mother, Anne Butler Carter Wickham,

1. *Richmond Dispatch*, July 24, 1888.
2. NARA; Ancestry.Com

was a first cousin of Robert E. Lee, whose mother Anne Hill Carter, was born at the expansive Shirley Plantation.

Williams C. Wickham grew up on the Hickory Hill plantation, a large estate compared to most in Virginia, and an appendage of the Shirley Plantation owned by Robert E Lee's mother, Anne Hill Carter Lee. His ancestors include one of Virginia's wealthiest landowners of the 1700s, Robert "King" Carter, named for his "autocratic business methods."

John Wickham, Jr. was a prominent Virginia attorney and an American Loyalist-one of few Loyalists to achieve national prominence after the American Revolution. He is best remembered for his role in the 1807 treason trial of former Vice-President Aaron Burr, whom President Thomas Jefferson had ordered arrested and indicted for treason. Suspected of trying to create an independent country in the center of North America and/or in present-day southwestern United States and parts of Mexico, Burr's version of events was that he intended to take possession of (and farm) 40,000 acres in the Texas Territory leased to him by the Spanish Crown. The evidence against Burr was weak, and Judge John Marshall found him innocent (not guilty). The trial, however, destroyed Burr's faltering political career.

John Wickham, Jr., eldest son of John Wickham Sr. and his wife Hannah Fanning, was born in the colony of New York in the village of Cutchogue. His father was a minister in the Anglican Church and a Loyalist, while his uncle Parker Wickham, also a Loyalist, was active in the local government.

After the American Revolution, Parker Wickham was banished from New York State under an act of attainder (the forfeiture of land and civil rights suffered as a consequence of a sentence of death for treason or felony). Despite vigorously declaring his innocence, Parker Wickham was never granted a trial and was sentenced to death if he returned to New York. The unfairness of this bitter event gave John Wickham, Jr. a life-long appreciation of the sanctity of a person's legal rights— regardless of political affiliation.

Although a first cousin of Revolutionary War hero Nathaniel Fanning, John Wickham, Jr. was heavily influenced by his uncle Edmund Fanning, a colonel (later a general) in the British Army. Fanning raised a unit called the "King's American Regiment," in which Wickham served as an ensign. While traveling through Virginia, Wickham was captured and tried as a spy, but was acquitted.

After the Revolutionary War, John Wickham, Jr. earned a degree in law from the College of William and Mary, studied under George Wythe and became a close friend of John Marshall-the fourth Chief

John Wickham, Jr. Wickham and John Marshall were thought to be Virginia's finest lawyers in those days.

(Shannon Pritchard)

Justice of the United States Supreme Court. Wickham moved to Richmond and experienced financial success helping British merchants collect debts from American businessmen. He married his first cousin, Mary Smith Fanning, and fathered two children. After his wife's early death at age twenty-four in 1799, he married Elizabeth Seldon McClurg, and they had seventeen children. McClurg was the daughter of Richmond Mayor and United States Congressman Dr. James McClurg, a member of the convention which framed the Constitution of the United States in 1787.

It was widely held that John Wickham, Jr. and John Marshall were in those days Virginia's finest attorneys. John Wickham, Jr., although a Richmond lawyer, soon adopted the life of a genteel planter—the life of

Elizabeth Selden McClurg was John Wickham, Jr.'s second wife.

(*Smithsonian Institution*)

hospitality, outdoor sports, and travel. He raised wheat as his cash crop. He was also an estate surveyor and emerging scientific enthusiast. Like others, he began interpreting his soil conditions with technical precision and analytic specificity. He studied cultivation techniques and belonged to Agricultural Societies.

The Carter family first started buying land—for what would become Hickory Hill—in 1735. By 1819 the Carters owned over 4,000 acres, and Robert King Carter gave 500 acres called Hickory Hill to his daughter Anne Butler Carter on the occasion of her marriage to William Fanning Wickham in December of that year.[3]

---

3. NPS Form 10-900 United States Department of the Interior National Park Service 0MB No. 1024-0018 National Register of Historic Places Registration Form, DHR No. 042-5792.

The original Hickory Hill mansion, constructed of wood, was built in 1820, with a four-acre ornamental garden laid out alongside. William and Anne raised wheat as their cash crop and grew Hickory Hill to 3,300 acres in size. The Hickory Hill property had long been an appendage to Shirley Plantation in Charles City County, much of it having come into possession of the Carter family by a deed dated March 2, 1734. The Carters were among the First Families of Virginia.

Anne Hill Carter Lee was the mother of Robert E. Lee. The Lee family visited Hickory Hill often—before, during and after the Civil War. Mrs. Robert E. Lee and her daughters left Arlington and stayed at Hickory Hill through much of the war. William Orton Williams, the childhood sweetheart of General Lee's daughter, Mary, proposed to her in Hickory Hill's large parlor. She declined, never disclosing her reasons, but it is thought that the war had hardened the sweet young man she had known into an angry, hard man. Orton was later captured and then hanged the following morning as a spy. General Robert E. Lee wrote that this cruel deed was done to Orton simply to get at himself.

John and Anne eventually expanded Hickory Hill to encompass 3,300 acres. Their modest original frame dwelling over an English basement grew with the plantation to become a brick 7,500-square-foot mansion in the Greek Revival style. Hickory Hill was one of the ten largest plantations in Virginia, amassing 275 slave workers on the property. At least 140 Shirley Plantation slaves were sent to Hickory Hill as dowry from two Carter sisters, Anne Butler Carter and Lucy Nelson Carter—on whose double marriage on December 9, 1819 at Shirley, these enslaved individuals were transferred to William Fanning Wickham and Edmund Fanning Wickham, along with the 3,000 acres of South Wales divided between the two Wickham brothers.[4]

Anne Butler Carter moved to Hickory Hill following her marriage to William F. Wickham. Their first child, Williams Carter Wickham, was born in Richmond in 1820, prior to his family's move into rural Hanover County. Williams Carter Wickham grew up on the Hickory Hill estate and, along with his father, watched as the Louisa Railroad was constructed through their working plantation. A stop was established there, appropriately named Wickham Station and their crops were loaded at its adjacent rail siding.

Grandfather John Wickham, Jr. also owned, raced, and bred racehorses—the best and most famous was named "Boston." A chestnut stallion with a white blaze on his nose, he was foaled in Richmond. Boston became one of the greatest racehorses of his time—and sired the great stud, "Lexington." John Wickham, Jr. initially owned the horse

---

4. Ibid.

Hickory Hill Plantation.

(Shannon Pritchard, OldSouthAntiques.com)

but lost him in a card game to Richmond native and friend Nathaniel Rives. Named after a popular card game–not the city–Boston was later known by the moniker "Old White Nose," because of his blazed face. After Wickham sold the horse to cover the $800 gambling debt, the horse became one of the most famous racehorses in American history. Wickham later placed a portrait of the famous horse in his home–in part to remind him of the wages of gambling. Boston, America's first great racehorse was inducted into the National Museum of Racing's Hall of Fame in 1955. His earnings from 1836 to 1843 were $51,700.[5]

After his death in 1839, John Wickham, Jr. was interred in Richmond's Shockoe Hill Cemetery. His son, William Fanning Wickham, born November 23, 1793 at Hickory Hill, also became a farmer. John Wickham's numerous descendants continued to be active in Virginia's affairs. His grandson Williams Carter Wickham became a Confederate cavalry general, and during the post war period, served as the first president of the Chesapeake and Ohio Railway. His granddaughter, Charlotte Georgiana Wickham, was the daughter-in-law of General Robert E. Lee and the first wife of William Henry Fitzhugh Lee, her second cousin through their shared Carter ancestry.

5. Brien Bouyea, sports@saratogian.com, @thepinksheet on Twitter; Thoroughbred bloodlines, http://www.bloodlines.net/TB/Bios/Boston.htm; http://www.tbheritage.com/Portraits/Boston.html

Boston was a famous racehorse owned for a time by Williams Fanning Wickham. As a two-year-old, Boston was lost by his breeder in a card game and was given to Wickham's friend Nathaniel Rives of Richmond to repay his debt of $800. He was named after a popular card game and later given the nickname of "Old White Nose". Boston had a willful temperament and was difficult to train.

(National Museum of Racing and Hall of Fame)

She was a first cousin of Williams C. Wickham and was the posthumous daughter of George Wickham (1816-1841) and Charlotte Georgiana Carter Wickham (1822-1843).[6] Her parents both having died when she was a baby, Charlotte was raised at Shirley Plantation by her maternal grandfather.

Williams Carter Wickham's father was William Fanning Wickham, and his mother was Anne Butler Carter (born in 1797 at Shirley Plantation, died in 1868), and a sister to Anne Hill Carter Lee, mother of Robert E. Lee. He is maternally descended from the Nelson and Carter (Robert "King" Carter) families. Williams married Lucy Penn Taylor, a great-granddaughter of John Penn, also one of the signers of the Declaration of Independence. Robert E. Lee was fond of visiting Hickory Hill. He once wrote a note to Wickham's father stating "I am

6. www.findagrave.com; Ancestry.com.

so glad that I stopped at Hickory Hill on my return to Lexington. It has given me pleasant thoughts for the rest of my life."[7]

Williams Carter Wickham's surviving siblings were John Wickham (1822-1847), Lucy Carter Wickham (1835-1923), and Anne Carter Wickham (1833-1834).[8]

At twelve years of age, William Fanning Wickham attended school at Parson Woodville near Stephensburg in Culpeper County. He graduated from Princeton College in Princeton, New Jersey. In 1829 he abandoned his practice of law—one of the most valuable in Virginia. He was considered a political moderate. He violently opposed secession, predicting that Civil War would end in ruin for the South. He hated abolitionists. Once Virginia seceded; however, he did all he could to promote the cause of the South. He was in favor of making peace under "honorable terms."[9]

William F. Wickham, believed in and benefitted from the Agricultural Societies' activities such as seed trading and estate surveying. He employed crop rotation and soil conservation methods. He quantified accounts of fertilizer improvements. His quantified accounts of field management and labeling demonstrated his developing character as a scientific agriculturalist. He fertilized using marl (sedimentary rock or soil consisting of clay and lime, used as fertilizer) in systematic fashion by the 1820s. "By 1828, his fields were being scrutinized for the bushels of marl they held; their productivity was calculated with consideration of cartloads of marl, bushels used per acre, and tons harvested per acre of wheat."[10] The primary crop at Hickory Hill was wheat, but corn, oats, fruits, and vegetables were also reaped. He purchased up-to-date machinery, including reapers and harvesters. He sent about 80 percent of his harvest directly to Richmond for marketing—withholding the remainder for the plantation. Most local planters sold their crop products nearby, but Wickham sent his commodities to Richmond to fetch a higher price.

---

7. Proceedings of the ... Annual Meeting of the Virginia State Bar Association, Report of the Twelfth Annual Meeting of the Virginia State Bar Association Held at Hotel Chamberlin, Fort Monroe, Virginia, July 17-19, 1900, pp. 82-84; Edited by Eugene C. Massie, Secretary, of the Richmond Bar, Richmond, Virginia, John T. West, Printer, 1900.
8. NARA; Ancestry.Com.
9. *Richmond Times Dispatch*, August 1, 1880.
10. Notes from the Ground, Science & Agricultural Improvement in the Early American Republic, Benjamin R. Cohen, Dissertation submitted to the Faculty of Virginia Polytechnic Institute and State University in partial fulfillment of the requirements for the degree of Doctor of Philosophy in Science and Technology Studies, February 25, 2005, Blacksburg, Virginia, 188-192.

William F. Wickham managed by "walking the fields," hiring men to oversee his slave labor force. He had 142 slaves, not all working the fields. For 3,300 acres, and distances from marl pits to fields of up to three miles, this traffic in marl manuring was both difficult and impressive. Over the years, production reached a peak of 1,500 bushels of marl per acre on 30 acres in the year of 1831. This volume required a tremendous amount of work, increasing his need for more slave labor. William owned 271 slaves in 1850 and 203 in 1860.[11]

William Fanning Wickham at age of 82
1793 — 1880
Great Grandson of
Capt. James and Hannah Smith Fanning

William Fanning Wickham (1793-1880) studied crop rotation and fertilizing and brought those skills to his plantation.

(Public Domain)

William Fanning Wickham kept diaries containing a record of crop collections and weather conditions between 1831 and 1836. The diaries noted a number of natural events that had devastating effects on crop yields at Hickory Hill. These include Hessian "fly in the wheat;" "violent rains and storms;" and "rust a scourge" during the summer of 1830. Meanwhile, on February 5, 1831, he remarked on "so cold a winter never seen in Virginia," with "5 freshes" (floods) since the middle of December; and, on February 12, "Wheat cannot be a good crop under any circumstances." The trials continued into early spring, with "thousands of wild geese–have to keep a boy in the wheat field to drive them away," as noted on March 1, 1831. Conditions had little improved by May 8, as Wickham wrote, "More fly than I ever saw before; many acres of wheat will not be worth replanting." On August 11, 1833,

---

11. 1850 and 1860 Virginia Slave Schedules; William Kauffman Scarborough, *Masters of the Big House: Elite Slaveholders of the Mid-Nineteenth-Century South* (Baton Rouge: LSU Press, 2003), 42-43.

Wickham wrote, "Worst crop [wheat] I ever made; the crops throughout the state are wretched." He added, "Seldom known so severe a drought." If anything, growing conditions worsened over the following year. On May 29, 1834 Wickham complained, "Wheat entirely destroyed . . . 4 feet higher than any fresh [flood] before" and "more than half the works/dykes are broken." The summer brought another drought, the "most destructive drought since 1822," according to Wickham on August 19. A week later on August 26, he noted, "5 weeks since rain. Whole county burnt up. Corn cannot make half an acre of crop." Finally, on August 26, 1836, Wickham reported quite the opposite problem: "Most incipient and violent rain I have ever witnessed–Little Page, South Anna, Ground Squirrel & every bridge on the South Anna has been carried away. South Anna 6 feet higher than the oldest inhabitants can remember." The sustained combination of extreme floods, severe winters, droughts, disease, insect damage, and wild geese, coupled with the nationwide Panic of 1837 financial crisis, is likely to have significantly reduced the plantation's cash income from its principal money crops. Wickham was probably forced to sell slaves to raise cash.[12]

In April 1852, at age 59, William F. Wickham traveled Europe, alone, aboard the steamer, "Pacific." Normally, but not always, the planter elite took their families with them on these sojourns, frequently in the company of neighboring planters. Wickham first visited England, where at Hyde Park, he marveled at "a scene that has no parallel in the world."[13] Spending May and June in Italy, he attested that the environment was "the loveliest country" he had ever seen.[14] William Wickham, however was disenchanted by the "beggary, uncleanliness, and squalid poverty he encountered everywhere on the Italian peninsula. He visited Geneva, Baden Baden, Antwerp, Brussels, before spending several weeks in France. Returning to the British Isles, he explored England and Ireland during the last six-weeks of his trip. Wickham was most enamored with England, which he labeled "a fairy land."[15]

12. NPS Form 10-900 United States Department of the Interior National Park Service 0MB No. 1024-0018 National Register of Historic Places Registration Form This form is for use in nominating or requesting determinations for individual properties and districts. Name of Property Historic name: Hickory Hill, Hanover County, Virginia.
13. W. F. Wickham to his wife, Anne, April 3, 16, 1852, Wickham Family Papers, Virginia Museum of History and Culture.
14. W. F. Wickham to wife Anne, June 22, 1852; Letter to daughters Mary Fanning and Lucy, June 28, 1852, Wickham Family Papers, Virginia Museum of History and Culture.
15. W. F. Wickham to wife, Anne Wickham, September 2, 18, 1852, Wickham Family Papers, Virginia Museum of History and Culture.

William F. Wickham was slow to embrace the church, being less pious than his wife. Writing from Paris during his 1852 European tour, Wickham admitted that his sabbaths "had not been all spent as you would desire," but he hastened to assure his "dearest love" that he had "enjoyed . . . no amusements, visited no spectacles, and in no matter violated it further than I have told you in my letters." Years later, in a letter of condolence to the widow of William C. Rives, Wickham expressed regret that he had not become a member of the church "early in life" as they had. "In affliction," he observed, "it is natural for every thinking being to have recourse to a higher power & to believe we shall be again with those we love in a happier world." Doubtless, the recent death of his own wife, Anne, had served to confirm his belief that solace could best be found in religion.[16]

On March 4, 1868 Robert E. Lee wrote William F. Wickham on the demise of his venerable wife, Anne Butler Carter Wickham, a niece of General Lee's mother:

> My dear Mr. Wickham, I grieve most deeply over the great sorrow that has fallen upon you and your house. Death in its silent, sure march is fast gathering those whom I have longest loved, so that when he shall knock at my door I will more willingly follow. She whom we mourn is among those whom I have longest and most dearly loved. She was the favorite of my mother, the object of my boyish affection and admiration, and has been cherished, fondly cherished, in the long years of manhood. She will always live in my memory, and the farthest recollection of her brings me nothing but pleasure.
>
> May He who has dealt the blow in mercy temper its affliction, and enable us to say, His will be done.
>
> Yours in true friendship.
>
> R. E. Lee[17]

William Fanning Wickham recorded that a Federal presence in Hanover County adversely affected slave behavior irrespective of the gender of the authority figure. "There are a great many hands in the house and from the state of the country, and the presence of the

---

16. William F. Wickham to Anne C. Wickham, July 21, 1852, VMHC; William F. Wickham to Mrs. W. C. Rives, April 28, 1868, Mrs. Rives to William F. Wickham, May 14, 1868, Wickham Family Papers, VMHC. William F. Wickham became a member of the Methodist church.
17. Wickham Family Papers, UVA.

Yankees below Richmond no discipline can be maintained among them . . . We get on as well as we can," Wickham lamented, "and that is like to be badly."[18]

In February of 1829, William F. Wickham put out a notice in the Richmond Enquirer of a twenty-dollar reward for the return to him of his slave, Cyrus. He described Cyrus as a dark mulatto, between 25 and 30 years of age, rather below ordinary height, prominent cheek bones . . . He also said that Cyrus had a large scar under one of his eyes, and that he owned a new suit of brown cloth . . . and a striped waistcoat, giving any information that could possibly help a person determine Cyrus's identity (and return him to Wickham). Cyrus was well known in Richmond, as he had lived there his whole life, and was married to a woman (assumedly also a slave) who lived at Mr. William McKim's. Wickham also stated that Cyrus was very intelligent and that he might attempt an escape in a vessel or steamboat. He requested that the masters of these boats not allow Cyrus onboard.[19]

Wickham never used the word "slave" in his message; however, he got his message across. He did go into much detail describing Cyrus, however. When advertising rewards for runaway slaves, an owner had every reason to be extremely precise in his descriptions, for the slaves would often go to great trouble to disguise themselves. By mentioning Cyrus's intelligence and the possibility of his escape by way of water, Wickham stated one of the possible ways for a slave to escape to freedom in the nineteenth century. If a slave could get to a boat, passage north would likely be much quicker than traveling at night by foot. Stowing away on a boat would allow a slave to hide and wait until arrival in the north, which was more desirable than being in a constant chase by their masters. Slaveholders needed the support of the masters of the steamboats to check for runaway slaves, for once the slaves were on the boats, there was little chance of getting them back.[20]

William Kennedy was an obscure, free black, tax-paying citizen of Henrico County, as evidenced by two receipts for taxes paid to the Henrico County Sheriff for 1853 and 1863, with the word "white" crossed out. (This taxpayer apparently had political influence.) A letter from William Fanning Wickham, who lived at Hickory Hill in Hanover County, sought Kennedy's help in a political campaign. On September 5, 1867, Wickham wrote:

---

18. Dixie's Other Daughters: African-American Women in Virginia, 1861-1868, Volume 1, 242.
19. *Richmond Enquirer*, February 3, 1829.
20. Ibid.

I enclose you ten copies of my address to the colored voters of Hanover, which you will oblige me by circulating where you think they will do good. You will perceive that I have expressed the idea that you expressed to me in our conversation at the Court House, "That it is important at this time that we should be represented by the most intelligent & honest men we can find." I will add, for the reasons I give in my address, that the representative ought to be one who will faithfully protect the rights & interests of the colored population & I will do that if I am elected with as much zeal as any one of themselves could do. This pledge I give & I wish it to be remembered, for I shall adhere to it. If anything brings you this way, I shall be pleased to see you at my house.[21]

Kennedy, it appears, was sort of a liaison between Wickham and the black community, since he was active in the Republican Party.

William F. Wickham died Wednesday evening of July 31, 1880 at one o'clock a.m., at his home in Powhatan County. He had been ill for nearly two months, but alarming symptoms did not arise until Friday before his death on Saturday. The funeral took place at Grace Church in Powhatan County, Sunday afternoon at three o'clock.

The original main house of Hickory Hill, completed by 1827, was completely destroyed by a fire in 1875. Williams Wickham's fine library, inherited from his father and added to by Williams and housed in a separate building, was spared. The damage was estimated at $7,000, while insured for $5,000. The main house was replaced by the present brick house, erected in a form reminiscent of the antebellum period.[22]

In an 1875 letter, William Fanning Wickham, "Fanny" Graham's elder half-brother, described the fire at Hickory Hill, the family plantation in Hanover County, Virginia, that destroyed a considerable portion of the house along with some family heirlooms and mementos. William Fanning Wickham wrote that "Mrs. Graham, who lost almost her entire wardrobe is as cheerful as if nothing happened. Her good temper exceeds anything I ever knew."[23]

This extensive Hanover County plantation has been the property of the Wickham family since 1820 when Robert Carter of Shirley left 1,717 acres to his daughter and son-in-law: Anne Butler Carter and William Fanning Wickham of Richmond. The Wickhams's son, Williams Carter Wickham of Hickory Hill, became a Confederate

21. William Kennedy Papers: 1853-1870. Virginia Historical Society. MssK3884a.
22. *Alexandria Gazette*, February 15, 1875.
23. Valentine Museum, Richmond, VA.

Portrait of "Aunt Betsy" [Christian] the valued nursemaid to the Wickham children.

(Valentine Museum)

general and legislator, and later served as president of the Chesapeake and Ohio Railway. Surviving the fire of 1875 were an 1857 brick wing and an important collection of antebellum outbuildings and farm buildings, including a Gothic Revival library. The spacious grounds are a remarkable example of antebellum landscaping, containing a romantic-style park with outstanding specimen trees, a geometric boxwood garden, and a tree-box walk of unusual height.

Hickory Hill, at one time encompassing nearly 3,500 acres, was one of the largest plantations in central Virginia by 1860. In 1850, the plantation was home to eight members of the Wickham family and an enslaved community of 191 African-Americans. A decade later, Hickory Hill was one of only two plantations in Hanover County, and nine in the entire state, on which more than 200 enslaved people lived and worked. A slave, "Aunt Betsy" [Christian], owned by Williams Carter Wickham, was a nurse to Wickham's children; she experienced a short period of freedom before her death in 1865. A painting of "Aunt Betsy" is housed in the Valentine Museum in Richmond.

The most important pillar of the Wickhams family's financial security was the increasing value and number of slaves at Hickory Hill. In 1852 there were two hundred slaves valued at $70,000, an average of $350 each at Hickory Hill. In 1860 there were 275 slaves, averaging slightly more than $650 each, worth $180,000 (Approximately $4.5 million in 2022 dollars). In eight years the value of the Wickham's slave property increased two-and-a-half-fold. Low crop yields were not something the Wickham family had to worry about. If the Wickhams had to endure several consecutive years of crop failures, they could always sell some of their slaves. The Wickham family was not alone, however. Slave owning in Virginia was not only for wealthy planters; it was widespread.

Along with grain crops, the enslaved workers cultivated a wide array of fruits and vegetables, likely for consumption on the plantation rather than as cash crops. A small amount of tobacco was grown as well, but it was never a premier staple crop at Hickory Hill.[24]

24. Gregg L. Michel, "From Slavery to Freedom: Hickory Hill, 1850-80," in *The Edge of the South: Life in 19th-Century Virginia*, eds. Edward L. Ayers and John C. Willis (Charlottesville: University of Virginia Press, 1991), 109-110; NPS Form 10-900 United States Department of the Interior National Park Service OMB No. 1024-0018 National Register of Historic Places Registration Form, DHR No. 042-5792.

CHAPTER 2
Family Heritage:
Williams Carter Wickham: Early Years

"I stand here ready to defend Virginia's every right;

but, at the same time,

determined to use every effort to preserve the Union."

William Fanning and Anne Wickham's son, Williams Carter Wickham (1820-1888), became a notable lawyer, judge, politician, soldier, and railroad executive. He was born in Richmond, on September 21, 1820, and moved to Hanover County with his parents in 1827. He grew up on the Hickory Hill estate, located near Hanover Court House, along the Pamunkey River.

Wickhams attended the Howard School—a boys' school near Alexandria, Virginia. The Howard School opened in 1831 and continued until 1834 with two teachers—the Reverend Jonathan Loring Woart (1807-1838) and his brother, the Reverend John Woart. The Episcopal High School opened in 1839 at the former Howard School location. Letters from the Reverend Jonathan Loring Woart (1807-1838) to William F. Wickham included progress reports for his two sons.

Williams also attended Thomas Hanson's private school in Fredericksburg and later enrolled at the University of Virginia in the Class of 1837 to study law. He and his near-relation Charles Carter Wickham boarded at Mrs. Lucy Brockenbrough's boarding house on Brockenbrough Hill, across the road from the university's academic village in Charlottesville. Her boarding home had a capacity for 12 students.[1]

Regulations for student dress at the University of Virginia were enacted and enforced—causing bitter feelings with some of the collegians and becoming a source of trouble with the faculty. These rules prescribed that the attire of students should be uniform and plain: "the coat, waistcoat and pantaloons of cloth of a dark gray

1. *Richmond Times Dispatch*, September 4, 1904.

mixture, known as Oxford gray broadcloth, at a price not exceeding six dollars per yard. The coat was required to be single-breasted, with a standing cape and swallow-tailed, the skirts of a moderate length, with pocket-flaps; the waistcoat single-breasted, with a standing collar, and the "pantaloons of the usual form." The buttons of each garment were flat, and covered with the same cloth. The pantaloons and waistcoat of this dress could be varied with the season without offense. For instance, the waist coat might be white and the pantaloons of light brown cotton or linen. Boots were absolutely prohibited; plain black neckcloths were prescribed for winter and white for summer, while no difference seems to have been made for the hat, which was required to be "round and black." A surtout (man's overcoat, similar to a frock coat)—of cloth of the price and color of the regulation dress was allowed, but not as a substitute on occasions of public examinations and exhibitions within the University. This uniform was strictly enforced for years, except during warm weather when the student was permitted to wear—within the "precincts—a light gown or coat of a pattern approved by the chairman. The uniform law was passed by the Board of Visitors on December 16, 1826; present were: Messrs. Madison, Monroe, Cocke, Cabell and Johnson. It was "repealed in 1845."[2]

Wickham enrolled in the optional military training offered by the university. He was furnished a uniform too; while those not taking the military option wore dark trousers, white shirt, tie, vest, and a white hat.

During Wickham's time at the university, professors submitted reports concerning students to the Chairman of the Faculty at the monthly faculty meeting. The Professor of Ancient Languages reported that Messrs. Rolin H. Kirk, Thomas M. Muldrow, Dr. M. Heriot, E. F. Montague, and Williams C. Wickham answered badly and that Messrs. John A. Strother and N. W. Smith are nearly always absent. The Professor of Modern Languages reported that Mr. N. T. Sorsby has always been absent and that Mr. Williams C. Wickham is idle. Williams C. Wickham was reported for inattention in Ancient & Modern Languages. The Chairman informed the faculty that Mr. Williams C. Wickham and Mr. Robert Hackett were in Charlottesville without uniform—Mr. Wickham wore a summer coat, and Mr. Hackett had informed the Chairman that some weeks ago he put a uniform entrusted to the hands of a tailor—and it was not yet finished. Wickham claimed his coat was also being repaired by a tailor. A motion was made, seconded, and passed that Mr. Wickham be

---

2. John S. Patton, *Jefferson, Cabell, and The University of Virginia* (New York: The Neale Publishing Company, 1906), 121-22.

reprimanded by the Chairman and that his father was to be written about the matter. A motion was made, seconded, and passed that Mr. Hackett be censured by the Chairman.[3] On December 19, 1837, Wickham was granted leave for two to three weeks to visit home. On March 14, 1838, he was reported for student misconduct (a uniform violation)—"as out of uniform yesterday in Charlottesville as to his vest, while his proper vest was sent for. He stated that he wore the silk vest he had on under the impression that it was allowed as summer clothing, and that he brought it with him from home. He was admonished that silk vests—as likely to lead to extravagance—were not allowed as uniform in summer even."

Upon graduating in 1841, Wickham read law under Judge James Lyons in Richmond and was admitted to the Bar in 1842. He then practiced law and became a planter, living at Hickory Hill. Much of his time was spent, however, managing the business affairs of Hickory Hill. He soon abandoned law for the life of a planter.

On January 11, 1848, Williams Carter Wickham married Lucy Penn Taylor (1830-1913) in Spotsylvania, Virginia. She was the daughter of Henry Taylor and Julia Leiper Taylor and was born at Hazelwood. She was the great-granddaughter of John Penn from North Carolina., one of the signers of the Declaration of Independence. They had five children together: John (1848-1848); Henry Taylor (1849-1943), who became an attorney and a Virginia state senator with an illustrious career, Anne Carter (1851-1939); Julia Leiper (1859-1873); and William Fanning II (1860-1900). In 1860, Williams's father owned 203 slaves; while Williams owned three.[4]

Williams Wickham was an interesting man. The children and his wife lived in the 1830 main house, while he generally lived in his separate, custom built, library and office building.

Williams Wickham was elected to the Virginia House of Delegates in 1849 as a Whig and was presiding justice of the county court of Hanover County for many years. In the Wickham household, a trusted slave named Robin Saunders served as the butler for the family. Another slave, Betsy Christian (called "Aunt Betsy") served as a nursemaid for the Wickham children. Robin died on November 5, 1861 at 69 years of age. Betsy died in 1865. Lucy Penn Wickham mused after "Aunt Betsy's" death: "I have changed my mind and like our old coloured [sic] nurses the best–tho Aunt Betsy does put as much

---

3. Jefferson's University—Early Life Project, 1819-1870 (JUEL), juel.iath.virginia.edu/. The uniform consisted of trousers, white shirt, tie, vest, and white hat.
4. 1860 Virginia slave schedules; *Richmond Times Dispatch*, September 4, 1904.

Williams Wickham married Lucy Penn Taylor in 1848

(Valentine Museum)

covering on in August as January. She was such a faithful kind friend to the children. She died this fall; it was a satisfaction to me that she had everything she wanted & I hope & believe she is in Heaven."[5]

On March 23, 1859, Williams's eighteen-year-old cousin, Charlotte Georgiana Wickham, married twenty-one-year-old William Henry Fitzhugh Lee "Rooney" Lee at Shirley Plantation. Charlotte was the daughter of George Wickham of the U. S. Navy (pre-Civil War) and Charlotte Carter Wickham. George Wickham was a brother of William Fanning Wickham (Williams's C. Wickham's father). Thus, Charlotte and Rooney were second cousins. The wedding was held in the same great hall where Rooney's grandparents were married—his grandmother was also born and reared there. Williams Wickham attended the wedding.[6]

Charlotte and Rooney settled down to farm at the old Custis estate, White House Plantation, a 4000-acre estate on the Pamunkey River in New Kent County, Virginia, which Rooney had inherited from his maternal grandfather, George Washington Parke Custis, in 1857. It had been the home of Martha Custis Washington prior to her marriage. Rooney spent most of his time tilling the land and refurbishing the plantation, which had fallen into disrepair.

In March 1860, Charlotte gave birth to Robert E. Lee's first grandchild, Robert Edward Lee. The flattered grandfather wrote:

> I wish I could offer him a more worthy name and a better example. He must elevate the first, and make use of the latter to avoid the errors I have committed. I also expressed the thought that under the circumstances you might like to name him after his great-grandfather, and wish you both, 'upon mature consideration,' to follow

5. Jane Turner Censer, *The Reconstruction of White Southern Womanhood, 1865–1895* (Baton Rouge: LSU Press, 2003), 70; Lucy P. Wickham to Bessie Shields, December 20, 1865, Wickham Family Papers, VMHC. Lucy, like other white women in the South, preferred white women for nursemaids, but they were hard to come by, and Lucy changed her attitude in observing Betsy. There is a portrait of "Aunt Betsy, painted in 1857, in the Valentine Museum in Richmond.
6. Douglass Southall Freeman, *R. E. Lee*, I, 389; Mary Bandy Daughtry, *Gray Cavalier: The Life Wars of General W. H. F. "Rooney" Lee* (Cambridge, Ma: Da Capo Press, 2002), 41; See "History of American Women, Charlotte Lee" (womenhistoryblog.com). Charlotte's parents (George and Charlotte Carter Wickham) both died when she was a baby. She was raised at Shirley Plantation by her grandfather, William Carter. Charlotte Wickham lived a life of wealth, yet her life was filled with tragedy, from the untimely deaths of her parents, to the loss of both of her infant children, to finally her own death in her early twenties. As a descendant of some of Virginia's most prominent families and living on one of the area's finest estates, Charlotte traveled in an elite social circle as she entered adulthood.

your inclinations and judgment. I should love him all the
same, and nothing could make me love you two more
than I do.[7]

Charlotte's health was never robust; the son she bore in March
1860—and the daughter she delivered two-and-a-half years later, Mary
Custis Lee both died in infancy. Rooney married again in 1867— this
time to Mary Tabb Bolling, and the couple had seven children.

During this time of increasing sectional tension, the Peace
Conference of 1861, a meeting of more than one hundred of the
leading politicians of the United States, was held in Washington, D.C.,
in February 1861. The purpose of the conference was to prevent—what
ultimately became—the Civil War. President Abraham Lincoln's
election in November 1860 led to a flurry of political activity. In much
of the South, elections were held to select delegates to special
conventions which empowered them to consider secession from the
Union. In Congress, efforts were made in both the House of
Representatives and in the Senate to reach a compromise over issues
relating to slavery that were dividing the nation. The Washington
Peace Conference of 1861 was the final effort by the individual states to
resolve the crisis. With the seven states of the "Cotton South" already
committed to secession, the emphasis on preserving the Union
peacefully focused on the eight slaveholding states representing the
upper and border South, with the states of Virginia and Kentucky
playing key roles.

The Montgomery Convention – May 4, 1861

The Montgomery Convention formally marked the beginning of
The Confederate States of America. Convened in Montgomery,
Alabama, and opening on February 4, 1861, the Convention organized
a provisional government for the Confederacy and created the
Constitution of the Confederate States of America. The Convention
named Jefferson Davis of Mississippi as provisional President of the
Confederate States of America and Alexander Stephens of Georgia as
Vice-President. The Convention also established dates for a formal
election for both offices; Davis and Stephens were elected without
opposition.[8]

---

7. John William Jones, *Personal Reminiscences, Anecdotes, and Letters of Gen.
   Robert E. Lee* (New York: D. Appleton and Company, 1874), 381.
8. Ellen Tucker, "The Convention and the Cause that Organized the
   Confederacy," February 2, 2021, https://teachingamericanhistory.org. The
   Confederate Constitution was modelled after the United States Constitution,
   but it explicitly mentioned slavery and provided for the internal trade in
   slaves (while prohibiting their importation from other nations.

The Provisional Congress of the Confederate States of America, a congress of deputies and delegates who were called together from the Southern States and became the governing body of the Provisional Government of the Confederate States of America (CSA) from February 4, 1861, to February 17, 1862. The Congress met in Montgomery, Alabama, until May 20, 1861, when it adjourned to meet in Richmond, Virginia, on July 20, 1861. It added new members as other states seceded; and it directed the election on November 6, 1861, when a permanent government was elected.[9]

The First Session of the Provisional Congress was held in Montgomery from February 4, 1861, to March 16, 1861. Members present from Alabama, Florida, Georgia, Louisiana, Mississippi, South Carolina, and Texas drafted a provisional constitution and organized a government. The Second Session of the Provisional Congress was held at Montgomery from April 29, 1861, to May 21, 1861. Members were present from Alabama, Florida, Georgia, Louisiana, Mississippi, South Carolina, Texas, Virginia, and Arkansas.[10]

The Virginia Secession Convention

In 1859, Williams Wickham was engaged in the pleasant pursuits of agricultural life when his senatorial district nominated him to be a candidate for the Virginia Senate. Wickham protested and tried to substitute a candidate with similar political views. Unsuccessful, he accepted the candidacy and was easily elected.[11]

Wickham was actively engaged in the 1860 Presidential Canvass–whenever he addressed any assemblage of his constituency, he stated that "the issue of that canvass was Union or disunion. I advocated the side of Union and opposed that of disunion."[12]

The Virginia Legislature met and passed a bill calling for a Secession Convention. Wickham published an address to his constituency—pointing out the dangers about to engulf them, and

9. *Journal of the Provisional Congress of the Confederate States*, Vol. I (Washington: Government Printing Office, 1904), 5-62, 271.
10. Ibid.
11. Cynthia Miller Leonard, *The Virginia General Assembly 1619-1978* (Richmond: Virginia State Library 1978), 436, 473; Jan. 24, 1861 Broadside, Wickham Family Papers, UVA.
12. March 20, 1861 speech by Williams C. Wickham to Virginia Secession Convention, University of Richmond, Boatwright Memorial Library, Digital Initiatives, Digital Scholarship Lab, The Library of Virginia, University Communications, Web Service, https://secession.richmond.edu/documents/images/index.php/proceedings.vol 2.0126.jpg.

warning them to "guard against the wiles of the dis-unionists, and the influence of the secession cry which was raised to entice them from the path of conservatism and moderation. I told them that disunion was no remedy for the ills upon us, and urged them to make every effort to maintain the rights of Virginia and yet to preserve the Union."[13]

In the county of Henrico, Wickham had attempted to recruit a friend—who held similar opinions to those he expressed—to be a candidate for the Secession Convention. Failing in that endeavor, Wickham consented to become a candidate. The citizens of Henrico elected him.[14]

The Virginia Secession Convention met from February 3–December 6, 1861, and elected John Janney its presiding officer. Early on, Wickham, as Chairman of the Secession Convention's Committee on Federal Relations—representing many Virginia conservatives at the Secession Convention—tried to find a way to avert secession by writing to General Winfield Scott in Washington on March 11, 1861:

> Mr. Lincoln's inaugural which in my opinion has been greatly distorted, from its true intention, by our people . . . . We have a noble band of conservatives who are bravely withstanding the powerful outside pressure that is being brought to bear upon them but our ranks are being sadly thinned by desertions, and we cannot say how long we will possess a majority of the Convention unless something is done to aid us.[15]

Wickham outlined the problem of the pro-unionists:

> South Carolina is kept apprised of our position and will seize the slightest pretext for a collision. Could I be permitted to advise I would urge upon the Administration to abstain from any effort to re-enforce the forts or to collect the revenues in the seceded States, and I would even go further and advise the withdrawal of the troops that are now there, as calculated to remove the thorn in the side and depriving them thus of any pretext for complaint. Such a course would reassure the weak and give additional strength to the strong; it would give quiet and rest from excitement to the people in those States, enable them to reflect on the consequences of what they

13. Ibid.
14. Jan. 24, 1861 Broadside, Wickham Family Papers, UVA.
15. Wickham to Winfield Scott, March 11, 1861, Abraham Lincoln papers, http://www.loc.gov/resource/mal.0800600

have done in passion, and I think tend greatly to bring about, what the conservatives of Virginia are so earnestly laboring for, a restoration of the Union. General, I know how gratingly such views may fall upon your military ear, and you must know how earnest I must think the need when I advise the non-enforcement of the law; but here is an emergency when the enforcement of a law may cause the destruction of all law in a vast portion of the country. The opinions I have here expressed are entertained by a large proportion of the conservatives of the Convention, for many of whom I am authorized to speak.[16]

Also on March 11, 1861, Wickham filed a minority report for the Committee on Federal Relations, which he chaired, stating, "Above all other things, at this time, they (delegates voting in the minority) esteem it of indispensable necessity to maintain the peace of the country, and to avoid everything calculated or tending to produce collision and bloodshed."[17]

Wickham's minority report further resolved:

That the people of Virginia are, under existing circumstances, unalterably opposed to the exercise of any species of force on the part of the Federal Government towards the States that have withdrawn themselves from the Union, and believing that any armed collision between the Federal authorities and those of the seceded States would render utterly futile the efforts in which Virginia is engaged, to reconcile the differences now existing between the States, and would cause the irrevocable dissolution of the Union, they earnestly insist that the Federal Government shall adopt a pacific policy towards those States, shall make no attempt to subject them to Federal authority, or to reinforce the forts now in possession of the military forces of the U. States, or to recapture the forts, arsenals or other property of the U. States within their limits, nor to resort to any measures calculated in the present excited state of feeling to provoke hostile collision; and on the other hand they invoke the seceded States to abstain from any act tending to produce such collision between them and the Federal authorities.[18]

16. Ibid.
17. *The Daily Dispatch*, March 12, 1861, Richmond, Virginia.
18. Ibid.

At the Convention, Wickham stated, "I stand here ready to defend Virginia's every right; but, at the same time, determined to use every effort to preserve the Union. I stand here acknowledging allegiance to Virginia first of all; but believing that that allegiance will be best discharged and the interests of the Commonwealth best promoted by the preservation of the Union."[19]

Wickham expressed the opinion that the impending crisis could be averted by amending the Virginia Constitution to preserve the Union. He cautioned that unless amendments were adopted, the Union would be broken.[20]

Wickham proposed popular votes within all states, or by conventions similar to Virginia's: "I presume the people of the Northern States, if they do not intend to grant this adjustment, will say that they do not, in their response to us by the popular vote, or by conventions similar to this. If the people cannot defeat the politicians, then the Union will have to go; but I believe if this question is ever brought fairly before them, they will defeat the politicians."[21]

The day after the attack on Fort Sumter, delegates of the convention poured out into the streets in Richmond to try to garner the newspaper "extras" just then arriving. Wickham read of the attack with grim dismay. Wickham was a strong Union supporter who had voted against secession. From a family that had long been Federalist or Whig, Wickham was both a planter and railroad investor, and saw Virginia's future in commerce and alliances with northern businesses. Wickham, an optimist, still hoped for some signal that the attack on Fort Sumter would not lead to war.[22]

At first the majority of the Convention delegates voted to remain in the Union, but stayed in session awaiting events. Conditional Unionists objected to Lincoln's call for state quotas to suppress the rebellion, and switched from their earlier Unionist vote to secession on April 17.

Delegate Williams C. Wickham of Hanover County, rose "to ask if it was not rather premature to ask [Confederacy President Jefferson] Davis to make the city his headquarters when, as yet, the ordinance of secession had not yet been put before the people of the state for

---

19. Ibid.,
   https://secession.richmond.edu/documents/images/index.php/proceedings.vol 2.0127.jpg.
20. Ibid., April 8, 1861,
   https://secession.richmond.edu/documents/images/index.php/proceedings.vol 3.0417.jpg.
21. Ibid.
22. Marie Tyler-McGraw, *At the Falls: Richmond, Virginia and Its People* (Chapel Hill: UNC Press, 1994), 132-33.

ratification. How embarrassing would it be to have the government to accept the invitation, only to have Virginians to reject secession and statehood in the Confederacy subsequently?"[23]

Williams C. Wickham sent a letter to the Editor of the *Richmond Whig* for publication,

> My Dear Sir—It is a matter of vital importance that the wisest means that can be devised should be adopted for bringing our people back as speedily as possible on the road to prosperity from which they were so heartlessly thrust by designing politicians, in the selfish endeavor to retrieve their own fallen fortunes: and who, careless of the sufferings they would cause to be inflicted on millions of their fellow-beings, drove them, by appeals to their passions and prejudices, to a course which has been productive of almost irretrievable ruin to every Southern State, and has in its results, falsified every declaration made by them in the advocacy of their rash designs. The first great step toward the attainment of this end is to revive in the hearts of our people that devotion to the Union which was as deeply implanted there before the war as in those of the people of any of the other states, but which has been either held in abeyance by the force of the Confederate dynasty or crushed out by the false teachings of the leaders of the secession movement. My own opinion is that the great mass of the people of this State have never lost their reverence or their attachment for the Government of the United States, and that they have only wanted freedom of speech and liberty of action to avow their attachment for it. The result of the contest has taught those who really wished for the separation that the power of the Government was too great to enable them to succeed in their unhallowed design of overthrowing it. and I think we may safely-say that the abstraction which declared that we had a central government, with the name and not the powers of a government, has met with a deserved and violent death. Almost everyone in Virginia accepts the result and is just prepared to contribute his portion towards the advancement of the common good of the country. The few that I do not, will, if permitted, I doubt not, leave their country for their country's good . . . All, then, that I believe to be necessary for the full development of the

23. Ibid., April 25, 1861,
    https://secession.richmond.edu/documents/images/index.php/proceedings.vol
    4.0556.jpg.

Union feeling in Virginia, is to reestablish the means of intercourse and interchange of opinion amongst the people of the State and thus give it an opportunity to exhibit itself, and I have no doubt that the State will stand forth prominent for her pride in the national glory, appreciation of the national prosperity, admiration for the national power, and devotion to the national interest*—all heightened by the terrible ordeal through which our people have passed. With a ready return to a proper allegiance to the United States Government, the people should at once be called upon to participate in the government, both State and Federal; thus being made to realize, as soon as possible, that they are their own governments, and giving them that tranquility which is the very life of an agricultural community . . . There is much for the State government to do, to aid in the re-establishment of prosperity and happiness. It has been for the four past years utterly diverted from its legitimate duties, and consequently our whole system has become deranged . . . The three great points of State policy that require immediate attention, are the reorganization of our system [of labor, the resuscitation of our internal improvement system, and the establishment of a financial monetary system. I do not propose to go into any discussion of these subjects, but merely mention them to show the importance to the welfare of the people of the State of an early recognition on the part of the general government of some authorities to exercise the functions of the State government; for, after all, it is to the State government that we must look for that legislation which will put in speedy operation the machinery by which the energies of the people will be directed to the general improvement of the country. Another most important subject which will demand the early and earnest attention of the States authorities when invested with governmental powers, is the question of a partition of the State. I cannot bear to contemplate the fact that Virginia should lose the noblest part of her ancient dominion, and I cannot but hope that, the immediate causes for the partition having been removed, the people of West Virginia, in common with ourselves, will wish to be reunited every portion of our old Commonwealth, and that they will consider favorably on overtures for that object. I am satisfied that, by the reopening of our lines of communication, the re-establishment of our post route, the recognition of a

Governor of the State, the regular meeting of our county courts, and the convening of a legislative body at as early a day as possible, we could, in an incredibly short time, get our whole system smoothly at work, and find our people better pleased with the government than they ever had been, and are more capable of appreciating the blessings that will flow from it. Nor do I believe that a vital blow has been inflicted on the prosperity of the Estate by the effects of the war; it is true that her loss in men and means has been enormous: even had there been stagnation alone for the past four years the effect would have been serious; but her people have shown an energy, which, had it been properly directed, would have advanced her material interests to a very high degree of prosperity-that energy will now be properly directed, and the whole population of the State with one accord, will bend themselves to the effort to bring the State forward to the highest state of mental, moral and physical improvement. One unquestionable benefit will flow to the State from the ordeal through which it has passed—the people will select wiser counsellors than those who have heretofore so grossly mismanaged their public affairs. I am most eager to see the State again on its march to prosperity, and I have the brightest anticipation of the future; I feel confident that so soon as tranquility is restored, we will see her, with the Union, and the Constitution as the polestar for her guidance, moving with steady steps to a position full of honor to herself and happiness to her people . . . Knowing how fully you will concur with me in these views and how faithfully you will labor to advance the welfare of the State and of the whole country. I am, truly your friend, Wms. C. Wickham.[24]

Western Virginia Republicans resented the unfair tax burden they felt was forced on western residents. These Republicans felt that the state's system of taxation was designed to favor the economic interests of eastern Virginian slaveholders, while hindering the development of the more free-labor oriented economy of the west. To add to their grievances regarding the levying of taxes, western Virginians protested that counties east of the Blue Ridge enjoyed most of the benefits resulting from any increased revenue. These benefits came in the form of roads, canals, and railroads used to transport slave-produced crops. Cyrus Hall spoke for the westerners, who favored an ad valorem tax

24. *Richmond Whig*, April 28, 1865, Image 4.

on slaves. Then, Williams C. Wickham answered for the easterners. Wickham's emphasis on preserving slaveholders' economic threat flowed out of his position, like Jeremiah Morton's, as one of the convention's few large planters.[25]

On April 4, 1861, the Convention voted against secession. Following the attack on Fort Sumter on April 12—and Lincoln's subsequent call for Southern troops to help put down the rebellion, on April 17 the Convention quickly voted to secede, subject to a statewide referendum scheduled for May 23. The statewide vote was conducted, the results supported secession.[26]

Following the state referendum favoring secession, Wickham spoke to his fellow delegates about his previous votes against secession, and his desire to change his vote:

> When the vote was taken on the adoption of the Ordinance of Secession, I voted in the negative; I believed that the proposition of the gentleman from Fauquier presented a far better mode of bringing the question, and, although it was defeated in the Convention, yet I thought it might be presented to the people as the course that would be pursued, if the Ordinance was not ratified by them; and as the action of this Convention was intended to be recommendatory–not final—I was unwilling, by my vote, to recommend a policy which I deemed unwise. But, sir, I am satisfied that today a very large proportion of the people of Henrico, with a full knowledge of the probable consequences of the act, are in favor of this ordinance; and, as I think it right that their wishes should be accurately expressed and carried out, and that the weight of their vote should go along with the Ordinance, I have no hesitation in asking the Convention to grant me the privilege of transferring my vote from the negative to the affirmative.
>
> Again, Mr. President, whilst I have differed from the majority of this Convention as to the mode in which a State should assert its independence, yet, with all my

25. William W. Freehling and Craig M. Simpson, eds., *Showdown in Virginia: The 1861 Convention and the Fate of the Union* (Charlottesville: UVA Press, 2010), 148; Alan Lawrence Golden, "The Secession Crisis in Virginia," Dissertation, Ohio State University, 1990, 179–80.
26. The actual number of votes for or against secession are unknown since votes in many counties in northwestern and eastern Virginia (where most of Virginia's unionists lived) were "discarded or lost." Governor Letcher "estimated" the vote for these areas.

devotion to the Union, I have ever acknowledged my allegiance as due, first of all, to the State of Virginia. Events that have transpired and are transpiring, render it clear that the Convention, in adopting that ordinance, have expressed the will of a large majority of the people of the State, and the State having assumed a position that will require the earnest and hearty co-operation of all her sons to successfully maintain, I regard it as a solemn duty, on my part, to give my humble aid in procuring unanimity of action and of thought among our people. I have the honor to command a troop of horse in the county of Hanover. Acting in conformity with the proclamation of the Governor, and with orders subsequently received from my superior officers, I have ordered that troop to prepare to take the field, and am on the eve of my departure from the city to take my place at its head, determined, on my part, to do all in my power to advocate the cause in which Virginia is engaged, and meaning to defend her flag wherever it may wave.[27]

Wickham regarded secession as a crime and believed that the South would ultimately be defeated and ruined.

Meanwhile, the Confederate Congress proclaimed Richmond to be new capital of the Confederacy, and Confederate troops moved into northern Virginia before the referendum was held. Soon, Union troops took Alexandria without opposition and held it for the duration of the war.

Following Virginia's secession, Captain Williams C. Wickham headed to join his Hanover Dragoons, which became part of the 4th Virginia Cavalry, which Wickham would soon command as its colonel.

Wickham was a gentleman of education and talent, great energy, and strong practical sense. With his limited military training during his years at UVA, he was a natural military man and a leader of men.

27. Ibid., April 18,1861,
    https://secession.richmond.edu/documents/images/index.php/proceedings.vol
    4.0257.jpg.

CHAPTER THREE

Wickham Goes to War

"You cannot tell how earnestly I long for
the conclusion of this war
that I may be again permanently at home where I had
a thousand times rather be than anywhere else."

–Williams C. Wickham
to his wife, Lucy,
November 3, 1861

In November 1859 Williams Wickham raised a local militia cavalry company, the "Hanover Light Dragoons," at Hickory Hill. He led this unit as its captain until the spring of 1861. The only military training he had was that which he had received at the University of Virginia. He was highly intelligent, studied war strategy and tactics, and drilled his militia regularly during the period before war erupted.

Wickham had dark hair and blue eyes, was solidly built, even husky, and probably stood about 5'8" tall. One of Stonewall Jackson's mapmakers, Capt. Oscar Hinrichs, described Williams Wickham as "short and bowlegged." Wickham was an excellent horseman, and Hinrichs also praised Wickham as having a "real horseman's soul and always is a capable officer."[1]

Wickham's company served under Col. George Richardson's Hanover County Regiment of Virginia militia. Wickham's unit was the only cavalry company of the contingent. Colonel Richardson required drilling and dress parades, during which Wickham's company always performed the best.

Hanover citizen Charles Morris recalled the initial assembling of the regiment for drills. The Hanover Court House was where the military assemblies, called "General Musters," occurred in the county and were great occasions of pride for the citizens. Initially, however,

---

1. Oscar Hinrichs and Robert K. Krick, *Stonewall's Prussian Mapmaker: The Journals of Captain Oscar Hinrichs* (Chapel Hill: UNC Press, 2014), xii, 178.

they were very amusing according to Morris. The officers of the county regiment, comprised of all the companies in the Militia district, met at the Court House several days in advance and were drilled by the commanding officer. On the great first day of assembling, Captain Mason's company paraded in one corner of the Court-Green, Captain [Sam] Perrin's in another, and so on. Morris recalled:

> The captains usually appeared in uniform, but the lower officers and the rank-in-file came in their everyday dress. The motley appearance was wonderfully ludicrous. The company formation, the utter ignorance and carelessness of nine-tenths of the company of all Military Revolutions' (as Sam Perrin called them) made the regimental formation and parade one of the most laughable things in the world.[2]

Morris continued:

> I was once Adjutant and Sargeant-Major to Col. George W. Richardson, colonel of the Hanover Regiment. He was a man of immense military feeling. Rather vain, eager for display, he always got himself up, regardless of expense, for those occasions—splendid horse, with gorgeous trappings—full uniform, gold epaulets, splendid sword and hilt, and above all a cocked hat and feather of the Continental character that made him look ten feet high. All his officers were required to have a 'Dress Parade' and, contrary to rule, concluded to have it before the regimental Revolutions, instead of at the close.[3]

At that time, there were twelve companies of militia in the regiment commanded by Colonel Richardson. Richardson held dress parades at Hanover Court House. At the 'tuck of the drum,' the companies filed off the Court-Green onto the road in front of the portico where the colonel had taken his proper place in all the pomp and circumstance of war. It took more than an hour to form the regiment by companies on the road—in the face of such confusion, tumult, and irregular front as was presented.

2. Charles Morris, "Memories of Hanover County," *Virginia Genealogical Society*, Vol. 23, No. 1 (1985), 18-20.
3. Ibid.

Morris asserted:

> Nothing could make the soldiers stand properly in line,
> or maintain proper position for even five minutes. When
> it came to opening ranks, as was required, some went
> forward, some backward at the word of command. On
> the right flank in line with the infantry, as part of the
> parade, was Capt. Wickham's company of cavalry, a
> mixture not hitherto known to Dress Parade, but was in
> uniform and presented a good appearance.[4]

Morris continued, "At last, the command was given, not to march
separately by companies and be dismissed, but to the regiment to
march by the left flank into the old field near the road. The distance
was about a quarter-mile ahead—there was a straight road running
through the field in which the regiment directed to form."[5]

Still, according to Morris,

> It took more than an hour to get the regiment into that
> position. But alas, after immense effort the formation was
> accomplished, and we could see the colonel with his
> escort all ready to come on the field, an unexpected
> circumstance brought all order to disarray. It was a piping
> hot day in July, the burning sun pouring down on the
> men at midday. Some folks had brought into the field
> sundry barrels of ice water, which were placed here and
> there convenient but out of way of operations. However,
> Morris derided, "this was more than the men could resist.
> In spite of remonstrance or command, of cussing or
> entreaty, the men made for the barrels by twos and by
> threes, by any number, falling out and coming back in a
> continual stream, until the barrels were empty, and as
> they had been whiskey barrels and the 'scent of the roses
> hung around them still,' many soldiers who came to drink
> stayed to smell and could never be recovered to the line.
> Meantime, the colonel with his escort stood in speechless
> amazement and anger. Colonel Richardson sent aide after
> aide to command and extort the officers to get their men
> in shape, but with no great result. At last, when he and
> his escort came galloping along the supposed front of the
> line, the effect of the splendid cortege and rapid review
> fell dead.[6]

4. Ibid.
5. Ibid.
6. Ibid.

Morris ended his observations:

> Meantime, Capt. Wickham's company was careening over the field performing all sorts of charges and Revolutions, and when the inert mass of the regiment began to move, it was with the utmost difficulty, and in obedience to no word of command, that some of us escaped being run over and mangled by the cavalry. I laughed till white with exhaustion from it, and from the heat; thought I should die. Colonel Richardson was thoroughly disgusted and soon left the field, with orders to the captains to march their companies to their separate grounds and dismiss them. But then came the aftermath, the various scenes of drunkenness, of quarreling and fighting, which seems characteristic of our people on all public occasions. I am glad to believe that such scenes are becoming less common in these days, chiefly due to the strong stand which has been made for temperance.[7]

When Virginia first called for volunteers to fight, Wickham and his Dragoons rode into Ashland, Virginia, and enlisted in the Confederate Army. In the fall of 1861, the Hanover Dragoons became Company G, 4th Virginia Cavalry, with Wickham serving as its captain.[8]

On March 16, 1861, Washington's Home Guards Cavalry, an unlettered company of Fairfax County, under Captain E. B. Powell, organized at Catts's Tavern, West End, Fairfax County. On April 20, 1861, Colonel Philip St. George Cocke mustered this unit into state service at Alexandria, Virginia. The company was assigned to Wickham's Squadron of Cavalry on July 29, 1861, and to the 6th Virginia Cavalry, Company F on September 12, 1861.[9]

On May 9, 1861, Virginia accepted Wickham's Hanover Light Dragoons into state service at Ashland, Virginia. The next day, Wickham's company began drilling; and on May 17, Lieutenant Colonel Richard S. Ewell mustered them into state service for one year at Camp Ashland, Slash Cottage, on the Richmond, Fredericksburg & Potomac Railroad, west of Ashland. The Hanover Light Dragoons and the Goochland Light Dragoons were stationed in Richmond on the evening on May 19, 1861. Though in Ashland only three weeks, Ewell had gained the respect of many of the officers there, including Captain

---

7. Ibid.
8. Ezra J. Warner and Wilfred Buck Yearns, *The Biographical Register of the Confederate Congress* (Baton Rouge: LSU Press, 1975), 262-63.
9. Special Orders No.276, Paragraph XVI, Adjutant & Inspector General's Office, Richmond, Virginia.

Wickham. Wickham was so impressed that on May 29, he wrote Richmond authorities, recommending that Ewell be promoted to colonel.[10] The Hanover County Dragoons was assigned to Wickham's Squadron Cavalry on July 20, 1861, and to the 4th Virginia Cavalry, Company G on September 4, 1861.[11]

On May 24, 1861, the Washington Home Guards reached Manassas Junction, Prince William County, Virginia; and four days later the Hanover Light Dragoons arrived. Mustered into Confederate service on July 1, 1861, these units were stationed in the rear between Island and Mitchell's Fords on the Bull Run River. On July 20, 1861, Captain Williams C. Wickham was assigned to command Wickham's Squadron of Cavalry (an unlettered Company).

Battle of First Manassas

Wickham's company was then assigned to Major Julien Harrison's Cavalry Battalion at Camp Ashland.[12] On May 27, they were ordered to Centreville.[13] They arrived at Camp Pickens, Manassas Junction, Prince William County, Virginia, on May 29, 1861.

As the Federal threat developed on June 1, 1861, Captain Wickham's and Captain Harrison's commands, both stationed at Fairfax Station, were ordered to Fairfax Court House. At 4:00 a.m., they started for Fairfax Court House, arriving by sunrise, too late for the 30-minute skirmish that had occurred between 3:00 a.m. and 5:30 a.m. During June and July, Capt. William Ball's and Wickham's companies picketed and performed reconnaissance along the Potomac River. They remained quartered at Fairfax Court House.[14]

The Hanover Light Dragoons was assigned as escort to the Alexandria Artillery on the morning on July 17, 1861. The first major action began on July 17, when the Confederate army abandoned Fairfax Court House about 8:30 a.m. Captains Wickham's, Ball's, and William H. Payne's companies were among those retreating. After being positioned on the Alexandria Turnpike with two cannons, Wickham's company covered the withdrawal to Mitchell's Ford that day.[15]

10. Donald C. Pfanz, *Richard E. Ewell: A Soldier's Life* (Chapel Hill: UNC Press, 1998), 124.
11. Special Orders No.248, Adjutant & Inspector General's Office, Richmond.
12. Special Orders No.127, Headquarters, Virginia Forces, Richmond, Henrico County, Virginia, on May 27, 1861.
13. Kenneth L. Stiles, *4th Virginia Cavalry* (Lynchburg: H. E. Howard Company, 1985), 3-4.
14. Ibid., 4.
15. Ibid., 5.

The Hanover Light Dragoons and the Washington Home Guards or Fairfax Cavalry, led by Capt. E. B. Powell, were assigned to Capt. Williams C. Wickham's Squadron of Cavalry on July 20, 1861. Wickham's Squadron of Cavalry was assigned to the First Brigade, Army of the Potomac, under Brig. Gen. Milledge L. Bonham. On July 21, 1861, the Hanover Dragoons was stationed in the rear between Island and Mitchell's Fords, on the Bull Run River, under the command of Capt. Williams C. Wickham. They were held in reserve until late in the day, when they were called on to press the beginning Federal retreat.

In a letter to his wife, Lt. William Brockenbrough Newton of Wickham's Cavalry Squadron recalled that just prior to the beginning of the great battle at Manassas, Capt. Wickham ordered everyone to pack hurriedly. Lt. Newton wrote,

> . . . in ten minutes baggage was packed, tents struck, and the wagons driven to the rear, and the whole command formed in line of battle. In a few moments, the glittering bayonets of the enemy lined the neighboring hills. From the heavy signal guns being fired at intervals along our line commencing at Germantown, and stretching along to Fairfax Court House, it was evident that the enemy were endeavoring to surround our little band.[16]

The Confederate strategy was aimed to deceive the enemy into believing that the Confederates intended to stage a vigorous resistance, while in fact, they were retreating slowly to Centreville. The Federals discovered the ruse and followed cautiously. Wickham's troopers, with Capt. Del Kemper's battery, were ordered to cover the retreat.

> They were the last to leave the village, and as we went out at one end of the street, his [the enemy] column appeared at the other. We halted at this place (Centreville) about 4 o'clock in the afternoon, again made show of battle, slept until 12 o'clock at the heads of our horses, and silently left the place, the enemy's pickets being within talking distance of ours.[17]

At daybreak, Wickham's horsemen crossed Bull Run, having marched slowly to keep pace with the retreating Confederate infantry. Trooper William B. Newton reported, "We found beds of leaves in the

---

16. *Richmond Daily Whig*, July 29, 1861; Judith W. McGuire, *Diary of a Southern Refugee, During the War* (Richmond: J. W. Randolph & English, Publishers, 1899), 55-56.
17. Ibid., 56.

woods, wrapped ourselves in our blankets, and slept for an hour or two, until roused by the roar of the enemy's guns, as he opened his batteries upon our lines. For two mortal hours, shot and shell flew thick along our whole line."[18]

The Union plan, intended only to draw the fire of Confederate artillery, revealing their locations. Confederate gunners were ordered not to fire a single shot until within point blank range. After firing began, two columns of Union infantry defiled to the right and left, making two separate attacks. Newton noted, "It was indeed a beautiful sight, as they came down in perfect order, and with the steady step of veterans. They came nearer and yet nearer, and yet no shot from our guns."[19] Confederate troopers thought they were going to retreat again. But shortly "a single shot from the Washington Artillery gave the signal of death, and for half-an-hour there was nothing but a continuous sheet of flame along the right of our line. The enemy fell back, rallied and charged again with a like result; again, they rested and rushed forward; but old Virginia was true to herself, and the gallant 1st [Virginia] and 17th [Virginia] regiments met them, though twice their numbers, charged them with the bayonet, and drove them back in utter confusion."[20]

The Confederate cavalry had been held in reserve, and although within range of the artillery, took no part in this action. The cavalry had battled for four hours the previous day. The action had:

> commenced at 8 o'clock of a sweet Sabbath morning. The enemy commenced with quite a heavy cannonade upon our right, which proved to be a mere feint to distract our attention, as his main attack was directed to our left wing. At ten o'clock the enemy had crossed the river on our left, and the fight commenced in earnest. From the hill on which we stood, we could see the smoke and dust, although at the distance of several miles from the fight waged on our left. Some thought our men had fallen back; others, that the enemy were retreating. It was an hour of painful interest.[21]

Meanwhile, by early July 1861, Union Brig. Gen. Irvin McDowell had amassed five divisions numbering nearly 36,000 troops in Alexandria. McDowell's plan was to march westward in three columns, and to make a diversionary attack on the Confederate line at Bull Run with two columns, while sending the third column around the

18. Ibid.
19. Ibid., 57.
20. Ibid.
21. Ibid., 57-58.

Confederate right flank to the south, cutting the railroad to Gordonsville, and threatening the rear of the Rebel army. Successful execution of this plan would result in isolating the Confederate force at Manassas from potential support from Gen. Joseph E. Johnston's army in the Shenandoah Valley, as well as troops from the south. McDowell reasoned that the Confederates would be forced to abandon Manassas Junction and fall back forty miles to the Rappahannock River, the next defensible line in Virginia, relieving pressure on Washington. From Alexandria, the Federal commander planned to proceed with 31,000 troops through Fairfax Court House and Centreville, before sending Col. Samuel P. Heintzelman's 3rd Division across the Occoquan at Wolf Run Shoals to unleash a surprise attack on Beauregard's right flank at Manassas. McDowell's forward movement began on July 16, and the next morning his forces reached the outskirts of Fairfax Court House.[22]

Confederate General Pierre G. T. Beauregard assembled some 21,000 Confederates—Virginia regulars and militia troops—along Bull Run to oppose McDowell. The majority of Beauregard's troops deployed behind Bull Run, guarding the various fords between the Warrenton Turnpike and the railroad bridge, twenty-five miles southwest of Washington. Beauregard posted two outposts to monitor McDowell's march south. At the first outpost was Bonham's 1st Brigade, positioned at Fairfax Court House, fourteen miles west of Washington and ten miles north of Manassas. The second outpost was manned by Brig. Gen. Richard S. Ewell's 2nd Brigade, located near Sangster's Station and along Braddock Road up to its intersection with Little River Turnpike, five miles south of Bonham's position.[23]

At dawn on the 17th, Colonel Radford was informed by Bonham of the approach of McDowell's forces at Fairfax Court House. Bonham followed Beauregard's orders to fall back along the preplanned line of retreat to Centreville, then Manassas.[24]

To strengthen his rear guard, Bonham split the cavalry into three parts. He assigned a squadron, comprised of the companies of Captains Williams C. Wickham and Joel W. Flood, to report to Col. Joseph B. Kershaw, commander of the 2nd South Carolina Infantry Regiment. He ordered Lieutenant Colonel Thomas Munford and his squadron to join Col. Thomas G. Bacon's 7th South Carolina Infantry Regiment, and three of Radford's companies to cooperate with Col. E. B. Cash's 8th South Carolina Infantry Regiment. Radford reported that Colonel

22. John Hennessy, *The First Battle of Manassas* (Lynchburg, VA: H. E. Howard, 1989), 9; Longacre, *Lee's Cavalrymen*, 8.
23. Ibid., 18.
24. *OR* 2/1:457.

Munford helped lead the retreat in "perfect order and to my entire satisfaction, bringing off everything."[25]

McDowell's Union force, unopposed, gained control of Fairfax Court House sometime after 9:00 a.m. on the morning of July 17, 1861. Realizing his troops were already tired from the summer heat and the long march from Alexandria, McDowell ordered them to march slowly westward towards Centreville. They unhurriedly followed the Confederate retreat.[26]

On the night of the 17th, McDowell came up with a plan for a reconnaissance the next day to determine if a turning movement around the Confederate right would succeed. McDowell ordered Brig. Gen. Daniel Tyler to march to Centreville and give the impression that he intended to cross Bull Run at Blackburn's Ford and then move to Manassas. The reconnaissance was to be conducted by Brig. Gen. Samuel P. Heintzelman's division. McDowell wanted to turn the Confederates to the right by crossing the Occoquan at Wolf Run Shoals and then cut the Orange and Alexandria Railroad.[27]

Although McDowell expressly told Tyler to take Centreville and remain there while watching the roads to Bull Run and Warrenton, Tyler exceeded his orders. McDowell cautioned him about not bringing on a general engagement. On July 18, taking a squadron of cavalry and two light companies of Col. Israel B. Richardson's brigade, with Colonel Richardson, Tyler proceeded on a reconnaissance down the road towards Manassas Junction all the way to Blackburn's Ford on Bull Run. He only detected a battery of artillery and some pickets on the opposite side. The opposite side of the ford was, in fact, defended by Longstreet's brigade, consisting of the 1st, 11th, and 17th regiments of Virginia Volunteers, with reinforcements available. Tyler ordered up artillery support and the remainder of Richardson's brigade to feel out the enemy, setting off the general engagement he had been ordered not to start. The Union attack commenced with thirty minutes of cannon fire, followed by an assault with three thousand infantry, which Longstreet's troops repelled with difficulty. After a few minutes, the Federal forces launched a second attack, which again was repulsed by Longstreet's skirmishers. After Longstreet beat back a third attack, he took the offensive—with artillery fire from the Washington Artillery—driving the invaders back towards Centreville.[28]

On June 19, Jubal Early reported to Gen. Beauregard at Manassas and deployed his regiment, the 24th Virginia Infantry, four miles east

25. Ibid., 457–58.
26. Hennessey, *The First Battle of Manassas*, 9.
27. Ibid., 9, 12–13.
28. *OR* 2:310–12, 461–62.

of Manassas Junction, where the regiment guarded the fords of Bull Run immediately above its junction with the Occoquan. At this time, brigades had not yet been formed; but in a few days, the regiments under Beauregard's command organized into six brigades: one made up of South Carolina troops under Brig. Gen. Milledge L. Bonham; another comprised of Alabama and Louisiana troops under Brig. Gen. Richard S. Ewell; a brigade of South Carolina and Mississippi troops under Brig. Gen. D. R. Jones; a brigade of Virginia troops under Col. George H. Terrett, subsequently replaced by Brig. Gen. James Longstreet; a brigade of Virginia troops under Col. Philip St. George Cocke; and a brigade comprised of the 7th and 24th Virginia, and the 4th South Carolina Regiments under Early's command. The 4th South Carolina had been sent to Leesburg in Loudoun County and did not join Early's brigade which was subsequently replaced by the 7th Louisiana Regiment.[29]

After this organization, the troops deployed as follows: the 4th South Carolina Regiment and Maj. Chatham R. Wheat's Louisiana battalion at Leesburg under Col. Nathan Evans; Bonham's brigade at Fairfax Court House, Cocke's at Centreville, and Ewell's brigade at and near Fairfax Station, all in front of Bull Run. Meanwhile, Brig. Gen. David R. Jones's brigade encamped on the south side of the Run near the railroad, at a place called Camp Walker, Longstreet's at the Junction, and the 7th and 24th Virginia Regiments of Early's brigade, camped separately, northeast and east of the Junction, three to four miles apart. The cavalry, consisting of Colonel Radford's regiment of nine companies and several unattached companies, mainly scouted and picketed with Evans, Bonham, and Ewell. One company on Early's right watched the lower fords of the Occoquan and the landings on the Potomac below the mouth of the Occoquan. There, another company subsequently joined it.[30]

Just prior to the great battle at Manassas on July 21, General Beauregard, commander of the Army of the Potomac, promised Colonel Radford, the most senior cavalry officer, the command of all of the cavalry; but on July 16, Lt. Col. James Ewell Brown Stuart of Gen. Joseph E. Johnson's army at Winchester was appointed to the post, receiving his colonel's commission and promotion with the support of Johnston. This rejection so soured Radford that he eventually decided to leave the army upon its reorganization in April 1862.[31]

29. OR 2/1:806, 822; Jubal Early, *Autobiographical Sketch and Narrative of the War Between the States*, 3–4.
30. Ibid.
31. Munford, "Reminiscences," *Cavalry Journal*, 280.

On the eve of the first major battle of the war, Colonel Radford commanded a mixture of cavalry companies, primarily from the 30th Virginia, but also including the "Chesterfield Troop" and the "Black Horse Troop". In September these became companies B and H, respectively, of the 4th Virginia Cavalry, and some independent cavalry squadrons, such as Capt. Williams Wickham's Squadron. Radford's combination of cavalry companies was assigned to Gen. Bonham's 1st Brigade of the Confederate Army of the Potomac under Beauregard. Bonham assigned Lieutenant Colonel Munford a squadron of the "Black Horse Troop" under Capt. William H. Payne and the "Chesterfield Troop," under Capt. William B. Ball. Munford's squadron was joined the day of the 21st by the Wise Troop (Company B of the 30th Virginia), led by Capt. John S. Langhorne and the Franklin Rangers (Company D of the 30th Virginia), under Capt. Giles W. Hale. Langhorne's company, had been detailed to the Loudoun Artillery in the morning but joined Munford about 5:00 p.m.[32]

After learning of McDowell's advance on Fairfax Court House, President Davis changed his mind about not ordering Joseph E. Johnston to Manassas, and at 1:00 a.m. on July 18th, he requested Adjutant and Inspector General Samuel Cooper, the senior officer, to telegraph Johnston to move his army immediately from the Shenandoah Valley to Manassas and support Beauregard. Johnston, without presidential approval and in direct contact with Beauregard, had been preparing to leave the Valley since the 15th. He easily slipped away from the overly cautious Maj. Gen. Robert Patterson and headed for Manassas Junction. Meanwhile, the delay caused by the slow march of McDowell's army from Fairfax Court House proved crucial in allowing reinforcing of Beauregard with Johnston's Army from the Valley.[33]

Before daybreak on the 18th, as he neared Bull Run Creek and under pressure from McDowell during the retreat, Bonham fell back across Bull Run at Mitchell's Ford. Radford occupied the position between Col. Philip St. George Cooke and General Bonham. In late morning, Capt. R. B. Ayres's Union artillery battery pummeled the Confederate forces at Mitchell's Ford crossing for two hours.

While the fighting raged at Mitchell's Ford, Heintzelman's reconnaissance showed the roads to be too narrow and winding to facilitate movement of troop columns and artillery. McDowell abandoned his plan for a surprise attack on the Confederate right flank and decided instead to make a diversionary attack with Gen. Daniel Tyler's 1st Division at the Stone Bridge on the Warrenton Turnpike.

32. *OR* 2/1:534–35, 552.
33. Ibid., 478; Hennessy, *The First Battle of Manassas*, 9.

McDowell planned to turn the Confederate left with the divisions of brigadier generals David Hunter at Sudley Springs and Samuel P. Heintzelman at Poplar Ford. From here, these two divisions could march into the Confederate rear. The brigade of Col. Israel B. Richardson continued to harass the Confederates at Blackburn's Ford, preventing them from thwarting the main attack. Major General Robert Patterson had expected to tie down Johnston in the Shenandoah Valley so that reinforcements could not reach Beauregard. McDowell's plan required close coordination but failed due to poor execution by his inexperienced officers and men. Nevertheless, the Confederates, who had been planning to attack the Union left flank, found themselves at an initial disadvantage.[34]

Early on July 21, McDowell began his attack, preempting Beauregard's planned attack of that very morning. At about 5:15 a.m., Israel Richardson on the Confederate right, fired a few harassing artillery rounds across Mitchell's Ford in his planned diversionary strike. It was hoped this would prevent the Confederates there and at nearby Blackburn's Ford from reinforcing the Confederates at Stone Bridge. Bonham and Radford, under fire, remained at Mitchell's Ford, holding the position against a possible Federal attack while Longstreet, not knowing of the pending action above the Stone Bridge, crossed Blackburn's Ford after receiving his attack orders at 7:00 a.m.[35]

Meanwhile, McDowell's planned flanking maneuver of the Confederate left began late, as a result of the entanglement of troops on the Warrenton Turnpike. By taking a wider detour than originally planned, Heintzelman missed the road to Poplar Ford, where he had been assigned to cross, and ended up following Hunter all the way to Sudley. Colonel William B. Franklin's brigade, leading Heintzelman's column, did not begin crossing at Sudley Ford until late morning. Heintzelman and Hunter did not begin crossing Sudley Ford until 9:30 a.m. Tyler reached the Stone Bridge about 6:00 a.m. and began demonstrating but failed to draw an expected response from the Confederates.[36]

From a hill on the Confederate right flank, signal officer Capt. Edward Porter Alexander observed the main Union column marching toward Sudley Springs. Using signal flags, he alerted Col. Nathan Evans at the Stone Bridge. McDowell's element of surprise was lost. All that stood in the way of the advancing 18,000 Union troops (only half that number had closed Bull Run until afternoon) was Evans's brigade. Evans headed for Matthews Hill and Henry Hill to intercept

34. *OR* 2:307, 489; Hennessy, *The First Battle of Manassas*, 27.
35. Hennessey, *The First Battle of Manassas*, 35, 43,
36. Ibid., 40, 44.

the Union column with 1,100 men; several companies of the 4th South Carolina had been left at the Stone Bridge. Evans was eventually reinforced about 11:00 a.m. by Bee's brigade and Bartow's—two Georgia regiments. The resulting clash on Matthews Hill was a bloody fight in which neither side could initially prevail. The battle went back and forth until finally, about noon, the Federals drove the Confederates off the hill, forcing them to retreat to Henry Hill. Meanwhile, Beauregard had been transferring troops from his center and right to block the Federals crossing at Sudley Ford, as he and Johnston headed for the main battleground.[37]

Fortunately for the Confederates, McDowell did not press his advantage and attempt to seize the strategic ground immediately, choosing instead to bombard Henry Hill from Dogan's Ridge with the batteries of Captains James B. Rickett's Battery I, 1st U.S. Artillery, and Charles Griffin's Battery D, 5th U.S. Artillery. The Confederates on Henry Hill held on against the Federal fire, preventing the Union army from reaching the Confederates' rear. Lieutenant Newton recalled, "We [Wickham's Squadron] were temporarily attached to Radford's regiment—ours was the first company, and mine was the first platoon. On we dashed in a gallop, and as we passed within range of a battery of rifled cannon a ball was fired at us which passed between Wickham and myself, knocking up a cloud of dust . . . We were ordered up to within five hundred yards of the enemy's artillery, behind a hill which afforded some protection against their destructive fire. For one hour the fire raged with incessant fury."[38] Finally, more of Beauregard's reinforcements arrived around noon. They were met by Generals Johnston and Beauregard, who had just arrived on the field themselves. Brigadier General Thomas Jonathan Jackson headed for Henry Hill on his own volition, having heard the troops there were in trouble.[39]

Noon also brought Brig. Gen. Jackson's Virginia brigade in support of the disorganized Confederates, accompanied by Col. Wade Hampton and six companies of Hampton's Legion and several companies of Col. J.E.B. Stuart's cavalry. Some of Stuart's command had been left in the Valley to watch Patterson. Jackson posted his five regiments on the reverse slope of Henry Hill, where they were shielded from direct fire, and was able to assemble thirteen guns for the defensive line, which he posted on the crest of the hill. Meanwhile, McDowell ordered the batteries of Ricketts and Griffin to move from

37. Ibid., 45–47, 62–64.
38. *Richmond Daily Whig*, July 29, 1861; McGuire, *Diary of a Southern Refugee, During the War*, 58.
39. Hennessey, *The First Battle of Manassas*, 45–47, 62–64.

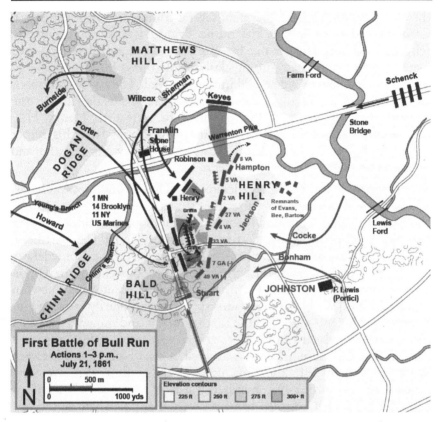

Hal Jespersen

Ridge to Henry Hill for close infantry support. Their eleven guns engaged in a fierce artillery duel against Jackson's thirteen, a mere 300 yards away. The Union pieces were now within range of the Confederate smoothbores and the predominantly rifled pieces on the Union side, which were not as effective weapons at such close ranges, with many shots fired over the heads of their targets. The battle raged on. Following Radford's orders, at about 3:00 p.m., Munford supported Colonel Radford on Gen. Thomas J. Jackson's counterattacking right flank.[40]

By 3:00 p.m., the tide of the battle shifted with Jackson's troops capturing Rickett's and Griffin's batteries on Henry Hill. The 4th Virginia regiment had taken [Governor William] Sprague's Rhode Island battery of six pieces at the point of the bayonet.[41] McDowell had two fresh brigades, one was Colonel William T. Sherman's, the other, Colonel Orlando Wilcox's brigade. McDowell was determined to reclaim his lost batteries. The fighting intensified on Henry Hill.

40. Ibid., 68–71.
41. *Richmond Daily Whig*, July 29, 1861; McGuire, *Diary of a Southern Refugee, During the War*, 60.

Finally, around 4:00 p.m., Colonel Oliver O. Howard's brigade arrived on the field after a fatiguing march. McDowell placed Major George Sykes's battalion of regulars on the west slope of Henry Hill to cover the potential withdrawal of the Federals on the hill. Realizing the futility of sending Howard against the Confederates on Henry Hill, McDowell directed him up Chinn Ridge to gain the Confederate left.[42]

Simultaneously, two of Bonham's regiments, the 2nd South Carolina under Col. Joseph Kershaw, and the 8th South Carolina, led by Colonel E. C. B. Cash, arrived and took position along the Sudley Road on the west side of Henry Hill. Other reinforcements arriving were Philip St. George Cocke's brigade and Capt. Del. Kemper's battery.[43]

Also, at this critical time Colonel Arnold Elzey's and Col. Jubal Early's brigades joined Cash and Kershaw. Johnston ordered them to attack the Union right. To the west of Sudley Road, Chinn Ridge had been occupied only briefly by Colonel Howard's brigade from Hentzelman's division. At 4:00 p.m., the two Confederate brigades that had just arrived–Early's and Kirby Smith's (now commanded by Col. Elzey after Smith was wounded)–drove Howard's brigade from Chinn Ridge. Beauregard then ordered his entire line on Henry Hill forward. This left Sykes's regulars the only organized Federal troops on the field. Driven from Chinn Ridge, Howard left the Regulars to cover the retreat. As the Union troops began withdrawing under fire, many panicked and the retreat turned into a rout.[44]

Radford soon crossed Bull Run just south of the Stone Bridge and headed for the turnpike until redirected by Johnston to head more eastward for the Cub Run bridge. Munford crossed at Ball's Ford and upon converging with Radford's forces, he found the enemy in "wild confusion" and charged, capturing more than twenty prisoners and several horses.[45]

After capturing the prisoners, Radford's and Munford's columns were met by a heavy volley of musketry, disabling four horses and slightly wounding four men. Two cannons on a hill beyond Bull Run then opened fire on the horsemen, killing Radford's brother, Captain Edmund Winston Radford of Company G of the 2nd Virginia; another officer, and five enlisted men also died. Dismounted troopers were sent after the guns. The Federals abandoned the guns and fled.[46]

---

42. Hennessey, *The First Battle of Manassas*, 74, 77, 102.
43. Ibid., 107–10.
44. Ibid., 110–11, 116.
45. *OR* 2:534; Longacre, *Lee's Cavalrymen*, 23.
46. Longacre, *Lee's Cavalrymen*, 24; *OR* 2:497, 533. Note: The Federal artillery fire probably came from guns of Capt. J. H. Carlisle's battery near Mrs. Spindle's house.

Next, Munford mistook Col. Joseph B. Kershaw's command and Capt. Del. Kemper's battery, at his rear, for the enemy. Withdrawing his command, Munford watched the mistaken 'enemy's" movements until Kemper opened fire upon the real enemy. Discovering his mistake, Munford recalled his squadron and joined Col. Kershaw. Upon Kemper's ceasing fire, Munford advanced, finding Major John Scott in command of Captain Eugene Davis's Company D, which had advanced along the turnpike to the bridge on Cub Run. Munford assumed command of the cavalry there and ordered them to dismount, while sending Captain William H. Payne's Black Horse Troop to Col. Kershaw for assistance. As soon as the captured cannons on Munford's side of the creek were hitched up, Maj. Scott, without consulting Munford, marched off with his Company D troops and the captured guns. Munford continued with the Black Horse and Chesterfield Troops until five more pieces of cannon, caissons, and forges were all hitched up. Munford later boasted as a result of his performance, that he "had the honor of delivering to his Excellency the President of the Confederate States ten rifled guns, their caissons, and forty-six horses."[47]

An ensuing attempt by Gen. Joseph Johnston to intercept the retreating Union troops from his right flank, using the brigades of Generals Bonham and James Longstreet, was a failure. The two commanders squabbled with each other; and when Bonham's men received some artillery fire from the Union rear guard and found that Gen. Israel B. Richardson's brigade blocked the road to Centreville, Bonham called off the pursuit.[48]

The Confederate victory of July 21 was followed by a day-long hard rain as Union troops passed through Fairfax Court House during the night strewing the roads with clothing, food, arms, and camp equipage. McDowell's men, along with panic-stricken northern civilians who had come down to watch the battle, continued their frantic retreat in the direction of Arlington and Washington. Both armies were sobered by the fierce fighting and high casualties, and realized that the war was going to be much longer and bloodier than either had anticipated.[49]

On the morning on July 22, 1861, the Hanover Light Dragoons was ordered to follow and observe the enemy, pick up stragglers, and secure relinquished property in the vicinity of Centreville, Virginia. They were accompanied by the 3rd South Carolina Infantry, the 7th

47. *OR* 2/1:525, 534–35.
48. Ibid., 476, 498.
49. Hennessy, *The First Battle of Manassas*, 121-22; William Marvel, *Mr. Lincoln Goes to War* (Boston, 2006), 149.

South Carolina Infantry, and a section of the Richmond Battalion Howitzers, 1st Company. These troops arrived at Centreville at 10 a.m. the same day.

The Hanover Light Dragoons was ordered to Centreville at 12 p.m. on July 23, 1861, and arrived at there at 2 p.m. the same day.[50] They were then ordered to Vienna, Fairfax County, Virginia, at 8 p.m. on July 23, 1861, and arrived at Camp Gregg, via Germantown, Fairfax County, Virginia, on the morning on July 24, 1861.

On July 25, 1861, the Organization of the First Brigade, First Corps, Army of the Potomac, occurred: Brigadier General M. L. Bonham, Confederate States Army, commanding; 2nd South Carolina Infantry, Colonel J. B. Kershaw; 3rd South Carolina Infantry, Colonel J. H. Williams; 7th South Carolina Infantry, Colonel T. G. Bacon; 8th South Carolina Infantry, Colonel E. B. C. Cash; 30th Virginia Cavalry: Hanover Light Dragoons and Washington's Home Guards or Fairfax Cavalry, Captain W. C. Wickham, Companies A, C, G, and H, Colonel R. C. W. Radford; Alexandria Artillery, Captain Del Kemper.[51]

After the first battle of Manassas the Hanover Light Dragoons was stationed at Mitchell's Ford, on the Bull Run River, in the evening on July 21, 1861. The Hanover Light Dragoons was stationed at Camp Gregg, Vienna, Fairfax County, Virginia, between July 26-31, 1861.

On July 22, Davis, Johnston, Beauregard, and Colonel T. J. Jordan (adjutant for Beauregard) held a conference at Beauregard's headquarters in Manassas to discuss the battle and what should be done subsequently. One option, that of crossing the Potomac and taking the fight to Washington City, was discussed; but Beauregard advised against it, warning that the crossing would be perilous due to the strong Federal fortifications along the river. The truth was that these fortifications did not even exist and were not even begun until General George B. McClellan was named commander of Washington and troops within the city on July 26.

Writing to his wife Lucy from Col. Cocke's brigade headquarters at Fairfax CH on September 1, 1861, Wickham recalled the recent visit to his camp by his younger brother Henry and his father William. He told Lucy, "tell Papa that we have gotten rid of the yellow jackets by our change of camp ground, and that if he comes up again, he will

---

50. Special Orders No.149, Paragraph I, Headquarters, Army of the Potomac, Camp Pickens, Manassas Junction, Prince William County, Virginia, dated July 22, 1861.
51. Special Orders No.169, Paragraph III, Headquarters, First Corps, Army of the Potomac, Camp Pickens, Manassas Junction, Prince William County, Virginia, on July 25, 1861.

escape being stung." Wickham stated, "I am still attached to Cocke's brigade and hope to remain so as it leaves me in a much more independent position than when attached to a regiment. I don't know how long it will be the case though. Col C. and myself will endeavor to make it permanent." Wickham related he now had his own blacksmith shop set up. He told Lucy that his activities were mostly confined to drilling and that she need not have any apprehension of danger to him. He asked her to have a suit made up for his manservant, Robin. He related that when his father visited, he didn't seem to appreciate the comforts of our military establishment. He stated that things are so much more comfortable now that they had moved their camp, and that the men "rejoice ourselves as living in a rather princely style."[52]

Even though Radford's 30th Virginia had been the first regiment mustered into service in September 1861, Stuart's regiment was designated the 1st Virginia Cavalry. In October, Radford's regiment was redesigned the 2nd Virginia Cavalry. It was the custom of the military to have the senior commanding officer assigned to the 1st Battalion, 1st Regiment, 1st Brigade, etc. As Stuart was promoted over Radford, it would be humiliating to have a commanding officer assigned to the 2nd Cavalry, and a subservient officer of lesser rank in charge of the 1st Cavalry. A few days later, Col. William E. Jones took over command of the 1st Virginia. Radford was infuriated and never forgave Stuart for preempting the naming of his regiment as the 1st Virginia. More likely, the beef was not the Cavalry designation, but Radford's being passed over as a senior colonel, with a junior colonel's being promoted.[53]

On September 5, 1861, Williams wrote Lucy from Fairfax Court House, in part, "I have written today resigning my seat in the Convention. And in the Senate and think I have taken my final leave of all political life, at which I know you will rejoice."[54]

On August 21, 1861, Beverly H. Robertson was appointed colonel, Provisional Army of Virginia.[55] On September 7, 1861, Colonel

52. Williams C. Wickham to Lucy Wickham, September 1, 1861, Wickham Family Papers, UVA. Robin was a trusted Wickham family slave, probably a son of the Hickory Hill household butler, Robin Saunders. Robin was trusted to travel, unaccompanied with passage paper signed by Wickham, by train from camp to Hickory Hill and back to deliver or retrieve packages or supplies. This Robin is not listed as one of 56 contrabands leaving with Union troops after a raid on Hickory Hill in June of 1863.
53. Munford, "Reminiscences," *Cavalry Journal*, vol. 4 (Sept. 1891), 279.
54. Williams C. Wickham to Lucy Wickham, September 5, 1861, Wickham Family Papers, UVA.
55. Special Orders No.303, Paragraph III, Headquarters, First Corps, Army of the Potomac, Camp Pickens, Manassas Junction, Prince William County, Virginia.

Beverly H. Robertson was assigned command the 4th Virginia Cavalry, disappointing Wickham.[56] Captain Williams C. Wickham, Hanover Light Dragoons, was appointed lieutenant colonel, 4th Virginia Cavalry, on September 11, 1861.

The 4th Virginia Cavalry Regiment completed its organization at Sangster's Cross Roads, Prince William County, Virginia, in September 1861. Its members were recruited from the counties of Prince William, Chesterfield, Madison, Culpeper, Powhatan, Goochland, Hanover, Fauquier, and Buckingham, and also the city of Richmond. The regiment was then under the command of Colonel Beverly Robertson, Lieutenant Colonel Williams C. Wickham, and Major William Henry Fitzhugh Payne.

Williams C. Wickham was named Lt. Colonel of the 4th Virginia Cavalry in September 1861.

(Shannon Pritchard)

McKinney's Company, under the command of Captain P. W. McKinney, was accepted in state or Confederate service at Buckingham Courthouse, Buckingham County, Virginia, on March 10, 1862, and was ordered to Richmond, Henrico County, Virginia, on March 19, 1862. The company was mustered in Confederate service for three years or the war at Richmond, Henrico County, Virginia, by Second Lieutenant W. H. Porter, infantry, Confederate States Army, on April 27, 1862, and was stationed at Camp of Instruction or Lee, Hermitage Agricultural Fairgrounds, between the Richmond, Fredericksburg &

56. Ibid.

Potomac Railroad and Deep Run Turnpike, two miles northwest of Capitol, Capitol Hill, Richmond, Henrico County, Virginia, on May 17, 1862. On May 23, 1862, McKinney's Company was assigned to the 4th Virginia Cavalry, Company K.[57]

On September 24, 1861, Stuart received a promotion to brigadier general in charge of all mounted forces; his appointment was confirmed in early December. Stuart now commanded all cavalry protecting the Alexandria Line. By October, Stuart commanded about 2,400 troopers, and as additional companies and regiments were added over the next few months, the number of horsemen increased rapidly, especially after including the newly created horse artillery.[58]

The battle of First Manassas was followed by eight months without a major battle in Virginia. Confederate cavalry was headquartered at "Camp Frontier," named after their region of responsibility, the front line of the Potomac River. In Brig. Gen. Irvin McDowell's Union army, discipline broke down and morale sank so low that it became impossible to undertake another offensive. President Lincoln called for 500,000 new volunteers for the army, and thousands of new recruits immediately began pouring into Washington at a rate of about ten thousand per week. Major General George B. McClellan, who had won a series of victories in western Virginia, replaced McDowell on July 26, 1861.[59]

The 4th Virginia Cavalry was officially formed on September 4, 1861. By September 19, the regiment assembled at Sangster's Cross Roads in Prince William County. Its members were recruited from Prince William, Chesterfield, Madison, Culpeper, Powhatan, Goochland, Hanover, Fauquier, and Buckingham Counties along with the city of Richmond.

The 4th Virginia Cavalry, organized as of September 27, 1861: Colonel Beverly H. Robertson, Lieutenant Colonel Williams C. Wickham, Major William H. Payne; Company A, Prince William Cavalry, Captain W. W. Thornton; Company B, Chesterfield Light Dragoons, Captain William B. Ball; Company C, Madison Cavalry or "Invincibles," Captain W. Thomas; Company D, Little Fork Cavalry, Captain R. S. Utterback; Company E, Powhatan Troop, Captain J. F. Lay; Company F, Goochland Light Dragoons, Captain A. M. Hobson; Company G, Hanover Light Dragoons, Captain W. B. Newton;

57. Special Orders No.118, Paragraph VI, Adjutant & Inspector General's Office, Richmond, Henrico County, Virginia.
58. McClellan, *Stuart's Cavalry*, 42; Longacre, *Lee's Cavalrymen*, 54–55.
59. *Battles and Leaders*, vol. 2:160; James A. Rawley, *Turning Points of the Civil War* (Lincoln: University of Nebraska Press, 1966), 58.

Company H, Black Horse Troop, Captain R. Randolph; Company I, Governor's Guards, Captain F. W. Chamberlayne.[60]

On October 27, Wickham first met Brigadier General James E.B. Stuart, writing Lucy, "I have just made the acquaintance of Gen. Stuart, who has command of all the cavalry and am very much pleased with him. He seems very intelligent and prompt and I have no doubt is one of the most efficient officers in the service."[61]

On November 3, 1861, Wickham wrote Lucy:

> We shall remain in the same uncertainty as to future operations and my opinion that there will be no fighting on this line is unchanged. I am getting vey restless at the inactivity of the army and am fearing that there is just want of ability in the higher departments of the Government. You cannot tell how comfortable I feel at the reflection that I have cut loose from politics and am free from all commissions. . . . The more I see of things the greater I think the folly and criminality of those who produced it, but there is no help now for I[me] but to fight it through . . . for the North it is a war for plunder and conquest. I cannot help hoping however (although I see no indication of it as yet), that the light of reason will show itself before long and that the people of both sections will see that they are committing "mutual suicide" and wasting their best resources in our unnatural strife that will result in the ruin of all and bring matters to our accommodation.[62]

Wickham liked Robertson but worried about his possible negative effects on the regiment, writing, "While I get on perfectly with [Colonel Beverly] Robertson and like him very much, yet I fear that an unfortunate habit that he has of complaining instead of making the best of everything and trusting to good temper and a willing discharge of duty to bring things right has impaired his influence and standing at Head Quarters and will operate against the regiment."[63]

---

60. Company G, by Special Orders No.248, Adjutant & Inspector General's Office, Richmond, Henrico County, Virginia, on September 4, 1861. Captain W. C. Wickham, Hanover Light Dragoons, was appointed lieutenant colonel, 4th Virginia Cavalry, on September 11, 1861, and First Lieutenant W. B. Newton, 4th Virginia Cavalry, Company G, was appointed captain, 4th Virginia Cavalry, Company G, on September 27, 1861.
61. Williams C. Wickham to Lucy Wickham, October 27, 1861, Wickham Family Papers, UVA.
62. Ibid., November 3, 1861, Wickham Family Papers, UVA.
63. Ibid.

The 4th Virginia Cavalry fought little for the remainder of the summer and fall. Captain William Ball led companies B, C, and E in a fight at Leesburg on October 21. During the remainder of the fall and winter, the 4th Virginia picketed along the Potomac, observing the enemy's movements. Wickham tried to reassure his wife, Lucy, that he was being careful in the fulfillment of his duties. Lucy always worried about his safety. On November 21, 1861, Williams wrote Lucy:

> You need not have any apprehension about my safety in any of these expeditions. I have a great facility for learning the topography of a country and the first thing I do when I go into a new part of it is first with the map and then by riding to make myself perfectly familiar with it so that it would be improbable for them to cut me off and then to use every precaution to ensure the safety of my men taking always forward only such numbers as can be best used for the purpose that I may have intended. The consequence is that whilst I have done more scouting and probably obtained more information of the enemy than anyone in the service, I have never had the slightest accident to occur to any one in any of my expeditions.[64]

On November 13, Williams wrote Lucy, telling her to instruct their son, Henry T. Wickham, who was hoping to become a soldier, "nobody can be made a good solder unless he is good humored. And ready to do pleasantly whatever he has to do and as he expects to be a soldier if the war lasts as long as I predicted, he must practice it in all things in advance."[65]

Wickham wrote Lucy from Camp Frontier in mid-December:

> We are still here in a state of uncertainty as to out winter assignments. I see that the convention has ordered the Governor in the reorganization of this militia to organize regiments of cavalry and I should like very much to get one of those and have them in camp for some time somewhere in our part of the country to instruct it and there take it into the field. If I could get a full regiment of cavalry, I would rather have it than any command in the army and I would make it a grand one, for I think my genius lays in that line. Rather than all that though I would prefer to be at home with you all, attending to our

64. Williams C. Wickham to Lucy Wickham, November 21, 1861, Wickham Family Papers, UVA.
65. Ibid., November 13, 1861, Wickham Family Papers, UVA.

own matters and leaving to them who made the fights the settlement of it. Whatever may be the result of this contest, I rejoice it is by no means certain, slave property is bound to be very insecure hereafter in Virginia and in probably all States. For years to come fanatics must be extremely treacherous, and I see anything but a prosperous future for the country in our day.

We had a grand display of cavalry day before yesterday near Centreville, and as [Colonel Beverly] Robertson avoids appearing under General Stuart whenever he can, having been his senior in the U. S. Army. I had charge of our regiment and it was decidedly the best on the ground.[66]

Wickham was unhappy about what he viewed as insufficient support of Virginia's soldiers by the Virginia Legislature. He drafted a legislative bill, "An act for the better organization of the active forces of Virginia," to improve conditions, and sent it to Confederate commander General Joseph E. Johnston. Johnston like the idea, and the bill was forwarded.

Wickham's bill proposed:

...all the companies of Virginia Volunteers now in the services of the Confederate States, whether artillery, cavalry, or infantry, shall be retained in the active services of the State, and shall continue to form a portion of the quota of Virginia in the Armies of the Confederate States, subject to such laws of the Confederate States as relate to the militia of the several states; On the day on which the term for which any such company was mustered into active service shall expire one fourth of the enlisted men of such company shall be discharged from the company and shall not be subject to any compulsory military duty for the twelve months next succeeding the day of such discharge. The men to be discharged shall be selected by the captain of their company with the approval of the colonel of their regiment with a proper regard to the necessities of the families of the men of the company; Hereafter, every Virginia company in active service shall consist of not less than one-hundred rank and file; for the purposes of supplying the deficiency that will be produced by the said discharge and for the purpose of filling the ranks of the several companies o the minimum number herein required, the drafts shall be

66. Ibid., Dec, 14, 1861, Wickham Family Papers, UVA.

made on the militia of the Commonwealth in the following manner. Immediately upon the passage of this act, captains of companies shall make requisitions to be approved by the colonel of their regiment and by the colonel to which the company belongs upon the Adjutant General of this Commonwealth for so as many as may be necessary to replace those to be discharge.[67]

Wickham had performed well in 1861. The next year brought challenges, including being wounded twice and captured as a prisoner.

---

67. Virginia Museum of History and Culture, Wickham Family Papers. Most of the elements of Wickham's proposed bill were changed by the Virginia Legislature.

Chapter Four

1862: Twice wounded
and taken prisoner

". . . our loss being slight, except in the wound inflicted upon
Lieutenant-Colonel Wickham, the country will be for a time deprived
of the services of a brave and zealous soldier and a most gallant and
meritorious officer."

–JEB Stuart reporting the action

at Fort Magruder.

On January 8, 1862, Williams wrote Lucy, "You cannot tell how
earnestly I long for the conclusion of this war that I may be again
permanently at home where I had a thousand times rather be than
anywhere else. He also wrote that his manservant, Robin, "has built a
built a wonderful shelter for the horses in their winter camp." He also
wrote his son, Henry, assuring him that the family horses were being
treated well. Williams told Henry:

> Robin has put up a capital shelter for Hal and Frank and
> they are almost as comfortable as if in a real stable. They
> are fat and sleek and ready for any work that they have to
> do. They are close to my heart and if I go out and say,
> 'Robin, have you fed the horses,' if he has not, both begin
> to neigh, but if he has not, they don't say a word; they are
> fine horses and I am very fond of them. They are all that
> I have here to pet and are very glad to have me pet them.[1]

By January 25, 1862, Colonel Beverly Roberson had moved the
regiment to Camp Ewell, two miles south of Manassas. Wickham, after
a short furlough, returned to Camp Ewell on January 29.

On February 4, 1862, Wickham wrote his wife from camp Ewell:

> I am making out very well, but am very tired of it and
> wish most sincerely I could get out of the army and be at
> home with you all. The bill in support of Virginia forces

---

1. Williams Wickham to Henry Wickham, January 8, 1862, Wickham Family
Papers, UVA.

[that Wickham originally summited to the Legislature] as passed by the Senate will be found utterly insufficient and will place us in the most crippled position in the spring campaign. I hope however that the House may improve it; if they do not and I find that my   anticipations of the evil consequences it will have on our army are about to be realized, I shall, if possible, get out of it as I have not the slightest idea of sacrificing myself in the useless effort to relieve the errors of such contemptable legislators.[2]

In mid-February, Wickham was on detached court martial duty which lasted several days. The regiment suffered through a snowstorm. Wickham's horse had a badly-hurt foot and Wickham felt that, in all probability, it was unrideable for two or three months. He wrote Lucy, "I have him in a very comfortable stable, but the poor fellow suffers very much with pain."[3] He also told Lucy that he was uneasy about the upcoming reorganization of his regiment that was part of the pending overall cavalry reorganization. Williams wrote:

[Beverly] Robertson by a most unfortunate habit of temper that he has, has made himself very much disliked by some of the companies, although he has provided better for his regiment in every respect and gotten more indulgences for his men than any other colonel in the services, and the consequence is that I am afraid that a kind of conflict between the State law and the Confederate law will be used to break up some of our companies. As it is decidedly the best regiment in the service, I should regret it very much, but it would offer me the opportunity of retiring from the service, which would suit my wishes.[4]

Wickham also told Lucy, "They are making another batch of democratic Generals. I wish most heartily that the democrats would have all the fighting on their hands. I am of another opinion that those who make the quarrels should be the ones to fight the battles."[5] Continuing, Williams told Lucy that Payne had returned to take his share of the work. He mentioned that "Nelson suits very well as a

2. Williams C. Wickham to Lucy Wickham, February 4, 1862, Wickham Family Papers, Virginia Museum of History and Culture.
3. Ibid., February 15, 1862, VMHC.
4. Ibid.
5. Ibid.

cook and makes my meals more comfortable and seems very well satisfied."[6]

Acting as rear guard for Lee's army, on March 9, the cavalry occupied Manassas. After burning the stores at Manassas, Stuart's horsemen followed Lee's army to the Rappahannock and picketed the front of the Blue Ridge to the Potomac River.[7]

With March coming to a close, the Confederates hurried to the Virginia lower peninsula to face the Union forces gathering at Fort Monroe. The bulk of Confederate forces travelled south, while the 4th Virginia kept vigilant for Union forces along the northern frontier. On March 28, Northern forces moved south along the Orange & Alexandria Railroad. Stuart ordered his cavalry to observe, but not bring on, a general engagement until the Confederate withdrawal across the Rappahannock had been completed. The next day, the Union forces continued south to Bealeton Station. As the Federal battle line formed one mile north of the station, Stuart ordered the 4th Virginia under Colonel Beverly Robertson to flank the Union left, threaten it, and then withdraw across the river crossing. The 4th held the Union forces before Bealeton Station until the evacuation had been completed. The 4th then crossed the river to the safety of Brig. Gen. Richard Ewell's troops four miles down the line. After the burning of the span crossing the river, the Union forces withdrew to Warrenton on March 29. Stuart ordered the 4th to join Colonel William E. Jones's cavalry in pursuit. The chase ended with 4th, 2nd, and 6th Virginias capturing some 50 Union stragglers.[8]

After resting in Richmond in early April, the 4th Virginia Cavalry, numbering 540 effectives, was ordered to Yorktown. Colonel Robertson set up camp about halfway between Yorktown and Williamsburg. Here, the regiment remained until the end of April. On April 2, the regiment was reorganized, and the unpopular Robertson was not re-elected, but was replaced by Lieutenant Colonel Williams C. Wickham. The 4th was one of the largest regiments in Stuart's cavalry corps.[9]

The Peninsula campaign was a major Union operation launched on the Virginia lower peninsula from March through July 1862, the first large-scale offensive in the Eastern Theater. The operation, commanded by Maj. Gen. George B. McClellan, was an amphibious

---

6. Ibid. Nelson was another Wickham family slave. He is listed as one of 56 contrabands who left with Union troops after a raid on Hickory Hill in June 1863 (Reference: Wickham Family Papers, VMHC).
7. Stiles, *4th Virginia Cavalry*, 9.
8. Ibid., 9-10.
9. Ibid., 10.

assault intended to capture the Confederate capital of Richmond by moving up the lower peninsula from the eastern tip near the entrance to Hampton Roads to Richmond, about 75 miles northwest.

The Confederate Army of the Peninsula was commanded by Brig. Gen. John B. Magruder, a popular leader who had held back Union forces in the area beginning in 1861. At the time that McClellan's Army of the Potomac arrived at Fort Monroe in early 1862, only Magruder's 13,000 men faced them on the Peninsula. The Confederate strategy of the early portion of the Peninsula Campaign became one of delaying, providing vital time for defenses to be built outside Richmond. General Magruder succeeded in the early stages of the Peninsula Campaign, partially by using elaborate ruse tactics to appear to have a much larger force than he actually had. Magruder had his troops marching back and forth behind the lines with great fanfare to appear to be a larger force. Magruder's efforts appeared to have the desired effect, as the ever-cautious McClellan moved very slowly with his forces, which were substantially larger than those of the defenders. Meanwhile, a long defensive line was being built outside Richmond.

As the Peninsula campaign developed, Confederate General Joseph E. Johnston moved his army east to reinforce Magruder and meet the challenge presented by McClellan's forces. The resulting battle of Yorktown lasted from April 5 until May 4, 1862. During this time, the Union forces were held at the Warwick Line across the peninsula from the James River to the York River.

Following the Confederate withdrawal from their Yorktown position, Maj. Gen. George B. McClellan was not prepared to mount an immediate pursuit with his entire force from the siege lines he had occupied for nearly a month. Initially, he was able to send forward only a portion of his army, led by the Third Corps of Samuel P. Heitzelman, to follow Gen. Joseph E. Johnston's Confederates. Heitzelman's divisions, led by Brig. Gens. Joseph Hooker and Phil Kearny, made contact with Johnston's army four miles southeast of Williamsburg. Hooker assaulted Fort Magruder, an earthen fortification alongside the Williamsburg Road but was repulsed. Confederate counterattacks, directed by Lieut. Gen. James Longstreet, threatened to overwhelm Hooker's men until Kearny's division arrived to stabilize the Federal left. A brigade of Brig. Gen. Darius N. Couch's IV Corps arrived to support Hooker's right. Brig. Gen. Winfield S. Hancock's brigade moved to threaten the Confederate left flank, occupying two abandoned redoubts. The Confederates counterattacked Hancock unsuccessfully, but his localized success was not exploited. Johnston continued his withdrawal up the peninsula that evening.

From its camp at Blow's Mill on Skiff Creek, the 4th Virginia covered the Confederate withdrawal to Williamsburg. The movement began on the evening of May 3. The weather was cold for the season, and the incessant rain hampered all movements. The 4th Virginia covered the Telegraph Road on the Confederate left with two other cavalry units.[10]

Meanwhile, discovering that the Confederates had retreated, McClellan ordered General George Stoneman's cavalry to pursue. Wickham made his stand four miles outside of Williamsburg on the Telegraph Road between King's and Queen's Creek. Wickham held the Federals back until an artillery barrage forced his withdrawal. Around 3 p.m. on May 4, Confederate horsemen had regrouped near Fort Magruder.[11]

The "Williamsburg Line" was a line of defensive fortifications across the Peninsula east of Williamsburg, anchored by College Creek, a tributary of the James River, on the south and Queen's Creek, a tributary of the York River on the north. A series of 14 redoubts were built along the line, with Fort Magruder (Redoubt Number 6) at the center at a key location. Redoubt No. 6, near the center of the Williamsburg Line, became known as Fort Magruder. It was shaped as an elongated pentagon, with walls fifteen-feet high and nine-feet thick. The earthworks were protected by a dry moat nine-feet deep. It mounted eight guns.

Fort Magruder, actually an elaborate earthen fortification, was named for General Magruder. It was the keystone of the Williamsburg Line—a third cross peninsula set of works located west of the Warwick Line; the second, was anchored by Mulberry Island, the Warwick River, and Yorktown.

In the early morning hours of May 4, the Confederates quietly withdrew from the Warwick Line, and, electing not to defend the Williamsburg Line, withdrew beyond it toward Richmond. The Williamsburg Line would be critical, albeit for a short time, in delaying a pursuit by the Union Army, giving the Confederates time to move west on the poor roads of the sandy terrain. About 24 hours later, McClellan discovered the move, and troops were soon moving toward Williamsburg on the only two main roads west–the Lee's Mill and Yorktown-Williamsburg Roads, which converged about 600 six-hundred-feet south-east of Fort Magruder.

On May 4, 1862, Fort Magruder was a major point of the first heavy conflict of the Peninsula campaign. The point at which the fort

10. Ibid., 10. Fort Magruder was named for Confederate General John B. Magruder.
11. Ibid.

was built had the strategic topographical advantage of being a very narrow piece of land, bounded on the west by Tutters Neck Pond and on the east by Cubb's Creek, restricting access to the town of Williamsburg beyond.

This fort was the focus of a concerted battle that raged for two days before Johnston disengaged his defenders. McClellan had been delayed long enough for Lee to assemble his defensive forces around Richmond. Wickham's 4th Virginia Cavalry, screening Confederate withdrawal, clashed with Union advance troops-George Stoneman's brigade, from Yorktown.

Confederate Gen. John B. Magruder intended to use the Williamsburg Line if forced to abandon the Warwick-Yorktown Line. When Gen. Joseph E. Johnston assumed command of the Confederate forces blocking Union Gen. George B. McClellan's advance from Fort Monroe toward Richmond, however, Johnston ignored the line and ordered a retreat up the Peninsula to the Confederate capital. On the evening of May 3, 1862, the Confederates withdrew from the Warwick-

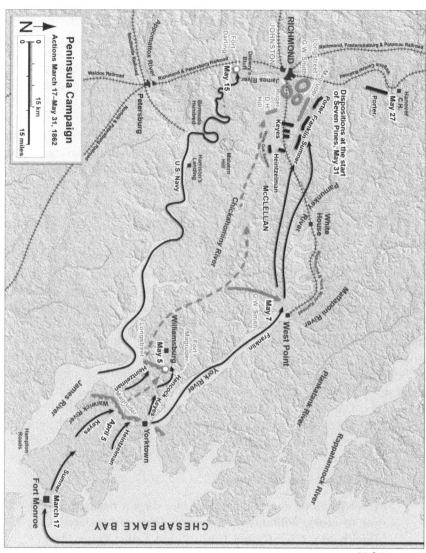

Hal Jespersen

Yorktown defenses in heavy rain and on muddy roads. When McClellan realized that the fortifications had been abandoned, he sent Gen. Edwin V. Sumner in pursuit. The Confederate rear guard, Gen. James Longstreet's division, had to slow the Federals and allow the Confederate artillery and wagon trains to advance toward Richmond.

General J.E.B. Stuart's cavalry watched for pursuing Federal troops. On May 4, cavalry engagements occurred between Williamsburg and Yorktown. A Confederate later recalled, "The roads were long strings of guns, wagons, and ambulances, mixed in with infantry, artillery and cavalry, splashing and bogging through the darkness in a

.river of mud, with frequent long halts when some stalled vehicles blocked the road."[12]

Stuart concentrated his strength on the Confederate left under Lt. Col. W. C. Wickham's 4th Virginia Cavalry, which clashed with Union Gen. George Stoneman's cavalry, including four batteries of horse artillery, along the Yorktown Road. Philip St. George Cooke, Stuart's father-in-law, commanded a Federal battery. When Stoneman detached Gen. William H. Emory to cut off a portion of the Confederate cavalry, Stuart and his horsemen became separated from the Southern forces. Stuart rode along the beach on the James River and then galloped up Quarterpath Road to rejoin the Confederate army.[13]

Two miles from Williamsburg, at the junction of the Yorktown and Lee's Mill roads, the advance of Brig. Gen. Phillip St. George Cooke's Command discovered a strong earthwork flanked by redoubts and manned by several regiments of Confederates about three o'clock in the afternoon. Cooke's force consisted of the 1st and 6th U.S. Cavalry regiments and Capt. Horatio G. Gibson's Battery (Company G, 3rd U.S. Artillery). The area was ill-suited to deploy from the march, with thick forest and marshy ground; but General Cooke ordered the deployment of Gibson's battery and the 1st U.S. Cavalry to attack the position. Captain John Savage's right-flank platoon had located a track through the woods which led to the Confederate left flank. The 6th U.S. Cavalry, under Major Lawrence Williams, was ordered to make a demonstration down this road to prevent the enemy flanking Union forces on their right side. Stoneman deployed the remainder of his force in a clearing a half-mile to the rear.[14]

The Charlotte Democrat reported:

> **In order to protect the Confederate wagon trains that had yet to cross Williamsburg, Joseph Johnston ordered Col. Wickham's 4th Virginia Cavalry and Col. Lucius Davis's 10th Virginia Cavalry and the 1st Company of Richmond Howitzers to position themselves as reinforcements. Wickham moved to the right of Fort Magruder, while Davis moved to the left, while a section of the Richmond Howitzers was positioned in an open field in front of the redoubts on either side of the fort.**[15]

---

12. Bill Coughlin, August 10, 2008. Woodland Park, New Jersey.
13. Bill Coughlin of North Arlington, New Jersey, August 10, 2008.
14. *OR* 11/1:424-27.
15. *Charlotte Democrat*, May 20, 1862.

George Stoneman arrived on the scene and quickly decided that the Confederates had too much artillery and infantry support and that his lack of infantry support made an attack by him futile, in his estimation. "I deemed it worse than useless to try to hold our position at the junction of the roads in front of strong earthworks and overwhelming force," Stoneman reported. Instead, he ordered his men to "withdraw and take up a defensive position."[16]

As soon as the Union cavalry began falling back, Wickham and the 4th Virginia charged the 1st U. S. Cavalry's rear guard. Captain Benjamin "Grimes" Davis wheeled a squadron about, countercharging Wickham, driving him and his regiment back.[17]

Amidst Wickham's cavalry charge near Williamsburg on May 4, 1862, during the battle of Fort Magruder, Colonel Wickham was severely wounded. During a hand-to-hand struggle while mounted, the 4th Virginia's regimental flag was captured by the 1st U.S. Cavalry. Colonel Wickham received a severe saber thrust through his side. Bugler Daniel F. Ball came to Colonel Wickham's aid, striking, knocking off-balance, and deflecting the attempted fatal wound aimed at Wickham by Federal trooper Lt. Col. William N. Grier of the 1st U.S. Cavalry. Though wounded, Wickham remained saddled until all was secure.[18] He was probably then taken to Williamsburg for treatment before moving with the army the following day heading back to Richmond. He was then sent home to Hickory Hill for a long recuperation. He did not serve again until June.

Stuart reported on the fight, "our loss being slight, except that in the wound inflicted upon Lieutenant-Colonel Wickham, the country will be for a time deprived of the services of a brave and zealous soldier and a most gallant and meritorious officer."[19]

Near 7 p.m., Brig. Gen. Winfield Hancock's advancing troops made contact with the Confederates at Fort MaGruder. As firing began, and with virtually no infantry, General George Stoneman proceeded forward, attacking with cavalry and mobile artillery under the command of Capt. Horatio Gibson. Wickham ordered his cavalry to charge, to the sound of cheers from nearby Confederates-Gibson's battery, which forced the Union to abandon their guns. The 1st U.S.

16. Adolfo Ovies, *The Boy Generals: George Custer, Wesley Merritt, and the Cavalry of the Army of the Potomac* (El Dorado Hills, CA: Savis Beatie, 2021), 60; *OR* 11/3:133, part1:423-27.
17. Ibid.
18. Carol Kettenburg Dubbs, *Defend This Old Town, Williamsburg During the Civil War* (Baton Rouge: LSU Press, 2002), 82. As severe as Wickham's near fatal wound was, I doubt that he stayed in the saddle until the day was over. I have been unable to find another source on this matter.
19. *OR* 23/1:443. Stuart feared that Wickham's wound may be mortal.

Cavalry, sent to protect the retreating bluecoats, rode straight into the Black Horse cavalry. Troopers from both sides clashed in hand-to-hand combat.[20]

Wickham turned to rally his troopers when Lt. Col. William N. Grier, 1st U.S. Cavalry, stabbed Wickham in his side. At the same moment, "bugler Daniel F. Ball partially slashed Grier, wounding him slightly and knocking him off balance," thereby affecting Grier's saber thrust, likely saving Wickham's life. Wickham remained "on the field in his saddle until it was evident no more duty was required of him against the enemy."[21] The 1st U.S. Cavalry captured the 4th Virginia Cavalry's flag. It was actually captured by one of Gibson's artillerymen, who was then accidentally sabered by one of the 1st U.S. Cavalry's troopers, who then claimed the flag. As the battle continued, Wickham was probably carried into Williamsburg to have his severe wound treated, most likely at one of the hospitals located in churches or private homes. The poor conditions of the roads back to Richmond precluded carrying the wounded via wagons. Due to the severity of his wound, Wickham was probably moved, with other wounded soldiers, to the wharf at King's Mill on the James for evacuation to Richmond via river transport.[22]

Major William H. Payne replaced the wounded Wickham on the battlefield. The next day, on May 5 near Fort Magruder, Payne was severely wounded through his jaw, throwing him from his horse. As Payne's troopers began retreating, cavalry private Dr. Edmund S. Pendleton observed that Payne was bleeding severely and would likely bleed to death. Dr. Pendleton rushed to assist Payne amid heavy enemy fire. He dragged Major Payne behind a tree, and "thrusting his fingers into his mouth, clamped a severed artery."[23] The two soldiers lay flat on the ground between two enemy firings, the air overhead so filled with bullets "that one could have caught a hatful by holding it up," Payne later recalled.[24] Payne was taken by ambulance into Williamsburg for surgery. Payne was then captured and taken to the

---

20. Robert Houghtalen, *I Am a Good Ol' Rebel: A Biography and Civil War Account of Confederate* (Bloomington, IN: AuthorHouse, 2016), 12.

21. *OR* 11/1:443. It is unlikely that Wickham remained on the field until he was no longer required there. His wound was likely too severe.

22. *OR* 11/1:444. The next day, Payne was seriously wounded in the face; William Nelson Pendleton, *Memoirs of William Nelson Pendleton, D.D.* (Philadelphia, J. B. Lippincott, 1893), 183.

23. Carol Kettenburg Dubbs, *Defend This Old Town, Williamsburg During the Civil War*, 123.

24. Ibid., 123, 125; *OR* 11/1:521-24; Mrs. William H. Payne, "Search for My Wounded Husband," VHS, 1910. Stuart reported that Payne had been killed. See *OR* 7/1:573.

hospital at Old Point, released on parole, and returned to Warrenton to recuperate.[25]

The Richmond Daily Dispatch reported that Wickham's wound "was very severe, but it is not thought to be mortal. He was attacked as he was attempting to draw his sword, after having fired his pistol. His charge was one of the most brilliant passages of the whole war."[26]

The Charlotte Democrat reported:

> The result of this fight was the entire repulse of the enemy, and reflected the greatest credit upon the gallantly of our troops. A fine iron rifled gun and three caissons were captured, the artillery horses having been killed or ridden off by the fugitive canonists, the pieces were brought off the field by the Howitzer company to whom the gun was given. The gun, a most excellent weapon, was used against the enemy during the entire fight of the following day. About 15 prisoners were taken in this engagement, nearly all of whom belonged to the 6th regiment of regular U. S. Cavalry.[27]

Lieutenant Richard Watkins of the 3rd Virginia Cavalry, wrote his wife, Mary, of his orders involving evacuating the wounded:

> On last Friday week before the rear guard of the army took up its march, I was ordered to Kings Mill Wharf on the James [River] in charge of all the sick of our Regiment. There I witnessed one of the saddest scenes ever witnessed in the army. Twenty-nine hundred sick men were lying on the cold wet ground awaiting the boats. I had forty or fifty under my charge which I succeeded in getting off very soon but my orders were to remain.[28]

Wickham was soon taken to his home near Ashland to recuperate. After a sharp contest, The Confederates around the fort managed to fend off the Union cavalry, and both sides backed off as darkness fell.[29]

25. Robert Houghtalen, *I am A Good Ol' Rebel* (Bloomington, In: AuthorHouse), 68
26. *Richmond Daily Dispatch*, May 12, 1862.
27. Ibid.
28. Lt. Richard Watkins to Mary Watkins, May 11, 1862, VHS.
29. Carol Kettenburg Dubbs, *Defend This Old Town: Williamsburg During The Civil War* (Baton Rouge, LSU Press, 2002), 82; OR 11/1; 444. A regimental history of the 6th New York Cavalry claims that Capt. William Sanders was the trooper who wounded Col. Williams Wickham. Ref: Donald C. Caughey and Jimmy J. Jones, *The 6th United States Cavalry in the Civil War: A History and Roster* (Jefferson, NC: McFarland & Company, 2013), 52.

The next day, what became known as the battle of Williamsburg began. Nearly 32,000 Confederates and 41,000 Union fought during the May 6 battle of Williamsburg, which was inconclusive.

William Henry Fitzhugh "Rooney" Lee wrote to his wife, Charlotte, on June 3, 1862:

> I went on a scout & was near the R. Road where the fighting near Hanover C.H. was going on. I made my way around & arrived on the Hills back of H[ickory] Hill in time to see the enemy advancing up the lane. I rode to the House for a minute. W[illia]ms was in bed, too sick to move. I saw the Ladies. I heard that your Grandpa was well. Cousin Tom & Renshaw were there, but mounted & were off in a moment.[30]

On June 9, 1862, just before beginning his famed ride around George McClellan, Gen. J.E.B. Stuart and Rooney Lee rode four miles from Stuart's camp to Hickory Hill to visit their wounded cavalryman. Stuart conferred with the still-recovering Williams Wickham, so as to benefit from Colonel Wickham's vast knowledge of the local terrain.

On June 29, 1862, while resting at Hickory Hill, Federal Brig. Gen. W. H. Emory's troopers overran the house and captured Colonel Wickham. Because of his severe condition, Wickham was paroled on the spot on the promise that he not bear arms until his exchange.[31]

The next day Wickham wrote Secretary of War, G. W. Randolph, "I beg your good offices in getting me released as soon as practicable from my parole not to bear arms against the United States until exchanged. [Beverly] Robertson's promotion makes me particularly anxious to be enabled to rejoin my regiment, which sadly needs my care."[32] Wickham was exchanged by special cartel for his wife's relative, Lieut. Col. Thomas L. Kane, of the Pennsylvania Bucktails.[33] Kane, an attorney and strong abolitionist, became a personal friend of Mormon Brigham Young and was helpful to the Mormons in migrating west to Utah.

Years later, William's son, Henry T. Wickham, recalled the events that occurred when he was 13 years old:

30. Lee Family Papers, Mss1 L51c355, Section 18, VMHC.
31. *OR* Series II, vol. 4:794-95; *OR* XI/3: 133, Pt. 1, 423-424, 427.
32. Ibid.
33. *OR*, Series II, IV:438. Kane was officially exchanged on August 27, 1862 under General Order 118 of the War Department, Adjutant General's Office, Union War Department, vol. 1:370.

On May 4, 1862, my father was desperately wounded at Williamsburg and was brought home. On May 27, occurred the battle of Hanover Court House, in which the Confederate forces were severely defeated. Part of them retreated by the River Road through Hickory Hill plantation. It was a memorable day for me. When the sounds of fighting came near there was much excitement at the mansion. Unnoticed, I crept away to the brow of the hill and witnessed, from a distance of about a quarter of a mile. The last stand of the routed soldiers. Next morning a Federal scout tied his horse and came up the walk holding a piece of paper in his hand. My grandmother advanced to meet him, and I was with her. He said, 'Is this Anne Wickham?' She replied, 'Yes.' He said, 'I want some of your good brandy.' She asked, 'How do you know I have any?' He said, 'This note says so.' She said, 'Why, you wouldn't read a lady's letter.' And he said, 'Stop preaching, old woman and bring me the brandy.' She said, 'If I bring you the brandy, will you go away?' and he said, 'I will, if you bring it back quickly.'

Henry T. Wickham's account continued:

So, she brought back the brandy, and he went away. Later in the day, the Federal picket line was extended beyond Hickory Hill and Col. Lawrence Williams, who was in command of the [Union] picket line and who knew about us, and who had learned that a wounded officer was there, came to the house. Nothing could have exceeded his courtesy, and he later brought General McClellan's staff surgeon, who after examination, said my father would die if the attempt to remove him was made, and took my father's parole as a prisoner of war. [Col.] Lawrence Williams was young, handsome, and dashing. He had a way with children. He came several times and would make his horse, which was a very fine one, jump over the yard fence for our amusement.[34]

Stuart sat with Colonel Wickham late into the night of June 9 and made his plans for the morning before drifting off to sleep in a chair in the "Big" parlor. Before sun-up Stuart and Lee were back with their troops ready to begin their ride. Scouts were sent out; 35 troopers were

---

34. *United States Congressional Record: Proceedings and Debates of the 76th Congress, Third Session*, Appendix, Vol 86, Part 17, August 6, 1940-September 27, 1940, 5892.

left to their sleep. When everything was in order, Stuart mounted with "Rooney" Lee and rode to nearby Hickory Hill, the home of Mrs. Lee's family and of Col. Williams C. Wickham of the Fourth Cavalry. After his wound at Williamsburg, the Colonel had been paroled by his captors, and had been permitted to return to the gracious old plantation, where he was recovering. With him and with the other members of the household, "Rooney" Lee had high converse. Stuart, for his part, went to sleep in his chair.[35]

Wickham, thus missed all of the fighting around Richmond, including the Seven Days' campaigns. After Norfolk and Yorktown were abandoned and after the destruction of the CSS Virginia, and after other bad news during the first half of 1862, many southerners became dispirited and saddened. The Union offensive on the lower Virginia peninsula threatened Richmond. Colonel Williams C. Wickham wrote to Confederate Congressman, William C. Rives, "Our happy country appears to be completely ruined. I was in Richmond yesterday and it is almost the universal opinion that the city will be in possession of the Yankees in a few days."[36]

On July 28, 1862, the Cavalry Division of the Army of Northern Virginia was created under the command of Major General James E. B. Stuart. There were two brigades: The First Brigade under Brig. Gen. Wade Hampton and the Second Brigade, under Brig. Gen. Fitzhugh Lee. The 4th Virginia Cavalry was assigned to the brigade of Fitzhugh Lee, along with the 1st, 3rd, 5th and 9th Virginia Cavalry and Capt. James Breathed's battery of Horse Artillery. Colonel Beverly Robertson was ordered to North Carolina to recruit and train new cavalry regiments, and Lieutenant Colonel Wickham was promoted to colonel, Robert Randolph to lieutenant colonel.[37]

By this time, Wickham was up and riding around Hickory Hill in preparation for returning to duty. Robert E. Lee was anxious for him to rejoin his army. Wickham was promoted to colonel on June 9, 1862. Wickham rejoined the regiment in late July. During the remainder of July and all of August, the 4th Virginia divided its time between picket duty along the Charles City front and camp instruction set up at Hanover Court House.[38] W. H. Payne was captured following his near fatal wound and held as a prisoner of war two or three months. As soon as exchanged, though not yet fully recovered, Payne returned to duty early in September, 1862. Having been promoted to lieutenant colonel, Payne was assigned to the temporary command of the Second North Carolina regiment of cavalry, which he held in Warrenton, Virginia, with about 3,000 wounded Confederate soldiers, and also a number of captured Federal prisoners.

The Second battle of Manassas was fought August 28–30, 1862, between Gen. Robert E. Lee's Army of Northern Virginia against Union Maj. Gen. John Pope's Army of Virginia. Following a wide-ranging flanking march, Confederate Maj. Gen. Thomas J. Jackson captured the Union supply depot at Manassas Junction, threatening Pope's line of communications with Washington, D.C. Withdrawing a few miles to the northwest, Jackson took up strong concealed defensive positions on Stony Ridge and awaited the arrival of the wing of Lee's army commanded by Maj. Gen. James Longstreet. On August 28, 1862, Jackson attacked a Union column just east of Gainesville, at Brawner's Farm, resulting in a stalemate but successfully attracting Pope's attention. On that same day, Longstreet broke through light Union resistance in the battle of Thoroughfare Gap and approached the battlefield.

Pope became convinced that he had trapped Jackson and concentrated the bulk of his army against him. On August 29, Pope launched a series of assaults against Jackson's position along an unfinished railroad grade. The attacks were repulsed with heavy casualties on both sides. At noon, Longstreet arrived on the field from Thoroughfare Gap and took position on Jackson's right flank. On August 30, Pope renewed his attacks, seemingly unaware that Longstreet was on the field. When massed Confederate artillery devastated a Union assault by Maj. Gen. Fitz John Porter's V Corps, Longstreet's wing of 25,000 men in five divisions counterattacked in the largest simultaneous mass assault of the war. The Union left flank was crushed and the army was driven back to Bull Run. Only an effective Union rear guard action prevented a replay of the First Manassas defeat. Pope's retreat to Centreville was, nonetheless, precipitous.

At about midnight on August 22, Stuart's troopers reached Catlett's Station, Pope's headquarters. Stuart ordered Colonel Wickham and his 4th Virginia to destroy the Waterloo Railroad bridge near Catlett's Station. Stuart sent Capt. W. W. Blackford, an engineer and Stuart's aide-de-camp, along to direct the operations destroying the bridge. Blackford recalled:

> the regiment was standing in columns-of-fours when Wickham and he received the order. Wickham and Blackford started together, approaching the column from the rear. As they reached the front in pitch dark,

Wickham then turned around and heading to the rear to give some orders, asked Blackford to await his return. Soon, as Blackford chatted at length with troopers near him, he began to wonder what was detaining Colonel Wickham. Suddenly, a flash of lightening occurred, revealing that the road in front of him was entirely empty. Blackford was shocked that Wickham had passed Blackford and his nearby companions of one company in the dark, proceeding to the front of the column and began leading his regiment forward, assuming Blackford would soon join him by his side.[39]

Blackford remembered, "There we were, feeling very foolish, one-half of the regiment gone with the Colonel and the guide on an important expedition and the other half with the Engineer officer left behind in the road. I could have cried for vexation, for I knew the importance of destroying the bridge before Pope sent troops to protect it." After waiting a short period hoping that Wickham would send someone and a guide to lead them, Blackford, not knowing the way, was forced to return to General Stuart. Blackford further remembered, that "upon recounting his woes to Stuart, his commander burst out laughing as Blackford discovered Wickham was then by his side." Wickham had just told Stuart that he had sent back several troopers looking for Blackford, but had not been able to find him or the rear of his column. After some delay, the group was reunited and began their march to burn the bridge. Because of the continuing rain downpours and enemy sharpshooters, the bridge could not be ignited. Stuart's report praised Wickham for being "energetic and thorough-going."[40]

The victorious Confederates scattered and looted Pope's headquarters. Stuart retired about 3 a.m. along the same route toward Warrenton, through Auburn Mills. The gray horsemen captured 400 prisoners, 500 horses, $500,000 in greenbacks, and $20,000 in gold. They presented some of Pope's private baggage, including a full-dress uniform coat and hat, as a trophy to General Stuart. They destroyed hundreds of tents, wagons, as well as the depot and some trains. According to Blackford, among the 400 prisoners was a woman dressed in a man's uniform. She wanted Stuart to release her, but he told her, "if she was man enough to enlist, she ought to be man enough to go to prison." So, in a state of great indignation, she was escorted off.[41]

39. W. W. Blackford, *War Years with JEB Stuart* (NY: Charles Scribner's Sons, 1945), 123-24.
40. Stiles, *4th Virginia Cavalry*, 17; W. W. Blackford, *War Years with JEB Stuart*, 123-24.
41. Stiles, *4th Virginia Cavalry*, 17, Blackford, *War Years with JEB Stuart*, 125-26.

At 1 a.m. on August 26, reveille sounded for Stuart's cavalry at Waterloo bridge. By 2 a.m., Wickham's regiment headed for Amissville. General Trimble headed toward Manassas Junction, while Stuart accompanied Wickham and the 4th Virginia as they were sent to the north side of the junction to cut communications with Washington and any escaping Federals. Wickham moved his regiment cautiously, not knowing the size of the Federal force occupying the area. About midnight, Wickham led his 4th Virginia in charging the junction through light musketry and cannon fire. Manassas Junction was secured without difficulty within 30 minutes. The capture of the vast stores at Manassas Junction supplied General Jackson eight cannons, complete with their ammunition, 175 horses, more than 300 prisoners, about 200 new tents, plus much in the way of commissary and quartermaster stores.[42]

On August 27, Fitzhugh Lee was dispatched to Fairfax Court House with the 3rd, 4th, and 9th Virginia Cavalry regiments to cut off the enemy's retreat. The 4th Cavalry marched parallel to the Orange and Alexandria Railroad, "riding over fences, across ravines, and through swamps." Plans to destroy the bridge spanning Cub Run, a tributary of Bull Run, were abandoned when a large Union force appeared.[43]

By sunrise on the 28th, the 4th Virginia reached Fairfax Court House; but discovering Federal infantry there, the regiment marched back to Centreville. That evening Wickham gathered hay for his horses north of Bull Run and bivouacked at Sudley Mill. Early on August 29, the 4th Virginia crossed Bull Run and took up position on General Jackson's left. On Saturday, August 30, the 4th Virginia observed the ongoing battle, then joined in the pursuit of the fleeing Federals. Darkness, combined with a hard rain, slowed the pursuit, eventually ending it.[44]

Wickham wrote Lucy from Sudley Mills on Aug 30, 1862: "The work though has played the mischief with my Regt, and my numbers are greatly reduced... I have never had half as much exposure or hard labor or lack of sleep or scanty fare as I have had for the last 14 days, and yet I was never better or stronger than I am today. I have taken 3 flags, horses, and cavalry equipment innumerable." Continuing, Wickham wrote, "...with 200 of my men, I charged the 12th Penn. Cavalry, 800 strong, routing them and scattering them all over the country, capturing a very large number of them... Gen. Ewell has lost

42. Stiles, *4th Virginia Cavalry*, 18.
43. Ibid.
44. Ibid., 18-19.

a leg. Tell Charlotte I have offered Rooney paper, but he seems too sleepy to write. He is well."[45]

Prior to sunrise on August 31, Stuart's cavalry was on the move again. Near Centreville, the 4th Virginia surprised a squadron of federals, capturing them all without firing a shot. The rains continued, making the roads into an almost impassible quagmire. Impeded by road conditions on September 1, Wickham managed to march his troopers through a thunderstorm toward Flint Hill. Fitz Lee's brigade reached Flint Hill, but having discovered that it was occupied by Union forces, and hearing shots in his rear, he withdrew. Wickham, who had been in the advance, then covered the withdrawal, driving off an enemy infantry regiment as the brigade retired to Germantown and encamped for the night.[46]

The following day, Fitz Lee's brigade occupied Fairfax Court House. On September 3, Fitz Lee's troopers demonstrated toward Alexandria. On September 5, the 4th Virginia, with the exception of Company H which had been sent along with Jackson for use as pickets, crossed the Potomac River at Leesburg. Wickham's regiment marched into Maryland at Edwards Ferry about 2 p.m. Arriving at Poolesville, the regiment skirmished with some federals before encamping in the vicinity of New Market.[47]

At dawn on September 14, the 4th Virginia crossed the Catoctin Mountains at Hamburg and continued on to Boonesborough, where the wary troopers rested until 4 p.m. Upon hearing firing at South Mountain, Stuart's cavalry rode up to cover the withdrawal of Confederates down from South Mountain. Covering the army's march, Fitz Lee's brigade, including Wickham's 4th Virginia, slowly moved toward Sharpsburg on September 15. Stuart's cavalry encamped that night atop Nicodemus Ridge. The next morning, Stuart ordered Fitz Lee to turn the Union right. Discovering that the approach was covered by Federal artillery, Fitz Lee's troopers withdrew to cover the Confederate left. The 3rd, 4th, and 9th Virginia Cavalry of Fitzhugh Lee's Brigade reached the field late in the afternoon of the 15th and took position on the extreme left of the Confederate Army. On the night of the 16th the brigade was massed near the river in support of the Horse Artillery. The troopers of the 4th Virginia did no fighting during the battle at Antietam on September 17 but were used as couriers and aides.[48]

45. Williams Wickham to Lucy Penn Wickham, August 30, 1862; Wickham Papers, UVA.
46. Stiles, *4th Virginia Cavalry*, 19.
47. Ibid.
48. Ibid., 20.

After resting on the 18th, Fitz Lee's brigade covered the Confederate retreat from Shepherdstown that evening. Stuart's cavalry was the last to cross into Virginia on September 19. The army rested, while Stuart established his headquarters near Charlestown, as his cavalry protected the Potomac against Federal intrusions. The aggregate strength of the 4th Virginia on September 30 was 768 men, while effectives numbered 411.[49]

During the first week of October, Stuart's cavalry rested and picketed from Harpers Ferry to Williamsport, skirmishing often with Federal patrols. On October 8, 1862, Robert E. Lee issued orders to Stuart to go into Maryland and Pennsylvania. Stuart was ordered to disrupt the Cumberland Valley Railroad at Chambersburg and destroy the railroad bridge near there. Lee concluded his order by urging Stuart to gather horses and other livestock on the raid. Stuart gathered 1,800 troopers and four pieces of horse artillery at Drakesville at noon on October 9, for his northern raid to Chambersburg, Pennsylvania. Colonel Wickham and 259 men of the 4th Virginia were chosen for the mission. Before sunrise on October 10, Stuart and his cavalry crossed the Potomac at McCoy's Ford, encountering little opposition as they marched rapidly, reaching Mercersburg around midnight. Stuart's troopers were detailed to roundup badly needed horses. Stuart's expedition reached Chambersburg after dark while rain fell, with the storm continuing through the night. Stuart's troopers destroyed the railroad station at Chambersburg, then encamped one mile outside town.[50]

Wickham recalled that Fitz Lee's contingent of Stuart's forces, with James Breathred's battery, stayed overnight at a farmyard just outside of Chambersburg. Wickham recalled that "he made his 'couch' in a covered wagon of such dimensions that no one accustomed to the corduroy roads of Virginia could even have dreamed of; it had in it 200 bushels of corn on the ear, and Breathred's boys, who were not accustomed to unlimited supplies of corn, won my admiration by the frequency by which during the night they brought me sliding from the top of the pile towards the tail of the wagon by their oft repeated returns for an additional feed for their horses." Wickham had a passion for seeing to it that his command's horses were often fed when possible; so, he appreciated the actions of Breathred's men in caring for their horses.[51]

---

49. Ibid.
50. Ibid.; *OR* 19/2:52, 55.
51. Williams C. Wickham to H. B. McClellan, March 6, 1883; Wickham Family Papers, VMHC.

At dawn on October 11, Stuart's column marched toward Gettysburg. West of the town, Stuart turned South, riding to Emmitsburg, where the troopers were greeted with cheers. Colonel Wickham recalled, "It was dull hard marching." Moving through the town, Stuart's column headed to Woodsborough and Liberty. They then marched due south to Barnesville by way of New London, New Market, and Hyattstown, Maryland. Crossing the railroad tracks south of New Market, the troopers again cut telegraph wires and destroyed rails. The column rode on through the night, reaching Hyattsville by first light. Twelve miles away at White's Ford were Union forces in pursuit of the rebels from multiple directions, seeking to destroy the raiders before they could cross the Potomac. Brigadier General George Stoneman guarded the area around Poolesville with a division of cavalry, artillery, and infantry. Stoneman sought to block Stuart's march route to the Potomac, while Colonel Alfred N. Duffie's command, along with Brig. Gen. Alfred Pleasonton's 400 horsemen, blocked the ford near the mouth of the Monocacy River. Seemingly oblivious to the threat, Stuart rode on, believing in "the great God of battles to release him from the hands of the Yankees." Stuart's adjutant, Major Henry B. McClellan, thought there would be a major fight before crossing the Potomac. Many of Stuart's troopers believed that capture was more probable than escape.[52]

Stuart ordered Colonel William E. Jones to form on the right side of the road and send a party forward toward Pleasonton's cavalry. He also ordered Wickham to take possession of White's Ford on the Potomac and arrange for the protection of the entire Confederate column when crossing the Potomac. Wickham promptly dispatched a squadron to the ford, running off a Union picket watching the crossing. Wickham then discovered a much larger formation of Union troops—perhaps a full brigade—was forming to attack his position. He realized he was in for a fight.[53]

Wickham dispatched his orderly John Lewis Talley back to Stuart with a request for two guns. Stuart hurriedly sent Major John Pelham and two guns to Wickham. Pelham quickly ordered up two of Breathed's guns, positioning them on a ridge overlooking the Poolesville-Monocacy Road. Breathred quickly unlimbered his piece "and soon threw the advancing line into confusion and drove them

52. David P. Bridges, *Fighting With JEB Stuart: Major James Breathed and the Confederate Horse Artillery* (Arlington, Va: Breathed, Bridges, Best, Inc., 2006), 101; Trout, Galloping Thunder, 119-21.
53. Ibid. Stuart, in his report of the mission, praised Pelham for his actions. Pelham was commander of the horse artillery, but in this action, Breathed's battery deserved the tributes.

back to the cover of the woods and repeated it whenever they appeared."[54]

Breathred's concentrated and accurate fire helped clear the way for the crossing of the Potomac. With guns in tow, Rooney Lee and the troopers made their way down to the riverbank. The horsemen and the cannoneers splashed across to the southern side—the captured horses close behind them. Wickham recalled:

> Breathed [Pelham] put his guns in a magnificent position on the hills just opposite the ford and never during the war did I see a more beautiful artillery practice than we then had on both sides of the line of Stuart's column. . . Infantry or dismounted cavalry were closing in and Breathed was so positioned as to enfilade each line and it was exhilarating to see he would by his well-directed shots cause each line to falter and recede as they came to the line of his range, thus keeping open a space through which he whole command safely marched and crossed the river.[55]

The Confederates forded the Potomac around midday following the two-hour skirmish and duel with Union Battery M, 2nd U. S. Artillery under Lt. Alexander Pennington. Stuart, reporting no losses during the expedition, praised the "coolness in danger and cheerful obedience to orders" of colonels Lee, Jones, Wickham, and Butler in his report of the mission.[56]

George McClellan, learning of the size of the Confederate raiding force, in a report to General-in-Chief Henry W. Halleck, remarked that "I have given every order necessary to insure the capture or destruction of these forces, and I hope we may be able to teach them a lesson they may not soon forget."[57]

The 4th Virginia and other regiments camped at Leesburg on October 12. Stuart's column stopped again at Snickersville on October 13, before returning to Charlestown the next day.[58] For the following week, the 4th Virginia resumed patrolling the Potomac, skirmishing with Union patrols. When Robert E. Lee moved his army back to the Rapidan-Rappahannock line, Stuart's cavalry covered Lee's left.

---

54. Ibid.
55. Ibid., 102; Thomason, *JEB Stuart*, 221-223.
56. *OR* 19/2:54.
57. *OR* 21/2:66.
58. Ibid., 20-21; *OR* 19/2:53; Arnold M. Pavlovsky, *Riding in Circles J.E.B. Stuart and the Confederate Cavalry 1861-1862* (Southampton, New Jersey: Arnold M. Pavlovsky, 2010), 496; Williams C. Wickham to Henry B. McClellan, March 6, 1883, Wickham Family Papers, VMHC.

Wickham commanded Fitz Lee's brigade due to Lee's having been disabled. Five regiments totaled less than one thousand mounted because of "greased heel" and "sore tongue" disease among the horses. The 4th Virginia had an aggregate of 878 troopers, with 467 present for active duty on October 29. The 4th Virginia made up almost half of Fitz Lee's brigade.[59]

On October 30, Stuart—with Wickham's troopers and six pieces of the "incomparable" John Pelham's horse artillery—crossed the Blue Ridge at Snicker's Gap and Castleman's Ferry. Under a bright sunshine, the gray horsemen rode into Loudoun County and bivouacked near Bloomfield and Upperville. On October 31 at Mountsville, Wickham encountered a Union regiment, capturing 70, wounding seven and taking two flags. The Confederate troopers drove the Union troopers down Snickers Gap Turnpike, with the 4th Virginia taking the lead as they approached Upperville. Wickham's regiment drove the Federals into the town during a brief, fierce fight, before withdrawing due to Union artillery fire-and with Federal infantry reinforcements approaching. Near dark, Wickham moved back to encamp at Union. General Stuart praised Wickham and his regiment for a noble showing that day.[60]

Beginning in early November, Wickham's 4th Virginia patrolled Fauquier, Stafford, and Prince William Counties. Wickham's adjutant reported that the regiment engaged in "very severe work in which it lost many men killed, wounded [and] captured." On November 2, Federal troops were reported in Union, so Stuart's cavalry was sent to investigate. Trooper George W. Beale reported, "the 4th Virginia was first to come up, and they were ordered ahead, and charged the Yankees in their encampment." Because of heavy Union artillery fires and reinforcements, Wickham's troopers withdrew across Beaver Creek Dam after the short engagement.[61]

The next morning around 9 a.m., the Federal cavalry moved toward Upperville. Wickham's horsemen fought all day to protect Maj. Gen. A. P. Hill's infantry moving by Ashby's Gap. Dismounting, firing from behind stone fences and downed rails, then withdrawing again, Wickham continued commanding Fitz Lee's brigade—due to Lee's having been disabled. The charge of the 4th Virginia retarded the Federal advance. Slowly withdrawing to the mountain pass, Wickham "displayed great zeal, ability, and bravery."[62] However, Colonel Wickham was wounded in his neck by a shell fragment. The 4th

59. Ibid., 21; *OR* 19/2:141.
60. Ibid.; *OR* 19/2:143, 145, Stiles, *4th Virginia Cavalry*, 21.
61. Ibid.
62. *OR* 19/2:143.

Virginia contested the road all the way to Ashby's Gap, where Capt. Woodridge, now in command of the regiment, held the mountain pass open until all the Confederates could pass safely to Front Royal.[63]

Wickham, after treatment, was sent home to Hickory Hill for convalescence. On November 11, 1862, from Culpeper Court House, Gen. Robert E. Lee wrote his first cousin and wife of Williams Wickham, Anne Butler Carter Wickham, at Hickory Hill:

> My dear Cousin Anne,
>
> I cannot help expressing my great regret that Wms [Williams] should again have been wounded. I regret it on my own account, on his & on hers; but I particularly regret it on account of the country, who at this time requires the services of all her sons. At the same time, I am filled with gratitude to the merciful Providence that turned aside at the proper moment the missile of death & which has on all occasions preserved a life so precious to those I love. I can say to you that I consider him one of our best Cavy officers. Prudent, firm & bold. His merits as a gentleman Patriot & Christian I need not enumerate to you. You can judge then how ill he can be spared from the Army. I trust he will soon be well enough to require us. I believe it is [his wife] pretty Luce that bribes him to come home on any ground. Please give my kindest regards to all your household, & accept the appreciation & love of your cousin. R E Lee[64]

Wickham continued to recuperate from his wound until early December, hustling back to his regiment before the battle of Fredericksburg on December 13, 1862. During the battle, Wickham's 4th Virginia covered General Jackson's right flank near Hamilton's Crossing. Due to the ground and location of the Federal advance, the 4th Virginia did little fighting, but they still lost one trooper killed and two wounded.[65]

Captain Charles Minor Blackford recalled that on the evening of December 12, Fitz Lee's brigade, including Wickham's 4th Virginia, had bivouacked in the woods five or six miles west of Fredericksburg. The troopers had no tents; the weather was cold, but not bitterly so.

---

63. Ibid.; *OR* 19/2:143.
64. The Papers of Robert E. Lee, 1830-1870, University of Virginia Special Collections, Charlottesville. The letter is not in Lee's hand. It was written in the time when the general was recovering from a fall that injured his hands and made writing difficult.
65. Stiles, *4th Virginia Cavalry*, 22.

Wickham had been seriously wounded at a battle at Fort MaGruder on May 4, 1862. This photo was taken just prior to the battle of Fredericksburg. Wickham told Capt. Charles Minor Blackford, "it's a damned shame I should have to suffer so much now and probably be killed tomorrow for a cause of which I do not approve. Remember, Blackford, if I am killed tomorrow, it will be for Virginia, the land of my fathers, and not for the damned secessionist movement."

(USAHEC)

Blackford recalled that Wickham's warming fire was just across the road from him. Blackford and Wickham were distant cousins, and were close, spending the evening of December 12, eating their supper out of the same skillet. They parted about 9 p.m., Wickham lay down on the ground near his fire to sleep. Blackford returned to his camp, checked the troopers, and retired near his fire.[66]

About 11 p.m., Blackford "was awakened by the sounds of groans" emanating from the area of Wickham's fire across the road. Hurriedly, he scampered across the road to Wickham, finding him in great pain. Wickham was again in pain from the wounds he had received during the battle of Williamsburg in May. His recurring pain was undoubtedly amplified by his cold and hard bed. Blackford recalled that Wickham was in bad humor, complaining, "Blackford, it's a damned shame I should have to suffer so much now and probably be killed tomorrow for a cause of which I do not approve. Remember, Blackford, if I am killed tomorrow, it will be for Virginia, the land of my fathers, and not for the damned secessionist movement."[67]

By this time, Wickham had decided to resign from the service. He believed that the South was going to lose the war and be ruined in the process. Many thousands of lives could be saved if a peaceful compromise, short of total surrender, could be achieved. He did not want to die for a cause he deemed illegitimate. On December 6, 1862, Colonel Wickham submitted a letter to Secretary of War James A. Seddon, tendering his resignation from the service. He cited his having received two wounds in the past several months and claimed his age was above the limit for conscription, thereby presenting himself with the opportunity of resigning.[68]

Wickham's request to resign was passed along to the chain of command for comments and or action. Brigadier General Fitzhugh Lee commented from Spotsylvania C.H: "I cannot think this is the proper moment in our Country's struggle for one of Col. Wickham's tried valor and known ability to retire from the contest. His long experience and high adaptability for command cannot but be felt by an excellent regiment he leads without a field officer as his wounds do not incapacitate him from active duty and he is under the age (maximum) contemplated by the 'Conscription Act.'" Lee went on to recommend disapproval of Wickham's request.[69]

---

66. Susan Leigh Blackford and Charles Minor Blackford, compilers., *Letters from Lee's Army* (Lincoln, Neb: University of Nebraska Press, 1998), 143.
67. Ibid., 144.
68. Letter from Williams C. Wickham to Secretary of War James A. Seddon, December 12, 1862; VMHC, Richmond, Va.
69. Brigadier General Fitzhugh Lee to Adjutant General C. H. Lee, December 6, 1862; VMHC.

Adjutant General C. H. Lee added that a surgeon's certificate had not accompanied the request and recommended disapproval. The Secretary of War formally disapproved Wickham's request on December 24, 1862.[70]

Wickham's 4th Virginia did not encounter any more fighting until after the New Year. During the first month of 1863, the 4th Virginia helped to picket the Rappahannock River. At this time, the regiment numbered 332 enlisted and twenty-one officers present of an aggregate of 753.[71]

---

70. C. H. Lee to Secretary of War Seddon, December 13, 1862 and Secretary of War Seddon's disapproval, December 24, 1862, VMHC.
71. Stiles, *4th Virginia Cavalry*, 22.

CHAPTER FIVE

1863: Spring Campaigns
Leading Up to Gettysburg;
Wickham Wants to Resign

"I am so anxious to get out of the war and be at home that although I had intended never again to have anything to do with politics and thought the time for giving notice is very short. I have today sent a card to the Richmond papers announcing myself as a candidate for Congress. It is the only accord left me for getting out as my resignation has looked blocked."

—Williams C. Wickham after Chancellorsville

Early in 1863, Colonel Williams C. Wickham, made clear his feelings about the war and wanting to retire from the service. On January 15 he wrote Lucy:

> Very soon after my return from home, I sent my resignation to the Sec of War, but it has recently been returned disapproved. I have again sent it to the President for his action but fear it will meet with the same fate. Then—I came to the determination to offer my resignation, first because I am very anxious to be with you all at home and think I have rendered service enough for full satisfaction of the claims of "duty;" next because I am heartily tired of this business and want to get out of it.—because I have been badly treated in the reorganization of the Brigades by having a Col. Senior to myself put into service while I was absent on account of a wound received whilst in command of the Brigade; and lastly because I am very fully persuaded that no matter what labor I perform or what ability I may display, I do not stand an equal chance with others for promotion, and I am not of that class that is willing to work without a fair chance for the honor. In short, I am unwilling further to risk my life to pin reputations to others; as then reasons though would not have benefitted me with the powers in

Richmond. I fear none, contenting myself with calling the attention of the President to the fact that in his proclamation again, [Alexander] Boteler and he took the proviso that officers in the army could at pleasure retire from the service. I am very doubtful of the success of my effort but can't help having a strong hope that in a few weeks I will be free from all military duty and be quietly at home with you all, then to remain uninterrupted.[1]

On January 15, 1863 Wickham wrote President Davis: "On the 6th ult., I tendered my resignation as Col of the 4th Va Cav and it was returned from the Sec of War, disapproved, ... my reasons were purely personal and I therefore deem it unnecessary to explain them."[2]

On Jan 26, 1863, Stuart had written of Wickham's earlier request to resign: "In the absence of any known sufficient reason for his resignation, I cannot consent to lose so valuable an officer as Col. Wickham from the army."[3]

By February 16, Stuart, Fitz Lee, and Secretary of War Seldon all provided negative endorsements of Wickham's request to resign. President Davis responded, "Not being aware of any requirements being made of Col. Wickham which are against the laws of notions of Humanity & of War ... resignation not accepted."[4]

Fitz Lee broke camp on February 9, 1863, marching to Culpeper Court House to relieve Wade Hampton's brigade. Wickham's 4th Virginia numbered 404 enlisted and 17 officers present out of an aggregate of 888 when it began picketing the Rappahannock River. By February 18, the regiment increased its ranks by 40 troopers and one officer, Lt. Col. W. H. F. Payne, and had marched to Spotsylvania County. Payne commanded the regiment for much of the following month because of Wickham's absence due to sickness.[5]

By February 26, Wickham had returned to his regiment, leading a reconnaissance down the north flank of the Rappahannock River. Crossing at U. S. Ford by swimming across, the 4th Virginia discovered Federals a few miles downriver; and their number being too strong, Wickham withdrew.[6]

1. Williams Wickham to Lucy Wickham, January 15, 1863; Wickham Family Papers, UVA.
2. Williams C. Wickham Service Record, NARA.
3. Ibid.
4. Jefferson Davis, *The Papers of Jefferson Davis: January–September 1863* (Lynda Lassell Crist, ed., 1998, LSU Press), vol. 9.
5. Stiles, *4th Virginia Cavalry*, 23.
6. Ibid.

On March 1, the 4th Virginia left Spotsylvania Court House, arriving in Culpeper two days later and was assigned to watch the Federal right flank. By the second week in March, Wickham's regiment numbered 412 men and were settled in Culpeper Court House, awaiting first light. The winter weather cleared as the armies on both sides positioned themselves for the upcoming spring campaign.

On March 11, 1863, Robert E. Lee wrote Wickham concerning a complaint he had received from a citizen concerning troopers improperly impressing the gentleman's corn. Lee noted that it was a single complaint, which he viewed as an indication of Wickham's proper instruction to his troops. He also complimented Wickham, "The care and attention you bestowed on your command as evidenced by its condition have not escaped my notice; and the almost singularity of this complaint shows that you & your agents have exercised with due caution of judgment the power of impressment ..."[7]

The day after the brutal fight of March 17 at Kelly's Ford, the 4th Virginia rested around camp fires, their tents having been sent away the previous day. The tents were returned by evening and used to shield the weary troopers from the cold and threat of snow that night. The troopers rested for two days. Lieutenant Colonel Payne, who had commanded the 4th Virginia while Colonel Wickham was on furlough, was transferred to command the 2nd North Carolina Cavalry on March 20 and led the regiment until his capture on August 30.

By the end of March, with reduced rations of eighteen ounces of flour and four of bacon per man, the 4th Virginia numbered only 373 effectives out of 900 on the rolls.[8]

The 4th Virginia Cavalry totaled 450 effectives in April, 1862. By July of 1863, the beginning of the spring campaign, active number had increased to 544. Of the 544 engaged at Gettysburg, about three percent would end up as casualties.[9]

On April 5, 1863 Lucy wrote Williams from Hickory Hill. She told him about a horrific train accident and the arming of slaves in Prince George County. She stated, in part:

> **Robert arrived safely ... Papa was over at the Quarters yesterday and saw him. He said he was very poorly ... two gentlemen came ... and were talking about an accident on**

7. Robert E. Lee to Williams C. Wickham, March 11, 1863, Valentine Museum, Richmond, Virginia.
8. Stiles, *4th Virginia Cavalry*, 25.
9. Ibid, 24.

the cars ... it happened about a quarter of a mile from the crossing towards the Ct House ... the 3rd car from the engine was thrown off and broken to pieces and track torn up ... There was no one in the car. The women and children were put in the two cars that got over. They sent up cars for the others. Genl. Stuart sent his regards to us. He was with two ladies—Capt. Louis Blackford and Dr. Carter ... they were down the next day ... Julia ... says she had only seen 300 Yankees that week. The 1st Maryland Cavalry were down then and two men had been to the house for butter, one very saucy, the other well behaved. They had taken Tom and John's and Julia's mules. Henry and William hid theirs in the woods. Julia says the people behave very well ... over in King George [County] the Yankees are arming the Blacks. It is too dreadful and painful to think of these things. I pray to God to give us Victory and Peace.[10]

Until the middle of April, with cold weather still persisting, the 4th's 410 troopers picketed the Rappahannock from its camp at Culpeper Court House. Marching out of Culpeper at first light on April 16, the 4th Virginia marched up the Sperryville Pike, bivouacking there on the 19th. Wickham's troopers numbered 499 that day. Fitz Lee's brigade left Sperryville on April 20, moving back to Culpepper through Woodville. The 4th Virginia encamped outside the court house on the Rixeyville Road and quietly picketed the Rappahannock for the following week.[11]

In April of 1863, Wickham and his command were actively engaged in the outpost conflicts preceding the battle of Chancellorsville. Prior to the opening of the campaign in 1863, while in command of his regiment at the front, he announced himself a candidate for the Confederate Congress from the Richmond district, writing on May 15 to the Voters of the Third Congressional District:

> In compliance with the request of friends from many parts of the 3d Congressional District, I announce myself a candidate for a seat in the next Congress of the Confederate States. Two years ago, I resigned certain political positions that I held, and since then, unless disabled by wounds, I have been constantly actively engaged. Now, I believe that energy and practical sense can be as potent for good in the councils of the nation as in the field. The people of the district know that if they

10. Raynor's HCA 2016-03 Historical Collections Auction.
11. Stiles, *4th Virginia Cavalry*, 25-26.

elect me all of energy and practical sense and of capacity that I possess will be devoted to the advancement of the best interests of the youthful confederacy. In this matter my duties in the field will require me to leave my interest in the hands of my friends.[12]

Without visiting the district during the canvass, on May 28, 1863, Wickham was elected by a sizable majority. Richmond voters rejected incumbent James Lyons. *The Richmond Enquirer* tried to label Wickham a "Unionist" because of his opposition to secession in 1861. Wickham, however, had satisfied all doubts as to his patriotism by raising a cavalry company for the war. Voters elected Wickham for the Confederate House of Representatives with 61 percent of the vote. Virginians also elected ex-Governor William "Extra Billy" Smith as governor. The colorful Smith replaced outgoing Governor John Letcher on January 1, 1864.[13]

As the 1863 elections for the Confederate Congress loomed, shortages—of food, goods, and forage; unpopular taxation; financial regulations; conscription and impressment laws; and the suspension of the writ of habeas corpus had led to doubts in some parts of the South that Jefferson Davis's leadership was capable of carrying the war to a successful conclusion. It was the never-ending casualties, however, that had affected many families and communities, leading many otherwise patriotic citizens to question the wisdom of war as a means of attaining Southern independence. An Augusta County, Virginia, a farmer likely spoke for many in his day journal entry for Christmas 1863: "There are many who were alive one year ago who are now in their graves, many of whom died of disease, others were killed in battle and were denied burial, in this unrighteous and desolating war."[14]

---

12. *The Daily (Richmond)Dispatch*, May 18,1863.
13. Smith was a brigadier general at the time, commanding a brigade. In 1827, Smith established a line of United States mail and passenger post coaches through Virginia, then expanded the business into the Carolinas and Georgia in 1831. It was in this role that he received his nickname, "Extra Billy." Given a contract by the administration of President Andrew Jackson to deliver mail between Washington, D. C. and Milledgeville, Georgia (then the state capital), Smith extended it with numerous spur routes, all generating extra fees. During the subsequent investigation of the Post Office Department, Smith's extra fees were publicized by U.S. Senator Benjamin W. Leigh, and he became known as "Extra Billy" in both the North and South. Smith was elected Virginia's Governor the first time in 1845.
14. John R. Hildebrand, ed., *A Mennonite Journal, 1862–1865, A Father's Account of the Civil War in the Shenandoah Valley* (Shippensburg, Pa.: White Mane Publishing Co., 1996), 28; John R. Hildebrand, "True Friends of the Confederacy," Virginia Tech, ejournal, *Smithfield Review*, 41, https://scholar.lib.vt.edu/ejournals/smithfieldreview/v21/sr_v21_hildebrand.pdf.

The results of the 1863 elections for the Second Confederate Congress reflected this growing unease among the voters, particularly in North Carolina and Georgia. In the Second Confederate Congress, 47 of the 107 House members were first-time representatives; in the Senate, three of its 26 members were newly elected. Twenty of the newly elected House members and the three new Senators held views that reflected the concerns of many voters that Southern independence would not be realized. They joined four or five incumbent House members and four sitting senators who shared their concerns. Together they constituted a loosely-knit peace coalition whose members believed that the time had arrived for the Confederacy to initiate peace negotiations with the Lincoln administration. Their position on the need for peace negotiations would receive little support; and they were viewed with suspicion by Davis, their congressional colleagues, and the general public.[15]

Elected to the Confederate Congress, Wickham, however, remained at his post in the army, leaving his seat in Congress vacant until the autumn of 1864. His election was considered a rebuke to President Davis's administration, who at that time was calling for a response to the Emancipation Proclamation by ordering officers to take no prisoners and to reward negroes for killing enemy soldiers. Fortunately, the Confederate Congress did not go along with Davis's proposed response to the Emancipation Proclamation.[16]

On April 27, the 4th Virginia marched to Brandy Station, setting up camp west of the railroad tracks. The following day, the Federals Crossed Kelly's Ford in boats and began setting up a pontoon bridge. General Stuart headed for the crossing at 9 a.m., planning an attack at dawn the next morning.[17]

On April 28, Major General Joseph Hooker led the Union army across the Rappahannock River near Fredericksburg. The Federals had crossed in force near Kelly's Ford, sending a heavy column across Germana Ford, on the Rapidan, and another towards Ely's Ford, on that river. The routes they were pursuing, after crossing the Rapidan, converge near Chancellorsville, whence several roads lead to the rear of the 4th Virginia Cavalry position at Fredericksburg.[18]

15. Ibid.
16. *Richmond Daily Enquirer*, May 28, 1863; Williams C. Wickham was elected to the Confederate Congress in May, 1863, but retained his command until October when he turned it over to Major General Thomas L. Rosser. He took his seat in Richmond on 9 November, 1863. Benjamin E Snellgrove, "The Confederate General", *National Historical Society*, 1991, pt. 6, p. 135.
17. Ibid., 26.
18. *OR* 25/1:796.

At daylight the next day, Wickham's command was in their saddle proceeding to Brandy Station, where they set up camp west of the railroad tracks. There, the 4th Virginia and the rest of Fitz Lee's brigade remained until ordered to Willis Madden's Tavern—sending out scouts, who upon returning, reported enemy crossing at Germana Ford. Wickham's 4th Virginia, with the rest of Fitz Lee's brigade, participated in the attack on the enemy's rear at Madden's, taking many prisoners. The 4th Virginia was then left on the Rapidan River to harass a Union column before withdrawing toward Raccoon Ford. Wickham's troopers rode all night in rain, crossed Rapidan Ford at daybreak on April 30, then marched to Spotsylvania County, while protecting the rear of Robert E. Lee's artillery—after a brief fight at 11 p.m. with a Union regiment about two miles from Spotsylvania Court House, where the 4th Virginia encamped.[19]

On May 1, Wickham was ordered to position his troopers on the left of the Confederate infantry line and to protect that flank, which he did until sometime after dark. He was then ordered to switch his position to cover the right flank of the army before Chancellorsville and to guard the River Road from Bank's Ford to the Childs's house, where the enemy was heavily entrenched. Wickham, joined by a small detachment of Colonel Thomas H. Owen's 3rd Virginia, remained on the right flank and continued to guard the River Road, until the enemy evacuated their position.[20]

Colonel Wickham reported capturing 241 prisoners and a large number of small arms, while losing one man killed, one wounded, and four men missing from a picket on the Hazel River.[21]

On May 2, Fitz Lee's cavalry covered the movement of General Jackson's corps as he turned the Federal right flank. Subsequently, Stuart's cavalry protected the flanks of Robert E. Lee's army, and held Ely's Ford Road in the enemy's rear. Wickham's and Owen were positioned on the extreme right.[22]

Chancellorsville

Colonel Wickham with his 4th Virginia cavalry and Colonel Thomas H. Owen's 3rd Virginia, were stationed between the Mine Road and the Rappahannock River. The rest of the Confederate cavalry was on Gen. Robert E. Lee's left flank. It was evident that a direct attack upon the enemy would be difficult and lead to great loss,

---

19. Ibid, 1048; Stiles, *4th Virginia Cavalry*, 26-27.
20. Ibid, 1048.
21. Ibid.
22. Ibid, 1047.

in view of the enemy's strength of position and superiority of numbers. Lee therefore, decided to turn General Joseph Hooker's right flank and gain his rear, leaving a force in front to hold Hooker in check and conceal the movement. The execution of this plan was entrusted to Lieutenant General Stonewall Jackson, with his three divisions. The commands of Major Generals Lafayette McLaws and Richard H. Anderson, with the exception of Brig. Gen. Cadmus M. Wilcox's brigade, which during the night had been ordered back to Banks's Ford remained in front of the enemy. Early on the morning of the May 2, General Jackson marched by way of the Furnace and Brock Roads, his movement being effectually shielded by Fitz Lee's cavalry, under General Stuart in-person.[23]

An aide-de-camp of General John Sedgwick's, captured by Colonel Wickham's regiment on the right near Banks's Ford, reported two corps, under command of Sedgwick. Robert E. Lee decided to hold Joseph Hooker in his works with Jackson's corps, and detach enough of other forces to turn on Sedgwick.[24]

"The cavalry was well-managed by Brigadier General Fitz. Lee, who seized Ely's Ford and held the road to within two miles of Chancellorsville—driving the enemy's cavalry from the former place. His men, without rations or forage, displayed heroism, rare under any circumstances, guarding the two flanks, accomplished an indispensable part of the great success, which God vouchsafed to us."[25]

The battle of Chancellorsville is considered by many historians as Robert E. Lee's greatest victory. The victory came at a terrible cost, however, as Maj. General Stonewall Jackson was mortally wounded in his left arm. The general survived; but his left arm was amputated and he was weakened by his wound. He died of pneumonia eight days later. Wickham felt that Jackson could be replaced but Robert E. Lee could not.

On May 8, Wickham wrote Lucy about the battle:

> The battle is at last all over and the enemy is crossing the river, and I am ordered again to keep up my old picket line so that I am now just where I was on the 1st of January. Since I left Culpeper C. House on the 29th ult, we have had a very hard time of it, but both men and horses have stood it well. I have lost but one man killed, and one wounded, and have some five or six missing. I have captured some 250 prisoners, including many

23. Ibid, 798.
24. Ibid, 888.
25. Ibid, 889.

officers, among whom was an aide of Gen. Sedgwick... I am disappointed in the results of the battle. I do not see that they bring us any closer to peace. I have only seen Gen. Lee for a moment after the close of the fights; he seemed in good spirits but I could not ask him about his opinion as to results. Stuart thinks it will have a powerful effect on public opinion in the North.[26]

Following Chancellorsville, Robert E. Lee and Jefferson Davis decided to carry the war into Northern territory again. The first northern invasion had resulted in the terrible battle at Antietam and subsequent retreat back to Virginia. An invasion northward would relieve Virginia of the presence of the enemy by drawing the Federals north of the Potomac. Also, Union troops might be moved away from the coasts of Virginia and North Carolina. In addition, the Federals might have to alter their Mississippi and Tennessee campaigns (Vicksburg, Mississippi, was then under siege by Ulysses S. Grant) to meet the new Confederate offensive. Equally important, ravaged by war for two years, Virginia was unable to feed General Lee's troops much longer.

After the battle of Chancellorsville, both armies reorganized. The Army of Northern Virginia, with additional men obtained by conscription, divided into three corps commanded by Lieutenant Generals James Longstreet, Richard S. Ewell, and Ambrose P. Hill. By the end of May, Lee had 76,000 men and 272 artillery pieces. Each corps had three divisions, with each division consisting of four brigades, except Longstreet's corps, which had three. The corps of the Army of the Potomac were about half the size of their Southern counterparts. On May 22, Maj. Gen. Joseph Hooker replaced his cavalry chief Stoneman with Brig. Gen. Alfred Pleasonton. Stoneman had been discredited at Chancellorsville, and Pleasonton had enhanced the effectiveness of the Union cavalry by virtue of his skills as a gifted administrator and organizer.[27]

Wickham's 4th Virginia was at Chancellorsville on May 9, reporting 449 troopers present for duty. That same day, Wickham ordered Capt. William. R. Smith, commanding Company H on detached duty in Fauquier County, to "collect your men immediately ... and proceed to join me near Chancellorsville with as little delay as possible." Smith was ordered to bring along Company A as well. On May 18, Capt. Jesse H. Heath wrote, "Stuart is collecting a great deal

26. Williams C. Wickham to Lucy, May 15, 1863, Wickham Family Papers, UVA.
27. Wert, *Cavalryman of the Lost Cause*, 240-41; Eric J. Wittenberg, *The Union Cavalry Comes of Age*, 237–38.

of cavalry for what purpose I do not know ...The men are all anxious for a big Pennsylvania raid and they will give fits if they do not go."[28] By May 19, Wickham's 4th Virginia's ranks had risen to 536 enlisted men, while the regiment remained in Spotsylvania County.[29]

On May 11, Gen. Robert E. Lee ordered Stuart to move his cavalry from Orange County north to Culpeper County in preparation for his planned invasion of the Keystone State. After his success at Chancellorsville, Lee planned to lead his army through the Shenandoah Valley for his second invasion of the North, where he was determined to capture horses, equipment, and food for his men. He was also hoping to threaten as far north as Harrisburg, Pennsylvania, or even Philadelphia, thereby influencing Northern politicians to give up their prosecution of the war. By May 22, Stuart had moved nearly 7,000 troopers from Wade Hampton's, Rooney Lee's, and Fitzhugh Lee's brigades to Culpepper; and by June 5, another 3,000 from Beverly Robertson's and William E. Jones's brigades joined them. Robertson's brigade camped southwest of Brandy Station near the John Minor Botts farm, while Jones came from the Shenandoah Valley. Lee's invasion plan called for Stuart to position his Confederate cavalry on the right flank of his army to screen the infantry and protect its rear.[30]

On May 15, Williams wrote his father:

> **"I am so anxious to get out of the war and be at home that although I had intended never again to have anything to do with politics and thought the time for giving notice is very short. I have today sent a card to the Richmond papers announcing myself as a candidate for Congress. It is the only accord left me for getting out as my resignation has blocked."**[31]

Lee's army was then at Fredericksburg, across the Rappahannock from Falmouth. He intended to march north to Pennsylvania. Hooker wanted to uncover Lee's plans. He knew that Lee was at Culpeper; but would he head north, or would he suddenly turn east and move toward Washington? Hooker assigned his entire cavalry corps-two brigades of infantry and four artillery batteries—to determine Lee's intentions by conducting a raid.[32]

---

28. Stiles, *4th Virginia Cavalry*, 27.
29. Ibid.
30. Heros Von Borcke, *Memoirs of the Confederate War for Independence*, vol. 2:264-65; OR 25/2:792.
31. Williams C. Wickham to William F. Wickham, May 15, 1863, Wickham Family Papers, UVA.
32. Wert, *Cavalryman of the Lost Cause*, 240.

When the brigade moved to Culpeper Court House on May 20, the 4th Virginia remained behind, picketing the lower Rappahannock for ten days during warming weather. The 4th Virginia, at this time with 590 effectives, was the largest regiment in Fitz Lee's brigade.[33]

Mumford's 2nd Virginia continued to picket the area along the Rappahannock until General Hooker had withdrawn across the Rappahannock on May 6. By May 20, the 2nd Virginia went back into camp near Culpeper Court House. The next day, a review of Fitzhugh Lee's brigade was held, followed on May 22 on John Botts's farm by a 4,000-man cavalry review by Stuart of the brigades of Fitz Lee, W. H. F. Lee, Wade Hampton, and the horse artillery of Maj. Robert F. Beckham. Shortly after the review, Robertson's brigade from North Carolina and William E. Jones's brigade from the Valley arrived, effectively doubling the size of cavalry under Stuart's command. Stuart scheduled another review for June 5, when it was expected that Robert E. Lee would attend.[34]

On May 31, 1863, Williams wrote to Lucy:

> After I had done all I had to do this morning I went down to Gen. Lee's, where I always find it pleasant, his staff being all nice gentlemen and had a most pleasant day dining with them and being an hour or more with the General, who is very well and in good spirits. In discussing the possibility of ending the war, Wickham thought that if we can beat them (enemy) at Vicksburg and Gen. Lee can get a fair chance at Hooker, I think it must wind up the war, the war I'm satisfied both parties are heartily tired.[35]

Robert E. Lee began marching his army north on June 3, as Wickham's 4th Virginia remained behind near Fredericksburg.

On June 5, General Stuart held another review of his corps on an open field near the little hamlet of Inlet Station, four miles northeast of Culpepper. The review was—not only a military parade—but also one of those magnificent pageants and splendid social events which the flashy Stuart loved to stage. The entire division passed in review with three bands playing and a flag waving at the head of each regiment. Then the column divided into brigades and regiments that performed drills. In a climactic finale, the troopers—yelling—their sabers drawn,

---

33. Stiles, *4th Virginia Cavalry*, 27.
34. Driver, *2nd Virginia Cavalry*, 80; McClellan, *The Campaigns of Stuart's Cavalry*, 261.
35. Williams C. Wickham to Lucy Wickham, May 31, 1863, Wickham Family Papers, UVA.

charged at the artillery, which was posted at intervals around the perimeter of the field. The artillery fired blank cartridges at the charging horsemen in a noisy conclusion. The day ended with another ball "on a piece of turf near headquarters, and by the light of enormous wood fires, the ruddy glare of which upon the animated groups ... gave the whole scene a wild and romantic effect."[36]

Not all were happy with these reviews. Some, such as Wade Hampton and the irascible "Grumble" Jones, considered them a waste of resources. Jones and his brigade had just arrived on June 3 and 4, and the men and horses were tired and needed rest. The review of June 5 did not allow for a respite.[37]

Robert E. Lee had been invited to review the troops, but he was unable to attend. General Lee ordered another review, and it was held on June 8. Lee surveyed all of his cavalry, some 9,500 troopers, at Inlet Station. According to Munford, Stuart was "as untiring on horseback as a Centaur—setting his steed as if part of his existence. No more dashing soldier ever drew a saber," Munford, however, complained, "In a fight, he was clearheaded, and inspired by word and example implicit confidence in his men; but his 'Leprechonian' tendencies would allow him to forget his men and horses. He kept [them] on picket all night–without rations—while he with jingling spurs and twinkling eyes reveled in the dance."[38]

The Confederate plan for the next morning, June 9, called for two full corps of infantry, under Lieutenant Generals James Longstreet and Richard S. Ewell, to march west into the Shenandoah Valley and then north towards Pennsylvania. Lieutenant General A. P. Hill's corps would temporarily remain on the banks of the Rappahannock to cover the movement. The cavalry command, under orders to screen Lee's invading forces, included the brigades of Brigadier Generals Wade Hampton, "Rooney" Lee, Beverly Robertson, "Grumble" Jones, Fitzhugh Lee (under Col. Thomas Munford due to Lee's bout with inflammatory rheumatism); and Capt. James F. Hart's battery of Maj. Robert F. Beckham's horse artillery. Lee wanted Stuart's cavalry to cross the Rappahannock at Beverly Ford, four miles northeast of Brandy Station, on the morning of June 9.[39]

Meanwhile, Gen. Joseph Hooker had ordered most of his cavalry and two brigades of infantry, totaling about 11,000 men and led by newly-appointed Federal cavalry commander Brig. Gen. Alfred

36. Von Borcke, *Memoirs of the Confederate War for Independence*, vol. 2:264-65.
37. Longacre, *Lee's Cavalrymen*, 188.
38. Thomas T. Munford to Anne Bachman Hyde, August 29, 1915, SHC, University of North Carolina, Chapel Hill.
39. *OR* 27/2:692.

Pleasonton, to attack the Confederates. Pleasonton devised a plan that assumed the gray horsemen were still near the village of Culpeper Court House, having heard of the Confederate cavalry's recent assembling there. His scheme consisted of attacks by two cavalry columns under Brigadier Generals John Buford and David M. Gregg. Buford, supported by infantry—would cross at Beverly Ford; while Gregg would cross at Kelly's Ford. The two Federal cavalry commands would then link up at Brandy Station. From there they intended to push to Culpeper. The plan was doomed from the start because Stuart was, in fact, bivouacked on Fleetwood Hill near Brandy Station; and Grumble Jones's brigade and Robert Beckham's artillery were camped just southwest of Beverly Ford itself. The Federals would find themselves trying to concentrate their forces while in the midst of Confederate cavalry.[40]

On the evening of June 8, 1863, a large Union cavalry column under Gen. John Buford positioned itself for a surprise move across Beverly Ford the next morning, where—unbeknownst to the Federals—no the Confederate cavalry was also planning to cross. Some six miles south at Kelly's Ford, General Gregg's 2,400-man Union cavalry division was also positioned to cross.[41]

On command, at 4:30 a.m. on June 9, Col. Benjamin F. "Grimes" Davis's 8th New York Cavalry led the Union column splashing across Beverly Ford in a thick fog. The battle of Brandy Station, the largest single cavalry battle of the Civil War, including about 2,000 Union infantrymen, had begun. The immense plains at Brandy Station were perfectly suited for such a cavalry engagement.[42]

General Buford was not expecting the presence of a Confederate force on the other side, but his attack surprised the Confederates. Many were still sleeping or cooking breakfast when the first shots were fired. Buford's attack was stalled by two guns from Hart's Battery; while Beckham's battalion—in imminent danger of being captured—made good an escape to higher ground at St. James Church, just as the surprised Confederates of the 6th and 7th Virginia Cavalry of Grumble Jones's brigade arrived on the scene. During the opening moments of the fight, Col. Grimes Davis was mortally wounded on Beverly Ford Road. Davis's 8th New York, now leaderless, began to retreat. Soon, the Federals regrouped and again attacked the Confederate brigades of Grumble Jones and Rooney Lee. Lee, at the

40. Longacre, *Lee's Cavalrymen*, 190; Stephen W. Sears, *Gettysburg* (New York: Houghton Mifflin, 2004), 64-66.
41. *OR* 27/1:949–52.
42. Major H. B. McClellan gives the Federal force as 10,981 and Stuart's as 9,536; McClellan, *The Life and Campaigns of Major-General J.E.B. Stuart*, 293.

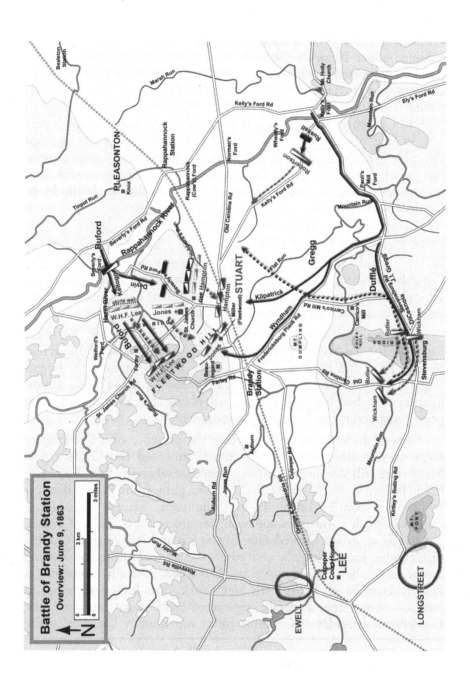

Battle of Brandy Station
Overview: June 9, 1863

Hal Jespersen

first sound of gunfire, moved his troopers from Welford's Ford just west of Beverly Ford to near St. James Church.[43]

General Stuart ordered Hampton, whose troopers at Brandy Station were awakened by the gunfire at Beverly Ford, to support Generals Jones and Lee, under attack at Beverly Ford Road. In accordance with Stuart's orders, Hampton left one regiment, the 2nd South Carolina under Col. Matthew C. Butler, in reserve at Brandy Station. His three remaining units, the 1st North Carolina, the Cobb Legion, and the Jeff Davis Legion, soon arrived at Beverly Ford Road and took position on the right of Major Beckham's horse artillery.[44]

Called to aid the 2nd South Carolina Cavalry at Stevensburg on June 9, Colonel Wickham led his troopers and a single piece of artillery to Stevensburg, marching by side roads through thick pine forests as shots were heard emanating from Beverly and Kelly's Fords.[45]

Both Gregg's and Buford's advances had been repelled by the Confederates. But Colonel Alfred N. Duffie, and 1,900 troopers under his command, had crossed Kelly's Ford in advance of Gregg that morning and marched inland. By 11 a.m., Duffie's progress had slowed due to weariness and unfamiliar roads and was just approaching Stevensburg, four miles south of Brandy Station. There, Duffie was met by Colonel Matthew Calbraith Butler's 2nd South Carolina, which had been held by Stuart in reserve. Alerted to Duffie's flanking movement by scouts, Butler recalled, "There was nothing left for me to do but to move without orders as rapidly as our horses would carry us and ... and check the advance."[46]

Realizing the urgency of the situation, Butler ordered Lt. Col. Frank Hampton and 20 troopers to sprint to Stevensburg and do whatever they could to delay the Union advance. He also dispatched Major Thomas J. Lipscomb and 40 horsemen to swing east, cross Mountain Road at Cole's Hill and approach Stevensburg from the north. Butler was counting on Frank Hampton to buy sufficient time for him to deploy his small force on commanding high ground known as Hansborough Ridge, just outside of Stevensburg. The woods and the sloping ground concealed the smallness of Butler's command.

Butler's 225 troopers were badly outnumbered, but he hustled his command down the Old Carolina Road. He now retained but 190

43. *OR* 27/2:721–22; Clark B. Hall, "The Battle of Brandy Station," *Civil War Times Illustrated* (May/June 1990), 35; Fairfax Downey, *Clash of Cavalry* (New York, 1959), 94.
44. *OR* 27/2:680, 721–22; U. R. Brooks, *Stories of the Confederacy* (Columbia, S.C., 1912), 145–46.
45. Stiles, *4th Virginia Cavalry*, 28; *OR* 27/2:680.
46. George Walsh, *Those Damn Horse Soldiers: True Tales of the Civil War Cavalry* (New York: Tom Dohterty Associates, 2006), 168; *OR* 27/2:683.

troopers as Colonel Butler detached 30 troopers to block adjacent Carrico's Mill Road. As leading elements of the 2nd South Carolina arrived in Stevensburg, a 6th Ohio Cavalry patrol was forced back east of a prominent ridge that sharply rose just east of the hamlet. Colonel Butler immediately decided to utilize Hansbrough Ridge as his defensive platform since this mile-long ridge blocked any enemy approach toward Stevensburg and Culpeper Court House, five miles beyond. Arranging his forces north to south on the ridge, facing east, Butler dispatched Capt. T. E. Screven with 60 troopers with orders to hold the northern section of the ridge; Colonel Butler secured the center of the ridge with an equal number; and Lt. Col. Frank Hampton held the southern section of the ridge with the remainder of the regiment. Hampton situated himself near the base of the Wishard Doggett house, then situated on the military crest of eastern Hansbrough Ridge.

Major Henry B. McClellan reported:

> **The woods concealed the smallness of (Butler's) numbers, and even on the road, the sloping ground prevented the enemy from discovering any but the leading files of Hampton's detachment. The enemy's advance was cautious, even timid. As Butler had anticipated, the first attempt was to break the line of his dismounted men on his left, and two such attacks were made, but both were repulsed by the close fire of his Enfield rifles."[47]**

Alerted that Federal cavalry threatened his rear at Stevensburg, General Stuart dispatched the 4th Virginia Cavalry from near Brandy Station toward Stevensburg as tactical support for the 2nd South Carolina. Soon, about 600 troopers commanded by Colonel Williams C. Wickham galloped toward Hansbrough Ridge. Wickham's force moved by way of "Mountain Road" from Norman's Mill to toward the "Hansbrough Gap," near the southern terminus of Hansbrough Ridge.[48]

As Wickham arrived, he sent Lt. Col. William H. Payne forward to alert Butler that reinforcements had arrived. Butler had requested that Payne report his dispositions to Wickham and to inform him and that he would gladly take orders from him. Wickham, who was senior to Butler, demurred, declining to assume command—probably due to

47. Ibid.; Clark B. Hall, "Stevensburg Phase, Battle of Brandy Station," https://www.battlefields.org/learn/articles/fight-hansbrough-ridge-june-9-1863.
48. Clark B. Hall, "Stevensburg Phase, Battle of Brandy Station"; Clark B. Hall, "Fight for Hansbrough Ridge: June 9, 1863," Battlefield Trust.

the strategic situation; Butler was firmly entrenched and knew the details of the terrain. Therefore, Butler requested that Wickham send two small squadrons to support Frank Hampton's squadron. The remainder of the 4th Virginia was to come into a line dismounted alongside the balance of Butler's regiment.[49]

Wickham's horsemen moved up in support of Hampton on Butler's right in an effort to stabilize the situation. Wickham's riders, however, constrained by the terrain from forming a battle line, became sacrificial lambs. "Wickham's regiment was in a position where it was impossible for it to act, enclosed as it was in a thick pine copse, on a narrow by-road," H. B. McClellan recalled, adding "where even a close column of fours could scarcely move. It was therefore necessary to turn the head of his column westward, toward Stevensburg."[50]

Wickham's men found themselves riding into the full fury of Duffie's advance. Without cover, Wickham's Virginians endured a hail of fire, then broke and ran. Major McClellan avowed that "there was not a finer body of men in the service ... But on this day, a panic possessed them. They did not respond to the efforts of their officers, and the enemy's pursuit was continued through Stevensburg and beyond ... where Colonel Wickham and a few of his men threw themselves into a field by a road-side, and by the fire of their pistols checked further pursuit."[51] Any other unit in the 4th Virginia's place would almost assuredly also have retreated in pell-mell fashion.

Duffie turned his attention to Lt. Col. Frank Hampton on the Confederate right, who, seeing the 1st Massachusetts approaching, met the charge with one of his own. Hampton and his men never had a chance. The weight of the Yankee onslaught overwhelmed them, scattering the command and sending Hampton to the ground with a mortal wound.[52] Hampton, a handsome man, had been slashed by a saber to the head and face, disfiguring him badly. He also had been shot in the stomach. He was taken to John S. Barbour's house, "Clover Hill," a mile west of Stevensburg, where he died that night.[53]

49. Ibid., Eric J. Wittenberg, *The Battle of Brandy Station: North America's Largest Cavalry Battle* (Charleston, S.C. History Press, 2010), 172.
50. George Walsh, *Those Damn Horse Soldiers: True Tales of Civil War Cavalry* (New York: Tom Doherty Associates, 2006), 169; H. B. McClellan, *The Life and Campaigns of Major General J.E.B. Stuart: Commander of the Cavalry of the Army of Northern Virginia* (Boston and New York: Houghton, Mifflin and Company, 1885), 289.
51. McClellan, *The Life and Campaigns of Major General J.E.B. Stuart: Commander of the Cavalry of the Army of Northern Virginia* (Boston and New York: Houghton, Mifflin and Company, 1885), 289. These occurrences in war happen, with no clear blame assigned.
52. Ibid.
53. Ibid.

Duffie followed this success with slashing attacks by the 1st Rhode Island and the 6th Ohio on Butler's main body, pushing it back through Stevensburg. "The enemy, having gained possession of the road ... from Culpeper," reported Maj. Thomas Lipscomb of the 2nd South Carolina, "... the right of our line fell back obliquely to the road leading from Stevensburg to Brandy Station. They were rallied and formed by Colonel Butler ... but the columns of the enemy pouring on the woods on his left, and threatening to gain his rear, compelled him (again) to fall back."[54] Union cannon fire erupted; one shell landing just 30 yards in front Butler, skipped and hit Butler and mortally wounded his horse. Butler was knocked off his horse with his right foot hanging by "a thread." "His was bleeding profusely, and Captain William D. Farley applied a tourniquet to keep Butler from bleeding out. Later, Butler's foot was amputated above the ankle.[55]

Major General Wade Hampton blamed the failures of Wickham's 4th Virginia Cavalry and Wickham himself at Brandy Station for the death of his brother, Lt. Col. Frank Hampton, who had been fatally wounded in the fight at Stevensburg, four miles south of Fleetwood Hill. Major General Calbrairh Butler insisted that he had asked Wickham to support Lieutenant Colonel Hampton, but Wickham failed to do so. Communications, as so often happen during battle, had broken down. The 4th Virginia had broken and run pell-mell during the fight, but so had many troopers of Frank Hampton's 2nd South Carolina. To his credit, Wickham had tried valiantly to rally his 4th Virginia, remaining on the field nearly alone. Hampton's grief over the loss of his brother may have caused him to overreact against Wickham.

For his part, General Stuart reported that all brigade commanders, including Wade Hampton, "were prompt in the execution of orders, and conformed readily to the emergencies arising." Stuart regretted that the 4th Virginia "broke in utter confusion without firing a gun, in spite of every effort of the colonel to rally the men to the charge. This regiment usually fights well, and its stampede on this occasion is unaccountable."[56]

Wade Hampton, who rarely criticized fellow officers, many years later wrote to a fellow soldier, "But for the fact that the 4th Virginia,

---

54. Ibid.
55. Ibid., 291; Samuel J. Martin, *Southern Hero: Matthew Calbraith Butler* (Mechanicsburg, PA: Stackpole Books, 2001), 74-75.
56. *OR* 27/2:683; 27/1:961. Frank Hampton was mortally wounded by a disfiguring saber wound across the face and head and a gunshot wound to the stomach. He died later the same day of the fight. Ref: Walter Brian Cisco, *Wade Hampton: Confederate Warrior, Conservative Statesman* (Washington, D.C.: Potomac Books, 2004), 117.

General Wade Hampton blamed Wickham and his 4th Virginia Cavalry for the death of his brother, Lt. Col. Frank Hampton.

(*Library of Congress*)

under the command of Colonel Wickham, broke and ran, my brother, Frank Hampton, would not have been killed that day."[57]

Wickham described the action at Stevensburg in his official report:

> Early in the morning, I was ordered to report to General Stuart, and, upon reporting, was ordered by Major (H. B.) McClellan to proceed to Stevensburg, and support the Second South Carolina Cavalry, the colonel of which reported that there was a heavy force of the enemy approaching. I was told that a piece of artillery would follow me upon nearing Norman's Mills.[58]

I received a message from Capt. (W. D.) Farley, of General Stuart's staff, that I had better come by the road on the left of the field than go direct to the village, as I proposed to do. Going forth at a trot, I found myself with the head of my column at the road from Stevensburg to Willis Madden's, about three-quarters of a mile from the village, in a road running through a thick pine copse, and on the flank of the Second South Carolina Cavalry.[59]

Receiving a message at the moment from Colonel [M. C.] Butler that he wanted more sharpshooters, I detached my first squadron, and sent it to him on the left, and ordered the rest of the regiment to be put in the road, with its head resting a quarter of a mile in the rear of the Second South Carolina, while I galloped to the front, to see the state of affairs.[60]

On reaching Doggett's House, I saw the enemy with a squadron formed in the road in column, and a squadron forming in line on the right, about 400 yards from me. Here, I found Lieutenant Colonel (Frank) Hampton, who had two very small squadrons with him, drawn up ready to meet a charge, if made. Finding no sharpshooters on the right, I dismounted a company, and threw them on the right. Before the arrangement could be completed, I found that the enemy were charging the Second South Carolina, which, without meeting the charge, had broken, and were rushing down on the rear of my column, which was just emerging from the pines.[61]

---

57. Manly Wade Wellman, *Giant if Gray: A Biography of Wade Hampton of South Carolina* (New York: Charles Scribner's sons, 1949), 109; U. R. Brooks, *Butler and His Cavalry in the War of Secession, 1861-1865* (Columbia, S.C.: The State Company, 1909), 169; Wade Hampton to Edward L. Wells, January 18, 1900, Wells correspondence at the Charleston, SC public library.
58. *OR* 27/2:743-44.
59. *OR* 27/2:731, 744. Captain Farley was mortally wounded in this fight.
60. Ibid.
61. Ibid.

Finding that my desire to put my right in front was thus frustrated, I wheeled my column by fours, and ineffectually endeavored to get my men to meet the charge, but the rush of the Second South Carolina Cavalry utterly demoralized them, and they broke and fled in confusion. After going some third of a mile, I succeeded in stopping some men, and again attempted to charge the enemy, who, upon seeing my stand, had halted, and were forming a line; but although the line wavered at the approach of only 6 who went forward to within 20 feet of it, the others would not follow, but again fled at the approach of a squadron of the enemy; nor for the next mile could all my efforts obtain the slightest halt in my fleeing squadrons. On reaching Barbour's gate, I turned in, and with me 3 or 4 officers and 5 or 6 men. These I immediately halted, and commenced firing at the flank of the pursuing squadron, which at once wheeled about, and retired through the village.[62]

The squadron sent to the left retired at Colonel Butler's command in good order, crossing below the mill, and going to the support of the artillery. The fifth squadron, though fleeing at first, went toward the mill, and, not being pursued, were rallied, and retired from under the enemy's artillery fire across the mill-dam. There were four regiments of the enemy's cavalry at Stevensburg.[63]

After much difficulty, I collected my scattered men, and, in connection with Major Lipscomb, then in command of the Second South Carolina, I ascertained that the enemy had passed off to the left, and were no longer in my front. My loss was 15 wounded and 27 missing. I took some prisoners, but not as many as I lost.[64]

I regard the conduct of my regiment, in which I have heretofore had perfect confidence, as so disgraceful in this instance that I have been thus minute in my report, that the major-general commanding, to whom I request that this be forwarded, may have the facts before him on which to base any inquiry he may see fit to institute.[65]

Major T. J. Lipscomb, who took over command of 2nd South Carolina Cavalry upon Col. Frank Hampton's being mortally wounded, submitted a report of the action, which was amended by Colonel Butler. The report stated:

> ... prior to the charge made by the enemy, and while establishing our lines, the command was turned over to Col. Wickham, of the Fourth Virginia Cavalry, who had

62. Ibid.
63. Ibid.
64. Ibid.
65. Ibid, 744-45. A court of inquiry was never conducted.

been sent by Gen. Stuart with his command and one piece of artillery to the support of Col. Butler, who had gone to the left, to establish sharpshooters along the crest of the wooded hills, which the enemy were threatening. Col. Butler informed Col. Wickman that the enemy were reported advancing in heavy force, and what disposition he had made of the small force under his command, and suggested to him to move his regiment up the road to the support of Lieut. Col. [Frank] Hampton, leaving the piece of artillery on the hill near Stevensburg, as he believed that would be the main point of attack. Col. Butler had no personal interview with Col. Wickham, but sent these messages through Lieut.-Col. [William H.] Payne and couriers. As soon as he had established the line of skirmishers and they had commenced firing, he moved rapidly toward where Lieut. Col. Hampton was stationed, on the right and in the road. Before reaching him, he met Adjutant Moore, who informed him that a heavy column of the enemy had charged him, and swept his little force before them. He turned at right angles to the right, and met the men about 300 yards from where they had been charged. They rallied and formed promptly, the enemy pursuing the Fourth Virginia Cavalry along the road toward Culpeper. The artillery was never placed in position beyond Norman's Mills, and was of no service, notwithstanding repeated messages from Col. Butler to bring it over and place it in position. Nor did Col. Butler hear from Col. Wickham.[66]

Rooney Lee had been severely wounded in his thigh during the battle of Brandy Station on June 13, 1863. On June 26, 1863, he was taken to Hickory Hill by his younger brother, Robert Lee, Jr., so that he could be with his wife, Charlotte Wickham Lee (half-sister of William and Edward Wickham), and his mother and sisters who were staying at Hickory Hill, while he recuperated from his wound.[67]

On June 26, a Union raiding party of about 1,200 Federal cavalrymen left the White House on the road to Hanover Court House, tearing up railroad tracks for four miles to Turnstall's Station. Upon arriving at Colonel Wickham's farm, Hickory Hill, they camped for the night. A small contingent was sent to capture Rooney Lee, having been told he was at Wickham's. At the time, Rooney Lee

---

66. *OR* 27/2:731.
67. Monte Akers, *Year of Desperate Struggle: Jeb Stuart and His Cavalry, from Gettysburg to Yellow Tavern, 1863-1864* (Philadelphia: Casemate Publishers, 2115), 122.

was staying in the plantation office with his nurse, brother Robert "Rob" Lee, Jr. About two weeks after arriving, Robert Jr. and Mrs. Wickham stepped out onto the front veranda after having just finished breakfast and heard shots ringing out in the Hickory grove down by the gate. She sent Robert to put a stop to the sport. While riding to the gate, Robert espied the raiders approach shortly before they reached the mansion. Wheeling his horse around, he raced back to his brother in the Plantation's office and attempted to remove Rooney quickly. Rooney protested that he himself had always paroled wounded prisoners and had no doubt the Yankees would do the same, not knowing that they were coming specifically to capture him.[68]

Rooney Lee was captured in the Hickory Hill Plantation office and carted away on a stolen wagon while his wife, two children, mother and sisters stood watching. William F. Wickham, upon returning to Hickory Hill shortly after the Federal raid, wrote Robert E. Lee about the happenings at Hickory Hill:

> I went to town last Friday at 8 o'clock & heard by telegraph that the Yankees had visited my house a few hours after I left there. I could not get home again till last evening. Their cavalry got here at 12 o'clock & left here at 5 o'clock. They carried off Genl W. H. F. Lee as a prisoner in my carriage. It seems to me a great outrage to have done so in the condition in which he was, but his wound was healing, & I do not think, further than the annoyance from the act, that he will suffer any serious inconvenience. I am told that he bore his arrest, as might be expected, with great composure. He was not treated with the least incivility, with exception of one or two words to my wife, by which rough men meant nothing, we have no reason to complain of the Yankees, further than their taking your son prisoner & their carrying off my horses & negroes of which I lost a good number. I have thought proper to give you this information, but from the letters of the ladies you might apprehend we had been treated with indignity. I feel confident that Fitzhugh will meet with kind treatment & with the attention that his situation requires. Charlotte, whose health is not good is dreadfully in distress, but I hope as she hears from her husband, as she did yesterday morning, that she will become more composed.[69]

---

68. Ibid, 123; *Richmond Daily Dispatch*, June 27, 1863.
69. William F. Wickham to Robert E. Lee, June 28, 1863, The Papers of Robert E. Lee, 1830-1870, Albert and Shirley Small Special Collections Library, UVA.

W. H. F. "Rooney" Lee was captured at Hickory Hill, where he had been taken to convalesce after his serious wound at the Battle of Brandy Station.

(Library of Congress)

Rooney Lee would be held in prison at Fort Monroe for nine months, during which time, his two children died of Scarlet Fever, and his wife died of what Robert E. Lee said was a broken heart.[70]

Robert, Jr. had escaped into the formal garden on the grounds and burrowed into the boxwood maze watching the whole affair unfolded, periodically creeping close to see if all was clear, but he was turned back several times. Meanwhile, Scott, their faithful manservant, led all but one of the officer's horses to safety. Afterwards, he was captured,

---

70. Akers, *Year of Desperate Struggle: Jeb Stuart and His Cavalry, from Gettysburg to Yellow Tavern, 1863-1864*, 123.

escaped, and returned. The Yankees, rightly or wrongly, believed that they had been taken across the Pamunkey River into Caroline County to their Uncle Williams Carter's plantation, "North Wales." Not content with their capture of the general, horses, wagon and other items looted from Hickory Hill, the Yankees sent a raiding party to North Wales to steal the officer's blooded horses. Not discovering them, they proceeded to beat the old gentleman to death, but he did not disclose the whereabouts of the boys' horses.[71]

Afterwards, even with the weight of Gettysburg upon him, Robert E. Lee, always the gentleman, wrote to his daughter-in-law, Charlotte (whom he referred to as daughter) while he was penned up in Hagerstown, Maryland waiting for the waters to fall so he could cross back into Virginia: "The consequences of war are horrid enough at best, surrounded by all the amelioration of civilization and Christianity. I am very sorry for the injuries done the family at Hickory Hill and particularly that our dear old Uncle Williams, in his eightieth year, should be subjected to such treatment, but we cannot help it and must endure it." While Rooney was held in a damp cell in Fortress Monroe, his children died of scarlet fever; and his wife Charlotte wasted away. General Robert E. Lee always expressed the opinion that she died of a broken heart.[72]

Rooney Lee's plight was a constant grief to his family, not least to his father. Robert E. Lee wrote Rooney's wife, Charlotte:

> I can appreciate your distress at Fitzhugh's (Rooney Lee) situation. I deeply sympathize with it, and in the lone hours of the night I groan in sorrow at his captivity and separation from you ... But we must bear it, exercise all our patience, and do nothing to aggravate the evil... I can see no harm that can come from Fitzhugh's capture, except his detention... I feel assure he will be well attended to. He will be in the hands of old army officers and surgeons, most of whom are men of principle and humanity.[73]

At first, in prison at Fort Monroe, Rooney Lee had been placed in a hospital and was well cared for. He had been allowed liberty to confine himself to the hospital on his assurance that he would not attempt to escape while there.[74] On July 15, however, Rooney Lee had

71. Ibid.
72. Robert E. Lee to Charlotte Wickham Lee. July 12, 1863; Douglas Southall Freeman, *R. E. Lee: A Biography* (New York: Scribner & Sons, 1934), 3.
73. Robert E. Lee to Charlotte Wickham Lee. July 26, 1863, Robert E. Lee, Jr., *Recollections and Letters of Robert E. Lee*, 34 (Kindle Edition).
74. *OR*, Series II, 6:69.

been ordered into close confinement and had been threatened with death by hanging—if the Confederate authorities executed Capt. W. H. Sawyer and Capt. John M. Flinn. These two Federal officers had been selected among the officers confined in Libby Prison and were sentenced to death for the killing of Capt. T. G. McGraw and Capt. William F. Corbin., who had been captured as spies within the Federal lines in Kentucky.[75]

Robert E. Lee never believed in retaliation, but he made no effort to intervene in his son's behalf. The Federal threat, however, had been effective in preventing the execution of Sawyer and Flinn. This event, in turn, had probably saved Rooney's life. All exchanges had been suspended, providing Rooney and his father with no idea of when he might be released. Rooney was still hopeful of an early exchange, but he would not be released until March 1864.[76]

Gradually, the restraints on Rooney Lee were relaxed at Fort Monroe, until he received so many friends and visitors that the authorities decided to send him to Johnson's Island Prison. Fortunately for Rooney, his orders were changed to send him to Fort Lafayette. He left Fort Monroe on November 13, 1863. Robert E. Lee told his family that this was a better situation, in as much "as any place would be better than Fort Monroe, with Butler in command." He added, "His long confinement is very grievous to me, yet it may turn out for the best."[77]

Still, the Federal authorities, admitting that Lee was not a spy, were not interested in exchanging him. In fact, they schemed to put impediments in his path to prolong his imprisonment. Enduring the stress associated with Charlott's sickly condition worsened. All of her vitality seemed to be slipping away. She died soon thereafter.[78]

Wickham liked Stuart, and apparently Stuart felt the same of Wickham. Wickham wrote Lucy of Stuart, "I went down to see Gen. Stuart and stayed with him yesterday on account of the storm, coming back today. I had a very pleasant visit. I am very fond of the Gen. and like him more and more every time [I] am with him."[79]

---

75. *OR*, Series II, 6:116, 1117; 5:691, 702; Douglas Southall Freeman, *R. E. Lee: A Biography* (New York: Scribner & Sons, 1934), 3:210-11.
76. Robert E. Lee to G. W. C. Lee, September 27, 1863, DU.
77. *OR*, Series II, 5:484-85, 495, 500, 516; Robert E. Lee, Jr., *Recollections and Letters of Robert E. Lee*, 40-41 (Kindle Edition); Douglas Southall Freeman, *R. E. Lee: A Biography* (New York: Scribner & Sons, 1934), 3:211.
78. *OR*, Series II, 5:706.
79. http://www.historyunderglass.net/confederate-general-williams-carter-wickham-war-date-autograph-letter-signed-2; The date of the letter is not known, but it is in 1863.

Chapter Six

1863: Gettysburg
and Fall Cavalry Reorganization

Meanwhile, despite the hard-fought battle at Brandy Station, Robert E. Lee saw no reason to delay his planned invasion of the North for more than a day. By June 10, Lee was convinced that Pleasonton's attack at Brandy did not signal a general offensive. That same day, Lee ordered Maj. Gen. Richard S. Ewell, who would lead the invasion vanguard, to resume his march from Culpeper to the Shenandoah Valley. Lee's infantry was on the move. Stuart's cavalry command remained at Brandy Station. Stuart tended to the wounded, culled unfit horses, sent troopers to find remounts, distributed captured weapons, and revamped his command to fill vacancies. He elevated Colonel John Chambliss to replace the wounded Rooney Lee. A week later, Robert E. Lee called on Stuart to join his northern marching army. Stuart and his cavalry had revenge on their minds, with Stuart reporting, "I am standing on the Rappahannock, looking beyond ... and feel not unlike a tiger pausing before its spring."[1]

Meanwhile on June 27, after the battle of Brandy Station, Lincoln replaced General Hooker with Maj. Gen. George Gordon Meade as commander of the Army of the Potomac.[2]

At the outset of Lee's northern invasion, Ewell's II Corps led the Confederate advance to Pennsylvania, while Longstreet's I Corps marched to Culpepper. A. P. Hill's III Corps remained at Fredericksburg until Hooker's intentions could be ascertained. Hooker, having been ordered to protect Washington, soon left the Fredericksburg area. J.E.B. Stuart's role was to operate on Lee's right flank and screen the Army of Northern Virginia's movements from the Union army. Pleasonton was ordered to determine Lee's movements by fighting through Stuart's screen.[3]

1. Edward G. Longacre, *The Cavalry at Gettysburg: A Tactical Study of Mounted Operations During the Civil War's Pivotal Campaign, 9 June–14 July, 1863* (Lincoln, Neb.: University of Nebraska Press, 1986), 93;
2. Sears, *Gettysburg*, 90, 123.
3. Ibid., 83–84, 94, 97, 105.

Wade Hampton's and Grumble Jones's cavalry brigades remained on the Rappahannock in order to maintain contact with A. P. Hill. Meanwhile, Stuart took Robertson's, Fitz Lee's (still under Munford), and Rooney Lee's troopers (under Chambliss) to guard Longstreet's right and front. Rooney Lee (replaced by Col. John R. Chambliss) had suffered a severe wound at Brandy Station and had been taken to Col. Williams Wickham's residence in Hanover County to recuperate, but a Union raiding party learned of his location and captured him. He was exchanged in March 1864. Fitz Lee was suffering a bout of inflammatory rheumatism of the knee, and Colonel Thomas T. Munford, a reliable, experienced cavalry officer, took over temporary command of Lee's brigade.[4]

The Battle of Aldie, June 17, 1863

The battle of Aldie occurred on June 17, 1863, in Loudoun County, as part of the Gettysburg campaign. Stuart's cavalry screened Gen. Robert E. Lee's infantry as it marched north in the Shenandoah Valley, behind the sheltering Blue Ridge Mountains.[5]

Late in the spring of 1863, tensions grew between Union commander General Hooker and his cavalry commander Alfred Pleasonton, because of the latter's inability to penetrate Stuart's cavalry screen. Pleasonton failed to gain access to the Shenandoah Valley to locate the Army of Northern Virginia, which had been on the move since the battle of Chancellorsville. On June 17, Pleasonton decided to push through Stuart's screen. To accomplish his goal, he ordered Brig. Gen. David McMurtie Gregg's division from Manassas Junction westward down the Little River Turnpike to Aldie. Aldie was tactically important because the Little River Turnpike intersected both Ashby's Gap Turnpike and Snicker's Gap Turnpike, which respectively led through Ashby's Gap and Snicker's Gap of the Blue Ridge Mountains into the Valley.[6]

Brigadier General Alfred Pleasonton did a poor job of bringing Gen. Joseph Hooker information on Lee's movements because he was unable to penetrate Stuart's screen. On June 16, Union General-in-Chief Gen. Henry Halleck wrote to Hooker, "The information sent here by General Pleasonton is very unsatisfactory." Through Maj. Gen. Daniel Butterfield, Hooker's chief of staff, Pleasonton was told to be

---

4. Longacre, *Lee's Cavalrymen*, 197; McClellan, *Campaigns of Stuart's Cavalry*, 296.
5. Sears, *Gettysburg*, 83–84, 94, 97, 105.
6. Mark Nesbitt, *Saber and Scapegoat: J.E.B. Stuart and the Gettysburg Controversy* (Mechanicsburg, PA, 1994), 46.

more aggressive in gathering information. On June 17, Pleasanton was ordered to "Drive in pickets, if necessary, and get us information. It is better that we lose men than to be without knowledge of the enemy, as we now seem to be." Pleasanton responded by sending a division toward the gaps in the Blue Ridge Mountains.[7]

Two turnpikes ran west from the town of Aldie, through Aldie's Gap in the Bull Run Mountains and to Ashby's Gap and Snicker's Gap in the Blue Ridge Mountains. Aldie's Gap allowed access to Loudoun Valley while the other two gaps were important vantage points for anyone wishing to view troop movements in the Shenandoah Valley. Knowing of Aldie's importance, Stuart posted Fitz Lee's brigade to the defense of the turnpikes. The lead elements of the brigade, the 2nd and 3rd Virginia cavalry regiments, arrived that morning. Col. Thomas Munford—still commanding Fitzhugh Lee's brigade—posted a picket line in Aldie and then retired the rest of the regiments to a farm northwest of town on the Snicker's Gap Turnpike.

The Union force sent to push through Aldie was Brig. Gen. David McMurtrie Gregg's division. The head of Gregg's column, a brigade under Brig. Gen. Judson "Kill-Cavalry" Kilpatrick, consisted of the 2nd and 4th New York, 6th Ohio, and 1st Massachusetts. Kilpatrick's column encountered the Confederate picket line and drove them back. The 1st Massachusetts pushed through. There, they came across the 5th Virginia regiment. The 1st, 4th, and 5th Virginia Cavalry regiments—the remainder of Munford's brigade under Col. Williams Carter Wickham—had just arrived west of Aldie. Wickham had ordered the 5th Virginia closer to Aldie to find a campsite. The Virginians drove the 1st Massachusetts back to Kilpatrick's main force east of Aldie.[8]

Wickham reported that he was ordered to move the 4th Virginia, the 1st Virginia, and the 5th Virginia, and Captain Breathed's battery through Middleburg to Aldie and encamp there with the rest of the brigade. Upon reaching Dover Mills, a small hamlet on the Little River west of Aldie, Wickham ordered Colonel Thomas Rosser's 5th Virginia to proceed to Aldie and select a camp. While the other horses were watering, Rosser sent Wickham a dispatch reporting that an enemy cavalry regiment was in his front, between Rosser and Aldie, and that he [Rosser] was about to attack them. Rosser posted a company of men, acting as sharpshooters, under Capt. Reuben F. Boston east of the William Adam farmhouse and then pulled the rest of his regiment back to a ridge covering the two roads leading out of

7. *OR* 27/1:42, *OR* 27/3:172.
8. *OR* 27/1:953.

Aldie. The 1st Massachusetts, supported by the 4th New York, mistook the movement west as a withdrawal and charged. Rosser's line held, and the Federals fell back. Rosser had secured the Ashby Gap Turnpike.

Wickham immediately positioned his 4th Virginia to cover his left flank on the road from Snickersville Pike. With the 1st Virginia and two of Breathed's guns, he went forward to support Colonel Rosser, who had driven the enemy back—but was forced to give way a little before a large force of enemy cavalry.[9]

A few well-placed shots from Breathed's guns checked the enemy's advance, but they were too late to save the 5th Virginia's sharpshooters, who had been pushed too far forward of support on ground where it was impossible for cavalry to aid them. This detachment of about 50 soldiers, under Major Rueben Boston, suffered heavy losses, and was forced to surrender. The enemy then turned their attention to Wickham's left, where Colonel Munford, commanding the brigade, met them with the 2nd and 3rd Virginia, reinforced by the 4th Virginia, and later by the 5th Virginia.[10]

Kilpatrick now turned his attention to the Snicker's Gap turnpike. The approach to Snicker's Gap was defended by the 2nd and 3rd Virginia regiments. The Confederates were dismounted, with sharpshooters posted behind a stone wall. The battle started with an artillery duel; then, as at Brandy Station, Kilpatrick's regiments were sent in piecemeal—slashed at by mounted horsemen and shot at by the sharpshooters. The 1st Massachusetts was trapped in a blind curve along the turnpike and torn apart.

The Federals threw in more reinforcements as the light faded, pushing Munford back. This coincided with an order from Stuart to withdraw, as more Federal cavalry was spotted near Middleburg, Virginia. Over at Ashby's Gap, the 6th Ohio overran Capt. Boston's company. By 8 p.m., the fighting trickled off. Kilpatrick had lost 305 men to Munford's 119, but the Confederates still held the roads leading to Ashby's and Snicker's Gaps.

Wickham reported that for the rest of the evening, he held his position—with the 1st Virginia and Breathed's guns—driving back Federal skirmishers whenever they attempted to advance. Wickham reported that "Captain T. T. Litchfield's sharpshooters were, as they always are, most efficient."[11] Wickham reported the 4th Virginia's losses were one killed, seven wounded, and nine missing.[12] The brigade,

9. *OR* 27/2:741-745.
10. Ibid.
11. Ibid.
12. Ibid.

under Colonel Munford, lost nine killed, 47 wounded, and 63 missing.[13]

Munford did not consider Aldie a defeat because his withdrawal coincided with an order from Stuart to retire, since more Federal cavalry had been sighted at Middleburg. Union casualties were 305 dead and wounded, with one colonel, three captains, five lieutenants, and 129 non-commissioned officers and privates captured, with their horses and arms, representing seven regiments. The Confederates losses were 119, including Lt. Col. James W. Watts, who was seriously wounded in the right arm and, henceforth, disabled. Watts had been riding at the head of the regiment with Munford when he ran at a fence, cleared it, and landed among the enemy. One trooper "saw him, standing in his stirrups knock a Yankee off his horse with his sabre," before he was shot by one of the blue horsemen. Aldie was the first in a series of cavalry fights along the Ashby's Gap Turnpike in which Stuart's forces successfully delayed Pleasanton's thrust across the Loudoun Valley, thereby depriving him of the opportunity to locate Lee's army.[14]

In the meantime, Colonel Wickham was positioning the 1st and 4th Virginia and Capt. James Breathed's battery to dispute any Federal advance up the Middleburg Road. As Rosser withdrew west, the 1st Massachusetts, with aid from the 4th New York, charged against what they had believed to be a retreat. Rosser's line held, and he mounted a countercharge in concert with a sharp volley from the sharpshooters that he had placed on his left. He drove the Federals back easily, securing his hold on the Ashby's Gap Turnpike. Munford then repositioned Rosser's 5th Virginia, 4th Virginia, and one gun from Breathed's battery so as to command Snickersville Road.[15]

Judson Kilpatrick turned his attention towards the Snicker's Gap Turnpike. An artillery duel ensued as more cavalry on both sides arrived. A furious fight erupted, which at first went in favor of Munford as Federal charges were met, stopped, and then forced back by the withering volley of sharpshooters entrenched along a stone wall. The 1st Massachusetts Cavalry was trapped in a blind curve on the Snicker's Gap Turnpike and was practically destroyed, losing 198 of 294 men in the eight companies that were engaged. One detachment of the 1st Massachusetts, under Maj. Henry Lee Higginson, was virtually wiped out in hand-to-hand fighting.

13. Ibid.
14. "Autobiography of St. George Tucker Brooke," 2, VMHC; *OR* 27/2:741; Whitehead, "Campaigns of Munford's 2nd Virginia Cavalry," 70–71.
15. *OR* 27/2:688, 739–41; McClellan, *The Campaigns of Stuarts Cavalry*, 297–98.

The tide of battle finally turned as Union reinforcements of David M. Gregg's cavalry charged into the fray in the fading light. Colonel William Stedman's 6th Ohio overran Boston's detachment on the Ashby's Gap Turnpike, capturing or killing most of his men. The fighting died down around 8:00 p.m. Stuart, who was not involved in the Aldie fight, ordered Munford to disengage, because his troopers were needed at another engagement at nearby Middleburg. The "engagement" turned out to be Stuart's near-capture by the 5th Michigan, while Stuart was dining with Brig. Gen. Asa Rogers at his residence.[16]

It was at Middleburg that Stuart's 250-pound Prussian aide, Major Heros von Borcke, was wounded in the neck by a Union sharpshooter. He recovered and returned to the army, but he was never able to resume the aggressive lifestyle he had lived up until then.[17]

Heros von Borcke died on May 10, 1895. Williams Wickham then said that von Borcke "was ever in the front rank of the charge and always in the rear of the retreat. No man in the Confederate Army did more faithful service than Heros von Borcke!"[18]

Munford wrote of capturing 168 prisoners and 137 horses, moving his dead and wounded back as he retired, while 30 to 40 Union dead were left on the field. Munford's total losses were 119, of which 58 came from Rosser's 5th Virginia. Munford also reported, "I do not hesitate to say that I have never seen as many Yankees killed in the same space of ground in any fight I have ever seen, or any battlefield in Virginia that I have been over." General Stuart added, "at Aldie ensued one of the most sanguinary cavalry battles of the war, and at the same time most credible to our arms and glorious to the veteran brigade of Brig. Gen. Fitz Lee." It was Munford who gallantly led Fitz Lee's brigade at Aldie, fully responsible for solid leadership on the field of battle and without the aid of Stuart.[19]

Both sides mostly rested on June 18; but the Federals did advance westward, with Stuart withdrawing toward Ashby's Gap. Wickham's command of 537 men, with—425 mounted—rested on the Snickersville Pike, where Wickham remained until June 21, when the brigade was replaced by infantry. Fitz Lee returned to health and assumed

16. *OR* 27/2:741; McClellan, *The Campaigns of Stuart's Cavalry*, 302–03; Thomas T. Munford to Robert E. Lee, March 18, 1866, Robert E. Lee Collection, Washington and Lee University; Thomas T. Munford to an unidentified Major, circa 1885, Munford–Ellis Papers, DU.
17. *OR* 27/2: 690.
18. Robert J. Trout, *They Followed the Plume: The Story of J.E.B. Stuart and His Staff* (Mechanicsburg, PA: Stackpole Books, 1993), 280.
19. *OR* 27/2:739–41; Thomas T. Munford to Robert E. Lee, March 18, 1866, Robert E. Lee Collection, Washington and Lee University.

command of his brigade on June 22. On June 23, Robert E. Lee ordered Stuart's horsemen into Maryland. The 4th Virginia marched to Union on the afternoon of June 23, while the brigade gathered at Salem.[20]

Stuart had sought guidance from Robert E. Lee for the raid into Pennsylvania and received vague suggestions from Longstreet and orders from Lee stating, "If you find that he [Hooker] is moving northward, and that two brigades can guard the Blue Ridge and take care of your rear, you can move with the other three into Maryland, and take position on General [Richard] Ewell's right, place yourself in communication with him, guard his flank, keep him informed of the enemy's movements, and collect all the supplies you can for the use of the army."[21]

Stuart had ordered the brigades of Beverly H. Robertson and Grumble Jones to guard the passes in the Blue Ridge Mountains, certain that they could join Lee before any general battle ensued. Robertson's brigade was a small one, consisting of two under-strength North Carolina regiments. Stuart despised Jones, and Robertson outranked Jones by date of promotion; thus, Robertson led the two brigades of 2,700 troopers on their mission. These brigades would not be able to do the necessary scouting and screening for Robert E. Lee that he needed. Stuart had been given wide latitude by Lee; a general engagement was not planned for Gettysburg. Lee's army, now in Pennsylvania, became blind to the disposition and movement of the Northern army. Stuart, under orders to report to Ewell, had taken a long circuitous raid around the Union Army and was not able to hook up with Ewell. The movements of the Federals had forced Stuart so far east that he had to cross the Potomac only 20 miles from Washington.[22]

Three cavalry brigades were assigned to march with Stuart; Fitz Lee's, Rooney Lee's (now under Chambliss), and Hampton's. The three brigades rendezvoused near Salem Depot on June 24, marched through Glascock's Gap, and proceeded to Haymarket the next morning. Wickham's command had left Union early that morning, and passing through Bloomfield and Upperville, arrived at Salem that evening. Encountering Federal infantry of Gen. Winfield Scott Hancock's II Corps, Stuart withdrew and went south and around them, camping at Gum Springs for the night. Stuart ordered Fitz Lee's

---

20. Stiles, *4th Virginia Cavalry*, 31–32.
21. Robert E. Lee to J.E.B. Stuart, June 22, 1863; *OR* 27/3:913.
22. Edward G. Longacre, *The Cavalry at Gettysburg: A Tactical Study of Mounted Operations during the Civil War's Pivotal Campaign, 9 June–14 July, 1863* (Lincoln, NE, 1986), 154.

brigade to Gainesville on the Manassas Gap Railroad, where it bivouacked for the night.[23]

Stuart's southeasterly detour around Hancock's army continued the next day, crossing the Orange and Alexandria Railroad at Bristoe Station before continuing to Brentsville. Turning north, Stuart's troopers headed for Wolf Run Shoals on the Occoquan River, where they spent the night. The next day, Stuart recrossed the Orange & Alexandria Railroad west of Alexandria, while he, Hampton, and Chambliss headed for the depot at Fairfax Station. Stuart ordered Fitz Lee's brigade to Burke's Station to cut telegraph lines and demolish tracks. Having completed his assigned task, Fitz Lee's brigade headed for Annandale, northwest of Stuart's position. Both raiding parties seized and plundered food goods and sutlers stores. Stuart and Fitz Lee let their hungry troopers eat for a while before resuming the march. Rejoining at Dranesville, Stuart and Fitz Lee's cavalrymen headed for the Potomac, crossing in darkness at Rowzwe's Mill Ford, north of Dumfries. Completing their crossing at 3:00 a.m., they were then in Pennsylvania. Esten Cooke recalled watching the rear guard's crossing from the Maryland side of the Potomac, "The picture was picturesque. The broad river glittering in the moon, and on the bright surface was seen the long, wavering line of dark figures, moving in 'single file;' the water washing to and for across the backs of the horses, which kept their feet with difficulty."[24]

Stuart immediately put his horsemen to work destroying the boats and docks on the Chesapeake and Ohio Canal, a major supply route to Hooker's army. Here, they captured 300 prisoners; and with the group taken at Fairfax Station, were sent under escort to Rockville, Maryland. While there, Stuart's hungry soldiers gathered rations for their empty haversacks and ate plenty. Corporal Charles E. Watts of the 2nd Virginia remembered," During this time it was necessary to stop and graze the horses several times because there was no food in the country." Rufus Peck of the 2nd Virginia recalled:

> **Eight packet boats had been sent up with provisions for Hooker's army, and when they came into the docks not knowing we were there, we turned the wickets and let the water out and burned the boats. We had been marching four days without any provisions at all, so we took what**

23. Driver, *2nd Virginia Cavalry*, 89; *OR* 27/2:688, part 3:913–915, 923; Stiles, *4th Virginia Cavalry*, 32.
24. Longacre, *The Cavalry at Gettysburg*, 154; Longacre, *Lee's Cavalrymen*, 205, 207; *OR* 27/2:693–94; John Esten Cooke, *Wearing of the Gray* (Bedford, MA, 1867), 235.

we could in our haversacks, before burning the boats. We took the mules, 24 in number, on with us[25]

The next morning, Stuart's raiders headed for Rockville, only eight miles northwest of Washington. In Rockville, Hampton's brigade spied a supply column of more than 150 wagons, laden with goods for Hooker's army. Hampton's riders corralled the train. William Blackford, riding at the head of the column, wrote, "you could see nothing but the long ears and kicking legs of the mules sticking above bags of oats emptied from the wagons." Stuart was very pleased; he could now take 125 (25 had been overturned) of the wagons in tow and deliver some quality goods to Lee's army. The wagon train slowed Stuart's speed as they continued north, but the grain and other materials were badly needed by soldiers and mounts alike.[26]

On the morning of June 29, Stuart's slowing pace brought his command to the Baltimore & Ohio Railroad at Hood's Mill and Sykesville, where the Confederate raiders destroyed tracks, the railroad bridge at Sykesville, depot buildings, and trains. They also had to chase off a Union patrol farther south near Cookesville. Stuart's column, dragging the captured wagons, headed north and by 4:00 p.m. approached Westminster, Maryland. Stuart realized by this time he could have been in Pennsylvania aiding Ewell. Entering town, Stuart encountered 95 determined troopers of Companies C and D of the 1st Delaware Cavalry of the VIII Corps. They were led by Maj. Napoleon B. Knight, with Capt. Charles Corbit and Lt. Caleb Churchman as company commanders. In Major Knight's absence, Captain Corbit led a charge of his men through the streets of Westminster to Washington Road. Expecting to overcome a small unit of Confederates, they found themselves facing a large body of General Stuart's veteran cavalry. The unwavering Federal troopers charged Stuart's advance guard, igniting a fierce skirmish. The Delaware unit, however, was quickly overpowered. Many were captured, including Captain Corbit and Lieutenant Churchman. Sixty-seven Union troopers were killed, wounded, or taken prisoner. Two Confederate officers of the 4th Virginia had been killed and four others were badly wounded chasing the 1st Delaware Cavalry from the field. Instead of proceeding into Pennsylvania to inform Gen. Robert E. Lee about the major Union troop movements, Stuart's cavalry was delayed long enough—as the result of the skirmish—to make it preferable to spend the night just

25. *OR* 27/2:694; Longacre, *Lee's Cavalrymen*, 207; Driver, *2nd Virginia Cavalry*, 89; Peck, *Reminiscences of a Confederate Soldier of Co. C of the 2nd Virginia Cavalry* (Fincastle, VA, 1913), 32.
26. William W. Blackford, *War Years with JEB Stuart*, 224; *OR* 27/2:694; Longacre, *Lee's Cavalrymen*, 208; Longacre, *The Cavalry at Gettysburg*, 155.

north of Westminster. Fitz Lee's brigade, with the 4th Virginia leading the advance guard, stopped at Union Mills, midway between Westminster and Littlestown on the Gettysburg Road. Stuart's scouts determined that Federal cavalry had encamped for the evening at Lillestown, seven miles north of Union Mills.[27]

The next morning, June 30, Stuart headed for Hanover, Pennsylvania, with Rooney Lee's brigade in the advance, Hampton in the rear of the wagon train, and Fitz Lee moving on the left flank. At 10:00 a.m., the head of the column approached Hanover and ran into the rear of Brig. Gen. Elon J. Farnsworth's cavalry brigade. The Union horsemen were heading straight for the gap in the mountains that Stuart intended to use. Upon seeing Stuart's column, the Union troopers demonstrated, as if preparing to attack. Chambliss's brigade, led by Lt. Col. Jefferson C. Phillips's 13th Virginia, promptly attacked and repulsed Farnsworth's horsemen. The Virginians drove the 18th Pennsylvania Cavalry pell-mell through Hanover, capturing a large number of prisoners and their ambulances. Behind the Union cavalry advance was a larger body of Meade's cavalry, which Stuart would have charged if his elongated column had closed up; but they were spread out. Besides, Stuart was now very anxious to proceed and reach the Susquehanna River as quickly as possible.[28]

Stuart faced a dilemma as his path intersected with the Federal horsemen of Kilpatrick's 3rd Division, who had an hour earlier entered Hanover, heading west for the 12-mile distance to Gettysburg. Stuart faced Kilpatrick's troopers protecting the center of Meade's army, while David M. Gregg covered the right and John Buford the left. Stuart was determined to keep his captured wagon train. Lacking the possibility of turning around, he had to face straight ahead and fight the blue horsemen to pass through town. Chambliss's regiment, under Chambliss, was counterattacked by Farnsworth's New Yorkers. To prevent Chambliss's horsemen from being swept back, Stuart brought forward two cannons from McGregor's battery, placing them to the left on Plum Creek. The guns kept the Yankee cavalry at bay, while Lt. Col. William H. Payne's 2nd North Carolina flanked them, attacking the remaining portion of the 18th Pennsylvania, scattering it.[29]

Payne pursued them, but he was soon stopped by reformed 18th Pennsylvanians and Farnsworth's New Yorkers. Unable to support Payne with either Hampton's or Fitz Lee's troopers—due to their

27. *OR* 27/2:694–95, part 3:396, 403–04; Longacre, *Lee's Cavalrymen*, 208–09.
28. *OR* 27/2:695.
29. McClellan, *Campaigns of Stuart's Cavalry*, 327-28; Longacre, *Lee's Cavalry*, 210.

positions covering the wagon train and about 400 prisoners—Payne and his North Carolinians had to withdraw. Soon the retreating Tarheels, without Payne—who had been wounded and captured—were fleeing town; and Chambliss's line appeared ready to collapse. Finally, about 2:00 p.m., the 1st Virginia Cavalry regiment arrived, along with Stuart's other four guns from Breathed's battery. Soon, Hampton had the guns set up at Mount Olivet Cemetery and began firing at a large detachment of horse soldiers, who seemed ready to attack. The shelling, along with the ready-to-charge Col. Pierce Young's horsemen of Cobb's Legion, discouraged the blue troopers from attempting to flank Hampton.[30]

Soon, Hampton had dislodged the Federal horsemen from their position. Meanwhile, Fitz Lee was facing part of George Armstrong Custer's brigade on his left. Part of Custer's Michigan cavalry brigade broke through Stuart's line twice on the Union right, but countercharges drove them off. The Wolverines soon moved over to the right side. As a precaution, Stuart formed his wagons in close quarters, prepared to burn them if he had to abandon them. Stuart's right, having been relieved by Hampton, permitted the cavalry commander to send Fitz Lee to move forward with the train, through Jefferson toward York, Pennsylvania. Pressured to join Ewell and Lee, Stuart held on until dark, then quietly slipped away. Kilpatrick, having had enough, did not hinder Stuart's movement north.[31]

As soon as the sun set, Stuart transferred custody of the wagon train to Fitz Lee and sent him on towards Jefferson. During the night march through Jefferson, the nearly 400 prisoners, many loaded in the wagons—and the wagon train itself—were a further hindrance. The mules pulling the wagons were starving and often unmanageable. Everyone was fatigued. Whenever the column stopped for any reason except fighting during the entire Pennsylvania march, the troopers and horses were fast asleep. When Fitz Lee reached the road leading from York to Gettysburg, he discovered that Ewell had retraced his steps and headed west. It appeared at that time that the Confederate army was concentrating its forces near Shippensburg. Meanwhile, after a short hiatus at Dover on the morning of July 1, Stuart pressed on towards Carlisle, hoping he could secure provisions for his starving troopers. One trooper remembered, "All the provisions we had on this

---

30. *OR* 27/2:696; McClellan, *Campaigns of Stuart's Cavalry*, 328–29; Longacre, *Lee's Cavalry*, 211; Longacre, *The Cavalry at Gettysburg*, 177.
31. *OR* 27/2:696; Edward G. Longacre, *The Cavalry at Gettysburg*, 174–178; McClellan, *Campaigns of Stuart's Cavalry*, 329; Longacre, *Lee's Cavalry*, 211.

march, except what some of us got at the boats [at Annandale], was
what we could beg from citizens. Some of us nearly starved."[32]

Stuart and his exhausted troopers pushed on and arriving at
Carlisle—he ordered some artillery shells fired into the Union-held
town. He ordered Wickham to burn the Carlisle barracks, the United
States Army's cavalry school. Wickham's 4th Virginia troopers burned
seven of the posts eleven buildings, destroying officers' quarters,
barracks, and stables. The total loss was later estimated at $47,600.
Stuart also destroyed a Federal supply depot. On the evening of July 1,
Stuart learned that Lee's army was concentrated at Gettysburg. He
immediately set out with his command for the scene of the main
battle. When he arrived on July 2, he and his men and horses were
exhausted from hard-riding and frequent-fighting, and were in no
condition to battle the Federal Army effectively. Rufus Peck recalled,
"As we had been marching so much and had so little rest since June 20,
we all laid down in a stubble field and were soon fast asleep." Peck was
so exhausted that the cannon fire during the night did not awaken him,
nor the fact that he had been dragged 30 yards by his horse seeking
grass. Rosser recalled, "Stuart had been marching constantly, almost
day and night, on scant forage and little rest for man or horse, for eight
days, within the enemy's lines, and while his conduct displayed a
daring almost to recklessness, he accomplished little, save the wear and
fatigue of long marches. He had undoubtedly impaired the strength
and vigor of his command."[33]

As the dark day of July 3 dawned, Wickham's 4th Virginia was
positioned in the vicinity of Hunterstown on the far left. Because of
this posting, Wickham's horsemen did not participate in the battle at
John Rummel's Farm. They could only listen to the sounds of the gun
and cannon fire.[34]

What happened when Stuart and Robert E. Lee met on the
evening of July 2 has long been the subject of controversy. As there
were no known witnesses at Lee's headquarters besides Lee and Stuart;
only Lee and Stuart knew what was said between them.

32. Peck, *Reminiscences of a Confederate Soldier*, 32; *OR* 27/2:696; McClellan,
    Campaigns of Stuart's Cavalry, 330; Longacre, *Lee's Cavalry*, 213; Longacre,
    The Cavalry at Gettysburg, 178.
33. Peck, Reminiscences of a Confederate Soldier, 32–33; Driver, 2nd Virginia
    Cavalry, 90; Thomas L. Rosser, Addresses of Gen'l T. L. Rosser, at the
    Seventh Annual Reunion of the Association of the Maryland Line, Academy
    of Music, Baltimore, Md., February 22, 1889, and on Memorial Day,
    Staunton, Va., June 8, 1889 (New York, 1889), 41. Rosser also despised
    Stuart, but only behind his back to his wife. Stuart probably never knew of
    Rosser's loathing of him; Wert, Cavalryman of the Lost Cause, 281.
34. Stiles, *4th Virginia Cavalry*, 33.

Regardless of Lee's admonishing Stuart or not—in preparation for the resumption of battle on July 3—Robert E. Lee ordered Stuart to protect the Confederate left flank, and attempt to move around the Union right flank. This flanking maneuver would, hopefully, draw Union strength away from the center, where Pickett was to attack. Lee ordered Stuart to attack the Federal rear if a breakthrough was achieved. If Stuart's horsemen could proceed south from the York Pike along the Low Dutch Road, they would soon reach the Baltimore Pike, the main avenue of communications for the Union army. They could then observe the Union rear and launch devastating attacks against the rear of Meade's army—perhaps even a breakthrough, if Lee's attack on the Union center was successful.[35]

Stuart commanded four brigades—led by Brigadier Generals Wade Hampton and Fitzhugh Lee, and Colonels John R. Chambliss and Col. Milton J. Ferguson, leading Brig. Gen. Albert G. Jenkins's brigade after Jenkins had been wounded the day before. The Confederates probably had no more than 3,400 troopers in action on July 3rd. Pleasonton's 3,250 horsemen opposed them.[36]

Ferguson's brigade led Stuart's column, followed at a distance by Chambliss and Hampton, with Fitz Lee's bringing up the rear. Between Chambliss's and Hampton's troopers were the batteries of Capt. Thomas E. Jackson and a section of Capt. Charles A. Green's Louisiana Guard Artillery, sent from Ewell's corps by Lt. Col. Hilary P. Jones. Left behind were batteries of Captains William M. McGregor and James Breathed, who were unable to obtain sufficient ammunition by the time Stuart left; they were ordered to follow as soon as their ordinance chests were full. Stuart proceeded along the York Pike for two miles; he then turned right onto a country road. He finally positioned his cavalry left of General Ewell's left, on a commanding ridge called Cress Ridge. Here, he had an open view of a wide plain of cultivated fields, stretching towards Hanover on his left and reaching the base of the mountain spurs among the Union-held position. The ridge's north end was covered with woods, which concealed his presence. Below, three hundred yards from the foot of the hill, on the plain below stood a large frame barn on John Rummel's farm. Stuart liked where he had stationed his forces.[37]

General David M. Gregg positioned his division at the intersection of the Hanover Road and Low Dutch Road, directly in Stuart's path. Gregg had two brigades, commanded by Colonels John B. McIntosh

35. *OR* 27/2:697–98.
36. Ibid., 698.
37. Longacre, *Lee's Cavalrymen*, 217; McClellan, *The Campaigns of Stuart's Cavalry*, 337–38.; Trout, *Galloping Thunder*, 290–91.

and J. Irvin Gregg, cousin of David Gregg. David Gregg positioned Irvin Gregg's brigade, supplemented by the newly-formed "Michigan Brigade" under Bvt. Brig. Gen. George Custer on the Baltimore Pike. Custer, on loan from Kilpatrick's division, requested to join David Gregg in the fight. Kilpatrick's other brigade, commanded by Gen. Elon J. Farnsworth, was stationed south of the Big Round Top-Emmitsburg Road skirmish line, on a wooded hill called Bushman's Hill.[38]

According to an unsubstantiated account by Henry McClellan, Stuart signaled his readiness to Lee by having Jackson's battery fire four cannon shots from the East Cavalry Field at about 11:00 a.m. This would have also alerted David Gregg to his presence had not Gregg already known it. Gregg, commanding about 3,000 cavalrymen, ordered McIntosh and Custer into a blocking formation, opposing Stuart's 3,500 horsemen. The two sides engaged in an artillery duel, with the Union gunners of Lt. Alexander C. M. Pennington's Battery M of the 2nd U. S. Artillery having a decided advantage because of their longer-range guns and superior ordnance. Stuart wanted to pin down the Union troopers and swing around their left flank. The Michigan horsemen, however, armed with Spencer repeating rifles with their increased firepower, prevented Stuart's flanking move. At about 1:00 p.m., Fitzhugh Lee's brigade made a direct charge, pushing back the Union skirmish line. Fitz's charge forced Stuart to commit Hampton to support him. Gregg ordered Custer to counterattack. Custer led the charge, shouting, "Come on, you Wolverines!" The fighting became furious with about 700 cavalrymen clashing at point-blank range. Custer's horse was shot out from under him; he quickly commandeered a bugler's mount. Stuart then sent in three regiments: Chambliss's 9th and 13th Virginia, Laurence Baker's 1st North Carolina, along with Hampton's Jeff Davis Legion, and squadrons from Fitz Lee's 2nd Virginia. This forced the Michigan troopers to retreat. The 2nd Virginia held the extreme left of the Confederate line northeast of John Rummel's farm.[39]

According to Pvt. Edward Colston of Company K of the 2nd Virginia, the mounted portion of the regiment moved to several locations but was not engaged that day. The dismounted troopers of the 2nd Virginia, however, were positioned on the extreme left of Lee's army. Here, two companies of the regiment fought with Federal

38. Longacre, *Lincoln's Cavalrymen*, 196–97.
39. McClellan, *The Campaigns of Stuart's Cavalry*, 339, 344; Jeffrey D. Wert, *Cavalryman of the Lost Cause*, 287. McClellan is in error here. Guns from Jackson's battery of horse artillery were there, but Charles Griffin's battery was not anywhere near this area.

sharpshooters, driving them back into the woods at the end of a large open field. Fitz Lee rode up to alert them that a squadron of between 15-to-20 mounted Union troopers was nearby. Lee ordered the Confederates to drive the Federal horsemen out of the woods, assuring them the enemy was only a small force. Fitz was wrong, and soon two regiments of Federal cavalrymen charged, nearly capturing Lee. Luckily, mounted Confederate horsemen came to the rescue, saving Lee and the dismounted troopers.[40]

When Stuart ordered the bulk of Hampton's brigade forward, Custer and Col. Charles Town led the 1st Michigan Cavalry into the fray. McIntosh led his regiment against the Confederate right flank. Hampton was seriously wounded with a saber cut to his head and a gunshot to his thigh. His brigade withdrew when they were assaulted on three sides.[41]

The losses from 40 minutes of intense close-quarter fighting on the East Cavalry Field were: 254 Union casualties, 219 of them from Custer's brigade; 181 Confederate. The fight was a strategic loss for Stuart and Robert E. Lee, whose hopes to attack the Union rear successfully were foiled. Lee sent word to Stuart that he was going to withdraw the Army of Northern Virginia and head for Virginia. Stuart, failing to attack the Union army rear, maintained his position until nightfall, when he withdrew to the York Pike, leaving the 1st Virginia on picket duty. Stuart sent Fitz Lee's brigade to Cashtown to protect the wagon trains congregated there. They were then to move on to Greencastle. He sent word to Robertson, who was on the right near Fairfield, to hold the Jack Mountain passes open.[42]

Meanwhile, southwest of Big Round Top Mountain, Brigadier Generals Wesley Merritt and Elon Farnsworth, under orders from Alfred Pleasonton, led two brigades on the left flank of the Union army. Merritt commanded the Reserve Brigade of Buford's division, while Farnsworth led a brigade of Kilpatrick's division. About 1:00 p.m., Farnsworth's 1,925 troopers arrived at their assigned position in a line south of George Bushman's farm, just as the Confederate

---

40. Edward Colston to Thomas T. Munford, April 15, 1886, Munford–Ellis Papers, DU; Edward Brugh to Thomas T. Munford, April 27, 1886, Munford–Ellis Papers, DU.

41. Longacre, *The Cavalry at Gettysburg*, 238. Wade Hampton, commenting on Stuart's Gettysburg Report, wrote Munford after the war, "I never read a more erroneous–to call it no harsher name–one that it was." Reference: Wade Hampton to Thomas T. Munford, December 18, 1897. Hampton was thought by many to be jealous of Stuart. At any rate, the two did not like each other. Ref: H. B. McClellan to Thomas T. Munford, February 20, 1904, Munford–Ellis Papers, DU.

42. *OR*, vol. 27, part 2, 699; McClellan, *The Campaigns of Stuart's Cavalry*, 341, 346.

bombardment of Cemetery Ridge commenced. Farnsworth's regiments were, west to east: 18th Pennsylvania Cavalry, 1st West Virginia, and the 1st Vermont. Battery E of the 4th U. S. Artillery occupied a small, rocky knoll in the rear, while the 5th New York Cavalry positioned itself in a nearby ravine to guard the artillery. Kilpatrick joined Farnsworth and they waited for Merritt's brigade, which arrived about 3:00 p.m., quickly straddling the Emmitsburg Road to Farnsworth's left.[43]

The Confederate forces to the east of Emmitsburg Road were infantry only. The four brigades of Brig. Gen. John Bell Hood's division—under the command of Brig. Gen. Evander W. Law—had escaped Round Top, through Devil's Den, and had regrouped back on Emmitsburg Road the day before. Initially, Law had only the 1st Texas Infantry facing Farnsworth to the south, but he was soon reinforced with the 47th Alabama Infantry, the 1st South Carolina, and Confederate artillery. To the west of the road, facing Merritt, was the Georgia brigade of Brig. Gen. George "Tige" Anderson.[44]

While Stuart was encamping on the York Pike during the evening of July 3, General Lee was withdrawing the main army to the west ridges of Gettysburg. Stuart did not know of Lee's movement until later that night, when he sought out Lee's headquarters. During the next day, a rainy July 4, Lee issued written instructions as to the order of march back to the Potomac, to begin at nightfall. The main portion of the 17-mile-long wagon train would be under the charge of Brig. Gen. John D. Imboden's relatively-fresh troopers and mounts, who had accompanying infantry and artillery. Lee sent Imboden on a cross-country route—marching west along the Chambersburg Pike, through the Cashtown Pass, turning south at Greenwood towards Marion, and passing through Greencastle to Williamsport. The brigades of Hampton (commanded by Gen. Laurence S. Baker) and Fitz Lee, including Wickham's 4th Virginia, were ordered to proceed by way of Cashtown, guarding the right flank and bringing up the rear on the road from Greenville to Williamsport. It rained all night, one thunderstorm after another, the rain often coming down in sheets. It was so dark that only during lightning flashes could anyone see what lay ahead. It would continue raining for 10 days.[45]

---

43. Jeffery D. Wert, *Gettysburg, Day Three* (New York, 2002), 272.
44. Ibid., 273–75.
45. *OR* 27/2:699; McClellan, *The Campaigns of Stuart's Cavalry*, 349; Eric Wittenberg, J. David Petruzzi, and Michael F. Nugent, *One Continuous Fight: The Retreat from Gettysburg and the Pursuit of Lee's Army of Northern Virginia, July 4-14, 1863* (New York, 2008), 3,5; Diary of I. Norval Baker, 18th Virginia Cavalry, VMI Archives.

Stuart had previously ordered General Robertson, whose two brigades (Jones's and his own) were on the right near Fairfield, to hold the Jack Mountain passes open—including two roads: one north, the other south of Jack Mountain (a peak in the Blue Ridge chain).[46]

In the order of the retreating army march, Gen. A. P. Hill's Corps preceded everyone else's across South Mountain through Monterey Pass; the baggage and prisoners of war were escorted by another corps. Longstreet occupied the center, and Ewell brought up the rear. The cavalry was dispatched as follows: two brigades (Hampton's and Fitz Lee's) on the Cashtown Road under Fitz Lee, with Munford commanding Fitz Lee's brigade. The remaining brigades, Jenkins's and Chambliss's, under Stuart's direct supervision, were to proceed by way of Emmitsburg, Maryland, guarding the retreating army. Stuart halted his command at dark, when it became hard to see in the heavy rain and dense woods. He halted for several hours and procured the services of a good local guide. Resuming the march at daylight, Stuart's troopers reached Emmitsburg a little after dawn. They stopped for a short time and procured rations. Resuming the march on the road to Frederick, they reached the small village of Cooperstown and paused to feed and rest the much-fatigued and hungry horses. After an hour, Stuart's horsemen continued, marching through Harbaugh's Valley, by Zion Church, and passed the Catoctin Mountain.[47]

The road then forked before debauching from the mountain—one fork leading to the left by Smithtown, the other to the right bearing towards Leitersburg. Here, Stuart purposely divided his command in order, more likely, to assure that at least half of the retreating cavalry would reach safety in Virginia. He sent Colonel Ferguson, commanding Jenkins's brigade, to the road on the right, while Chambliss's brigade, accompanied by Stuart, took the left road. Stuart's column met resistance from some of Kilpatrick's cavalry at the pass in the mountain; but with the aid of his artillery, he drove them away. Ferguson also met resistance, broke through, but was directed by Stuart to retreat and followed his path.[48]

Just before nightfall, Stuart sent dependable Pvt. Robert W. Goode of the 1st Virginia to inform Robert E. Lee of his position and what Lee needed to look out for en route. Stuart, after waiting for Colonel Ferguson to come up, proceeded towards Leitersburg in darkness.[49]

46. *OR* 27/2:699.
47. *OR* 27/2:700; Driver, *2nd Virginia Cavalry*, 92; McClellan, *The Campaigns of Stuart's Cavalry*, 349–51.
48. *OR* 27/2:700; McClellan, *The Campaigns of Stuart's Cavalry*, 351.
49. *OR* 27/2:700; McClellan, *The Campaigns of Stuart's Cavalry*, 351–52.

Fitz Lee's brigade, under Munford, was the last to leave Gettysburg on July 5. His mission was to act as rear guard for Lee's army as they retired along the Cashtown Road, heading for a crossing of the Potomac at Williamsport. The next day Munford's troopers skirmished with Union cavalry at Greenwood.[50]

Meanwhile, on July 5, Kilpatrick's cavalry, including Custer's brigade, reached the road between Emmittsburg and Fairfield where Ewell's train was moving towards Williamsport. The Union troopers captured and destroyed a large number of wagons and took 1,360 prisoners. On the 6th, Col. John Irvin Gregg, chased Imboden's trains, albeit at a pace leading some to believe that he really did not want to fight. At Greenwood, the Confederate caravan turned south, and Gregg's advance came up against Imboden's rear guard, including the 2nd Virginia. A small skirmish ensued, with the Federals claiming they took 100 prisoners and "a large quantity of wagons."[51]

On the morning of July 6, Stuart, having been notified by Fitz Lee at Leitersburg that Kilpatrick's cavalry had headed towards Boonsboro, immediately set out for the town. Jones had nearly been captured the previous night while separated from his brigade when it was attacked by Kilpatrick's troopers. Jones arrived from Williamsport, where he had taken the portion of his train that had escaped capture (60 wagons were lost–some reports put the figure much higher). Jones informed Stuart of Imboden's arrival at Williamsport. Having then reached Cashtown, Stuart ordered Jones to proceed on the Boonsboro Road a few miles and then head for Funkstown. Jones was then to hold Funkstown, covering the eastern front of Hagerstown. Munford was relieved by Fitz Lee on July 7, taking command of his brigade and concentrated them at Funkstown. In an all-night fight, Stuart's troopers attempted to drive Federal cavalry from Boonsboro; neither side gained the upper hand. Stuart's exhausted troopers camped near Funkstown. Fitz Lee's brigade remained at Funkstown until July 10, then marched through Downsville to Hagerstown on July 12. Chambliss's and Robertson's commands proceeded directly from Leitersburg to Hagerstown. Kilpatrick was heading to Hagerstown to confront Stuart, while Buford was starting for the wagon trains at Williamsport. Meanwhile, Stuart diverged from Jones's line of march at Cashtown and proceeded with Jenkins's brigade by way of Chewsville towards Hagerstown.[52]

---

50. Driver, *2nd Virginia Cavalry*, 92.
51. McClellan, *The Campaigns of Stuart's Cavalry*, 352–53; *OR* 27/1:917, 1019; Longacre, *The Cavalry at Gettysburg*, 250–51; Driver, *2nd Virginia Cavalry*, 92.
52. *OR* 27/2:701, 703; McClellan, *The Campaigns of Stuart's Cavalry*, 356-57; Driver, *2nd Virginia Cavalry*, 93.

The next day, July 8, Stuart proceeded to Downsville on the road to Sharpsburg, joined there by Brig. Gen. William T. Wofford's infantry brigade of Longstreet's corps. Stuart positioned Jenkins's cavalry in front of the retreating Confederate infantry. The Confederate vanguard then approached Hagerstown, only a few hours march to Williamsport. Stuart covered the front of Lee's army in its march back to the Potomac at Williamsport. There, Lee's army constructed a formidable line of earthworks from Williamsport, downriver four miles to Falling Waters—and waited for the swollen waters of the Potomac to recede. The Federals had earlier destroyed a pontoon bridge at Falling Waters; another would have to be built. Trooper Charles Blackford wrote, "The rise in the river prevents the wagon train from crossing."[53]

Fitz Lee led his brigade against Union cavalry the next day at Boonsboro; but finding them too strong, he retreated back to Funkstown. On July 10, a large Federal cavalry force drove Fitz Lee away, his brigade falling back to Downsville. The next day, Lee's troopers were driven from Downsville. Sergeant Parker wrote from Washington County, Maryland on July 11:

> We have been fighting regularly for three days. The first day had five men wounded from our squadron; second day none hurt; had one killed in our squadron yesterday... The river has been up so we could not cross none of our men, only in ferry boats... Our troops are now forming a line of battle in sight of us. We are expecting a big fight.[54]

As Stuart arrived at Chewsville, he learned that Kilpatrick's Cavalry was nearing Hagerstown from Boonsboro and that Chambliss's brigade needed reinforcements. He dispatched Jenkins's brigade forward hurriedly, and arriving at Hagerstown, Jenkins found it in the possession of Federal cavalry. His brigade made a flank attack, while Jones launched artillery fire from further up on the left. A small body of Confederate infantry, under Brig. Gen. Alfred Iverson, held the north end of town, aided by Robertson's and Chambliss's cavalry. Stuart was worried about the trains, which were congregated at the foot of a hill near the Potomac at Williamsport, just six miles from Hagerstown. The river was too swollen by recent rains for a crossing, so it was imperative that Stuart arrive there rapidly. Stuart pressed an

53. *OR* 27/2:702-03; Blackford, *Letters from Lee's Army*, 189.
54. Wright, *Lee's Last Casualty*, 110; Driver, *2nd Virginia Cavalry*, 93.

intense attack at Hagerstown against Kilpatrick's cavalry. Kilpatrick sent two brigades on ahead for Williamsport, holding only one brigade under Col. Nathaniel P. Richmond to hold off Stuart. Kilpatrick's skirmishers fought street-to-street before being forced out of town, heading for Williamsport and the Confederate trains. Just as the town cleared, Stuart heard the sound of artillery fire from Williamsport.[55]

Stuart's cavalry, except for two brigades under Fitz Lee, was just clearing Hagerstown, when Stuart ordered Chambliss to pursue Kilpatrick's troopers immediately. Again, Munford, commanded Fitz Lee's brigade during this period. Robertson's two regiments and Jenkins's brigade kept to the left of the road, paralleling Chambliss. A portion of Stuart's horse artillery also headed for Williamsport. Soon, part of Chambliss's leading brigade, the 9th and 13th Virginia, charged the Union horsemen of Kilpatrick, followed by a flank attack begun by Jenkins's brigade; they were stalled by the many post-and-rail fences, however. They were delayed long enough for the Federal riders to rally along a crest of rocks and fences, from which they opened up with artillery, raking the road. Jenkins's horsemen dismounted and deployed over difficult ground, finally dislodging the blue-clad troopers, while Confederate mounted troopers pressed them. The Union cavalry made one countercharge but was repulsed by Col. James B. Gordon, commanding a portion of the 5th North Carolina Cavalry. Colonel Lomax's 11th Virginia of Jones's brigade joined in, sending the Union cavalry stampeding for the rear. Lomax's troopers charged down the turnpike with sabers drawn, under supporting Confederate artillery fire.[56]

Kilpatrick's horsemen headed for Williamsport, followed by Stuart's command, reaching the edge of the river crossing town just as darkness began to set in. Before relief could reach them. Kilpatrick, with Buford's help, had planned on capturing and destroying the Confederate wagon trains there. Buford had already been in a fierce fight less than a mile from Williamsport when Kilpatrick arrived and positioned his troopers on Buford's right. Fitz Lee's horsemen arrived in the vicinity of Williamsport by the Greencastle Road. The Federals were being attacked in the rear by Jones's troopers, artillery, and some infantry. At the same time, Confederate infantry began to move on Kilpatrick's right flank. Buford sent word to Kilpatrick that he was about to retire, fearing that the Confederates would move down the Sharpsburg Pike, cutting off their retreat. Slowly the Union soldiers retreated, fighting off Confederate attacks until dark, when Kilpatrick

---

55. *OR* 27/1:1006–07, part 2:701–02; McClellan, *Campaigns of Stuart's Cavalry*, 357–58.
56. *OR* 27/2:702; McClellan, *Campaigns of Stuart's Cavalry*, 358.

and Buford merged, proceeding to encamp near Jones's Crossing. Stuart had saved the main wagon trains. The Federals lost an aggregate of nearly 400 men, while Stuart reported losses of 254, exclusive of Jones's brigade, from which no report was received.[57]

One trooper of the 2nd Virginia was in good spirits despite the loss at Gettysburg, "Well here I am [in Williamsport] in sight of dear old Virginia. The wagon trains have pretty much all arrived and the troops are but a little way behind, all marching in perfect order and without molestation by the enemy. There are only two regiments of infantry here at this time, but all the wagons, and they [wounded troops] are crossing the river quite rapidly."[58]

From July 8-12, severe fighting took place between Stuart's cavalry and the divisions of Buford and Kilpatrick at Boonsboro, Beaver Creek, Funkstown, and on the Sharpsburg Road. The cavalry fought mostly dismounted, aided on both sides by small bodies of infantry. Stuart reported an aggregate loss of 216 troops in these hotly-contested engagements, while Buford, Kilpatrick, and Col. Pennock Huey reported a total loss of 158. Stuart successfully delayed the advance of the pursuing Federal army until General Lee had established a strong position. On July 12, Stuart uncovered Lee's front; but the pursuing Union forces found it too strong to attack.[59]

General Imboden pressed two local ferries into service; and as soon as the wounded were treated and fed, those who believed they could walk towards Winchester were ferried across the river to Virginia. Eventually, three additional ferries were built and began carrying wounded across. A new pontoon was constructed at Falling Waters for crossings there; the majority of Lee's army would cross there. The bulk of the infantry, artillery, and wagons, however, were not able to complete the crossing to Maidstone, Virginia until July 14.[60]

Captain Charles Blackford of the 2nd Virginia wrote from Williamsport on July 12, "There is now a pontoon bridge at Williamsport, and by tomorrow there will be one at Falling Waters, below this point. It happened there was a large amount of timber at Williamsport and out of it we built twenty boats and on them built a pontoon bridge in four days." Blackford crossed the next day at Falling Waters during a violent rainstorm. He wrote that most of the soldiers and wagons had crossed that day. Fitz Lee's brigade was the last to

57. *OR* 27/1:708, 928, 935, 995, part 2:702; McClellan, *The Campaigns of Stuart's Cavalry*, 359-61.
58. Blackford, *Letters from Lee's Army*, 188.
59. McClellan, *Campaigns of Stuart's Cavalry*, 363-64; Wert, *Cavalryman of the Lost Cause*, 296-297; *OR* 27/1:118, 925, 936, part 2:716.
60. Wittenberg, Petruzzi, and Nugent, *One Continuous Fight*, 25.

cross in a persistent rain before the rear guard of the 2nd Virginia. Buford's cavalry kept "a very sharp cannonade upon us. After we crossed, our rear guard, under the command of [Brig.] Gen. [James J.] Pettigrew, of South Carolina, was sharply attacked and the General was killed."[61]

On July 13, Fitz Lee's troopers posted on the west bank reconnoitered Union positions. During the evening, Fitz Lee's regiments manned Longstreet's entrenchments, while the infantrymen slogged through pouring rain to cross the Potomac at Falling Waters. Adjutant Tayloe described the crossing, "It was quite a picturesque sight when we crossed to see men wading the River up to their necks, and then a train of ambulances, and then two or three regiments of Cavalry one below the other."[62]

On July 14, both Buford's and Kilpatrick's divisions pursued the Confederates to Falling Waters, capturing many prisoners and abandoned property that was left behind. When Lee's army crossed the Potomac by 8:00 a.m., Stuart's cavalry acted as rear guard, making an obstinate resistance near Falling Waters, where the main crossing took place. The next day, Buford's and Kilpatrick's divisions, having arrived at Falling Waters too late, moved to Berlin to obtain supplies. The pursuit of Lee's soldiers through Loudoun Valley to the Rappahannock River would be made by Union cavalry in detachments.[63]

Trooper John W. Lakes wrote his wife after crossing back into Virginia, "I never had my saddle off of my horse one hour at a time for three weeks and the most sleep that I got was on my horse's back. We travelled more at night than in the day ... we lost every wagon we had while we was [sic] in Md and Pa. What the Yankees did not get we lost in the river... cows, sheep and bread is all we live on."[64]

Trooper I. Norval Baker of the 18th Virginia recalled the terrible condition of the horses before they crossed into Virginia, "the green flies were around us all the time and orders were not to unsaddle or unbridle our horses and be ready for duty at all times. Our blankets were under our saddles and soaked with water and the green flies were working under the rawhide covering of our saddles and ulcerated backs of our horses." After crossing into Virginia, the troopers were ordered to unsaddle their horses. "Our horses' backs were raw with ulcers one

---

61. Blackford, *Letters from Lee's Army*, 190, 193; *Autobiography of St. George Tucker Brooke*, 32. General Pettigrew was actually mortally wounded, dying three days later.
62. Driver, *2nd Virginia Cavalry*, 93–94.
63. *OR* 27/1:917.
64. Driver, *2nd Virginia Cavalry*, 94; John W. Lakes letter, July 15, 1863, Collection of James I. Robertson, Virginia Tech, Blacksburg, Virginia.

and two inches deep and full of maggots." After a thorough cleaning and drying out of blankets, saddles and horses' backs, "it took months before the horses backs were cured."[65]

The Army of Northern Virginia's trek into Pennsylvania had been hard on the troops and horses. They had escaped back into Virginia, but the cost had been horrific. Despite the hardships experienced, Wickham's 4th Virginia suffered relatively light losses of only 17 troopers missing or captured during the campaign. Never again, with the exception of Jubal Early's raid near Washington in 1864, would the South be able to mount an attack in the North. Soon, they would be fighting the fall campaigns of Bristoe Station, Mine Run, and North Anna.

Back in Virginia, with the main army at Bunker Hill, the 4th Virginia picketed the Shepherdstown area with its brigade. On July 16, Fitz Lee's brigade encountered Federal troops at Kearneysville, driving them back before the fight ended at sunset. The following day, the Union force moved to the north side of the Potomac. On July 19, the 4th Virginia, camped at Leetown, reported 425 troopers mounted and 48 dismounted out of 949 on its rolls.[66]

Meanwhile, Wickham had submitted a resignation request earlier (on July 14, 1863) after his election to the Confederate Congress, but J.E.B. Stuart and Robert E. Lee did not want to lose his services. Secretary of the Commonwealth, George W. Munford, notified Wickham of his election on June 27 to the Confederate Congress. On July 18, 1863, Stuart forwarded Wickham's resignation request, noting, "Respectfully forwarded with the earnest desire to prevent the loss of the Confederate army of so valuable an officer—Col. Wickham has displayed fine ability, zeal, and bravery as an officer and has been recommended for promotion. I feel deeply that his absence to the councils of the nation deprives the cavalry service of its best colonel."[67] Wickham's request was finally submitted to the Secretary of War August 1, 1863. On July 16, 1863, President Davis declined his request for resignation.[68]

On July 22, trooper Pvt. Lawson Morrissett of Company B wrote that the 4th Virginia "left camp before daybreak," rode to Berryville and then Millwood. Next, the regiment crossed the Shenandoah River at Berry's Ford, encamping near the river. The following day, the regiment moved on to Front Royal, passing through Chester Gap before proceeding to Flint Hill. Wickham next bivouacked his troopers

---

65. Diary of I. Norval Baker, 18th Virginia Cavalry, VMI Archives.
66. Stiles, *4th Virginia Cavalry*, 34.
67. Williams C. Wickham Service Record, NARA.
68. Ibid.

near Gaines's Cross Roads. Morrissett wrote, "with nothing to eat but blackberries," the 4th Virginia left the cross roads on Friday morning for Rixeyville. By July 25, Stuart's cavalry occupied the Rappahannock line. Trooper Sgt. John A. Holtzman wrote to the pleasure of the men, corn for the horses had finally arrived.[69]

On July 28, Wickham's 4th Virginia was at Brandy Station, with 313 serviceable horses, 531 troopers present, out of 963 on the rolls. The Gettysburg campaign had been hard on the Army of Northern Virginia, including the 4th Virginia Cavalry. Although the regiment had not participated int the cavalry fight at Rummel's Farm, Stuart praised the troopers of the 4th Virginia. By the end of July, the regiment had 398 mounted men, while continuing to occupy Bandy Station. Like the entire cavalry corps, the 4th Virginia's troopers were worn out and weary.[70]

On August 1, Wickham's command moved its encampment to Salem Church. During August, all was relatively quiet along the Rappahannock line for the 4th Virginia. On August 4, Wickham's troopers were involved in a small skirmish at Culpeper Court House, losing one trooper captured. By mid-August, the regiment numbered 21 officers, and 387 enlisted men present out of 953 aggregate on the rolls. Located in Spotsylvania County, Wickham's regiment suffered because of the desolate countryside, which had been brought on over military trafficking that had occurred there since the onset of the war. Food was reduced to "three crackers and a greasy spot a day." The horses were only allotted about a pound of corn per day, with five pounds being the limit, and at times none at all. One soldier described the horse as "graven images and are living on their constitutions and the hope for a better day." The entire brigade was suffering badly, with no improvement in sight.[71]

The 4th Virginia marched between Fredericksburg and Bowling Green, with some on picker duty and the rest in camp. On August 29, Wickham's regiment had 988 men on the rolls, with 533 present for duty. Throughout the month of September, the 4th Virginia marched about Culpeper County working the picket line. The regimental adjutant reported the regiment as being "in a good state of discipline and efficiency." Capt. Robert Randolph reported on September 7 that he was "tired of (the) monotonous camp life," and that the regiment had not rested this much since the start of the war.[72]

---

69. Stiles, *4th Virginia Cavalry*, 34.
70. Ibid.
71. Ibid., 35.
72. Ibid. Randolph was promoted to major on September 4, 1863.

Cavalry Reorganization

General Robert E. Lee feared that Wickham would resign from the army and take his seat in the Confederate Congress. Lee wrote his wife, "Wickham still continues in the service, but I fear is getting tired of it."[73] In reorganizing the cavalry corps, consideration may have been given to promoting Wickham to brigade command in order to entice him into remaining in the service. Prior to the reorganization, many expected Col. Thomas Munford would receive a brigade, but Munford was passed over for Wickham. For whatever reasons, Wickham received the coveted promotion and brigade. The command of the 4th Virginia passed to the skillful hands of Lt. Col. W. H. F. Payne, a brave, fine officer.

Munford seethed: "This reminds me vividly of my own services in our war. Gen. Wm. C. Wickham was Colonel of the 4th Virginia Cavalry of the 2nd Brigade Cavalry. I was Senior Colonel. Wickham was elected to Congress. Stuart had endorsed and recommended me to command the Brigade and I was commanding it, but Wickham, being a Congressman-Elect got himself made Brigadier and held both offices and drew the pay of both. I did his work ..."[74]

By Special Order 226, from the headquarters of the Army of Northern Virginia, dated September 9, 1863, the cavalry divisions were reorganized as follows:

Hampton's Division:

William E. Jones's brigade: 6th Virginia, 7th Virginia, 12th Virginia, and 35th Battalion Virginia Cavalry.

Laurence S. Baker's brigade: 1st North Carolina, 2nd North Carolina, 4th North Carolina, and 5th North Carolina. Baker would not lead the brigade due to a disabling arm wound inflicted on August 1. Colonel James B. Gordon was promoted to brigadier general to command the brigade.

M. C. Butler's brigade: Cobb Georgia Legion, Philips Georgia Legion, Jeff Davis Legion, 2nd South Carolina. Butler was in South Carolina, recovering from a leg amputation after Brandy Station. Pierce M. B. Young assumed temporary command of the brigade.

73. Robert E. Lee to his Mary Anna Randolph Custis Lee, September 4, 1863, Lee Family Papers, Mss1L51 c 475, Section 23, Virginia Historical Society, Richmond; Stiles, *4th Virginia Cavalry*, 36.
74. Thomas Taylor Munford to James Longstreet, Feb. 19, 1899, Glen Irving Tucker Papers, Southern Historical Collection, University of North Carolina.

Williams C. Wickham received his promotion to brigadier general during the cavalry reorganization of September 1863. The capable William H. Payne took command of the 4th Virginia cavalry as its colonel.

(Hanover County Historical Society)

<u>Fitzhugh Lee's division:</u>

W. H. F. "Rooney" Lee's brigade: 1st South Carolina, 9th Virginia, 10th Virginia, and 13th Virginia.

Lunsford Lomax's brigade: 5th Virginia, 1st Battalion Maryland Cavalry, 11th Virginia, and 15th Virginia.

Williams Wickham's brigade: 1st Virginia, 2nd Virginia (under Munford), 3rd Virginia, and 4th Virginia.[75]

Trooper Richard Watkins of the 3rd Virginia Cavalry wrote his wife, Mary, that Wickham now commands his brigade. "His appointment gives general satisfaction. His profanity is the only objection to him. We hope that the dignity of his position ... will induce him to amend his habits in that respect. How sad it is ... that some of our officers set such examples before the men."[76]

On September 13, Union cavalry commander Maj. Gen. Alfred Pleasonton attacked and defeated J. E. B. Stuart's cavalry at Culpeper Court House, situated halfway between Richmond and Washington, D.C. This Union victory opened the Culpeper region to Union control, ushering in the Bristoe campaign. During this campaign, several significant cavalry actions occurred, including the battle of Auburn on October 14 and the battle of Buckland Mills on October 19, 1863.[77]

Lieutenant Colonel William R. Carter, 3rd Virginia Cavalry, recorded in his diary for October 1, 1863, that the 3rd Virginia moved their camp from Orange Court House to Mrs. Frazier's farm, about 2-and-a-half miles from Orange Springs. General Wickham was seriously injured by a fall from his horse while galloping across the field near Orange Courthouse. Colonel Carter recorded, "Wickham's horse fell with him and hurt him quite seriously. He fell upon and bruised his left leg."[78] Colonel Tom Owen of the 3rd Virginia took over command of Wickham's brigade for the Bristoe and Mine Run campaigns.

On October 11, Stuart attempted to assault the Federal rear at Brandy Station in order to gain the high ground at Fleetwood Hill.

75. *OR* 29/2:707–08; McClellan, *The Campaigns of Stuart's Cavalry*, 371–72.
76. Richard Watkins to his wife, Mary, December 30, 1863, VHS; Jeff Toalson, ed., *Send Me a Pair of Old Boots & Kiss My Little Girls: The Civil War Letter of Richard and Mary Watkins, 1861-1865* (New York: iUniverse Books, 2009), 217-18.
77. "Bristoe Campaign," NPS.
78. Walbrook D. Swank, ed., *Lieutenant Colonel William R. Carter, CSA* (Shippensburg, PA: Burd Street Press, 1998), 91; *Charleston (South Carolina) Daily Courier*, October 7, 1863.

Stuart sent the 12th Virginia to attack Union cavalry near Fleetwood Hill, but a Union cavalry squadron struck the flank of Stuart's 4th and 5th North Carolina, routing them and forcing their retreat. The Federals established a strong position on Fleetwood Hill and were able to thwart all Confederate attacks with artillery. Regardless of their success, at nightfall the Federal cavalry, under Pleasanton, recrossed the Rappahannock River to safety.[79]

During the cavalry fight at Brandy Station, Maj. Gen. Fitzhugh Lee's cavalry division and two brigades of infantry forced Union Brig. Gen. John Buford back across the Rapidan River at Morton's Ford. Trooper Capt. Richard Watkins of the 3rd Virginia recalled Fitz Lee. "Genl Fitz Lee has rather distinguished himself and is rapidly gaining the confidence of his Division ... He is certainly one of the most reckless daring men I ever saw ... He is always in the thickest of the fight and above all the noise and confusion his full rich voice can be heard cheering on the men. But ... like all others, he has his weakness. He drinks to excess and rumor says the habit is growing ... that persisted this habit will soon ruin him."[80]

On October 12, Stuart left Thomas Rosser's 5th Virginia with only one piece of artillery near Brandy Station, with orders to picket the Rappahannock. He ordered Col. Pierce Young to move Maj. Gen. Matthew C. Butler's brigade from James City to Culpeper Court House. He then proceeded with the remainder of his command toward Warrenton, 15 miles southwest of Manassas in Fauquier County, Virginia. Stuart had succeeded in screening Gen. Robert E. Lee's army from the prying eyes of the Union cavalry. Meade mistakenly thought Lee was at Culpeper Court House, and on the afternoon of the 12th, he dispatched the II, V, and VI Corps with Buford's cavalry for Culpeper, intending to fight Lee there. Meade's advance struck Rosser's regiment mid afternoon, forcing Rosser to fall back in the face of a vastly superior force. He fought a stalling action as best he could while retreating, delaying the Federal advance from reaching a wooded ridge called Slaughter's Hill, north of Culpeper Court House, until nearly nightfall.[81]

Meanwhile, Young had arrived from James City, bringing five pieces of artillery. Young dismounted every available man and positioned his guns in advantageous positions. Rosser's troopers joined his line of battle. Severe cannon fire surprised Buford's approaching cavalry, ceasing their advance. Buford bivouacked for the night, as did Rosser and Young. Rosser's troopers lit many campfires in an

79. *OR* 29/1:442–44, 448.
80. Richard Watkins to Mary Watkins, October 21, 1863, VMHC.
81. H. B. McClellan, *The Campaigns of Stuart's Cavalry*, 383.

attempted ruse to fool Buford into thinking that the Confederate force was larger than it appeared. During the night, Meade received information that General Lee was in fact moving on the Orange and Alexandria Railroad, so he moved his army to confront the Confederate commander. Buford also moved back across the Rappahannock River.[82]

On October 13, General Lee ordered Stuart to conduct a reconnaissance toward Catlett's Station, southwest of Manassas on the O&A Railroad. Lee's main army concentrated at Warrenton, and when Stuart reached within eight miles of Catlett's Station and Warrenton Junction, he discovered Meade retreating toward Manassas. Stuart spotted a large number of Federal wagons near the railroad between Warrenton and Manassas; however, two Federal corps along the road protected the wagons. Stuart realized that he could not attack with his cavalry command alone. He sent his inspector general, Maj. A. Reid Venable, to Robert E. Lee with the information, but Lee responded by sending a courier to Rosser telling him that Auburn was in the Federals' hands. Stuart then realized that he was cut off from the main army, stranded between two Federal corps. He had two choices: fight through or ride around the Union forces. He chose to hide his two brigades of cavalry and seven artillery pieces until Lee could arrive to attack the Federals. Stuart found a small secluded valley for this purpose, just 175 yards from where the Federals bivouacked for the night.[83]

Before dawn on October 14, Stuart heard a volley of musketry on Warrenton Road and assumed that it was General Lee advancing to attack. Responding, Rosser assaulted the Federals camped near him with cannon fire and then attempted to break through the Union lines. Lee was not attacking, however, and Stuart suffered substantial losses while breaking free of the Federals and proceeding toward Warrenton.[84]

Wickham suffered an injury—after falling off his horse, his horse then fell on his leg. Wickham's brigade—under Thomas Owen due to Wickham's injury—moved out on Friday, October 9, to cover the Rapidan River, encamping that evening at the Honorable Jeremiah Morton's farm. They remained in camp the next day until evening, when Federals crossed the Rapidan at Morton's Ford in considerable force and captured some of Lomax's pickets. They then recrossed to the north side of the Rapidan. The next morning, October 11, Owen's command crossed the Rapidan at Raccoon Ford, finding the enemy in

82. Ibid, 384.
83. *OR* 29/1:448.
84. Ibid.

a battle line at near Stringfellow's house. Fitz Lee ordered Owen to charge the enemy's battery and take it. Owen dispatched his entire command to complete the task. During the fight, Owen ordered the 4th Virginia to charge the Union sharpshooters. Success came at cost—Captain William B. Newton of Company A of the 4th Virginia was killed leading a charge. Captain Phillip D. Williams of the 4th was mortally wounded.[85]

The main Confederate body pushed the Federals back toward Stevensburg. Fitz Lee's division rode to position itself for an attack on the Union flank. Upon running into strong Federal artillery, Lee decided not to attack. The enemy soldiers advanced outside Stevensburg. Lee sent in each regiment in to attack; but with strong sharpshooter support, the Federals beat the gray horsemen back each time. Finally, a charge by the regrouped 4th Virginia drove the Federals back. Joined by Stuart's main force at Brandy Station, Fitz Lee's brigade drove the Federals back across the Rappahannock. Owen assigned the 2nd Virginia to picket and proceeded to encamp at John Botts's farm.[86]

Stuart's horsemen had won the fights at Raccoon's Ford and Stevensburg but paid a heavy price. Valiant Captain William B. Newton of Company A of the 4th Virginia was killed leading a charge at Raccoon Ford. Company H suffered ten killed and the loss of 20 horses. As the Federals retreated, Fitz Lee's division, without the 4th Virginia, pursued them.

On the morning of October 12, Owen moved to Miller's Hill, below Brandy Station in support of the 2nd Virginia. At midday, he moved his troopers toward Jeffersonton, crossing the Rapidan River at Starke's Ford. Fitz Lee ordered Owen to move toward Hedgeman River and cross at Fox's Ford, which he accomplished without difficulty. Owen drove in Federal pickets and took possession of the heights overlooking the ford and the roads leading to Warrenton Springs and Bealeton Station.[87]

On October 13, Wickham's brigade saddled up about 10 a.m. to go on a scout around Catlett's Station on the Orange and Alexandria Railroad. Owen encountered Federals in heavy force near Auburn protecting their trains. After a brief exchange, Owen withdrew and went into camp four miles from Catlett's Station. The next day, Owen led Wickham's troopers via New Baltimore and Gainesville to Langyher's Hill and went into camp. The following day, October 15, Owen moved to Manassas, where he encountered Federal forces, and

85. *OR* 29/1:471.
86. *OR* 29/1:472; Stiles, *4th Virginia Cavalry*, 36-37.
87. *OR* 29/1:472.

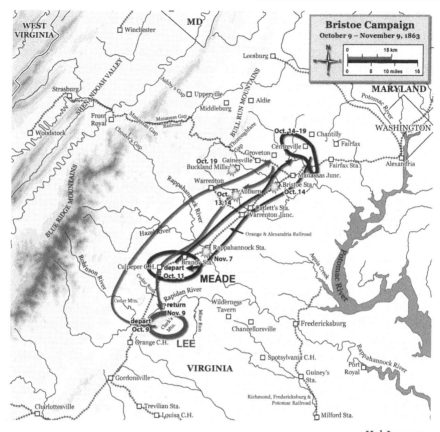

Hal Jespersen

dismounted his sharpshooters. Along with sharpshooters from Lomax's brigade, they engaged the enemy in a sharp fight, driving them across Bull Run to their entrenchments. Remaining in place until dark, Owen then withdrew, leaving pickets and encamping near Manassas.[88]

The next day, all remained quiet until late evening when the Federals recrossed the river and Owen went into camp near Manassas Junction. On October 17—learning that the Federals had threatened to advance from Groveton—Owen moved Wickham's brigade first to Gainesville and then toward Groveton. Owen dispatched skirmishers—who drove the enemy back—and proceeded to Ellis's place, encamping near Langyher's Mill. The next morning, Owen led his troopers to Langyher's Hill, encamping there all day and evening, while leaving the 4th Virginia picketing at Gainesville.[89]

88. Ibid.
89. Ibid.

A few days later, Stuart's and Fitz Lee's commands withdrew from Bristoe by separate routes, planning to meet in the vicinity of Warrenton. On October 18, Brig. Gen. Judson Kilpatrick attacked Stuart's outposts, forcing the Confederate cavalry commander to withdraw his troopers to the south bank of Broad Run at Buckland on the Warrenton Turnpike. Here Stuart planned to make a stand until Fitz Lee could join him. Rosser's brigade camped in the area of Haymarket for the night. Early on October 19, Gen. Wade Hampton's cavalry division, which included Rosser's brigade, joined in defending Buckland against Kilpatrick's attacking cavalry. Stuart, commanding Hampton's division in his absence, received a suggestion from Fitz Lee that Stuart withdraw from Kilpatrick thereby enticing him to follow. At a given signal Stuart would turn and attack Kilpatrick, while Fitz Lee would attack from the south against the Federal left flank.[90]

Stuart sent Hampton's division to Chestnut Hill, only two-and-a-half miles northeast of Warrenton. The unsuspecting Federal cavalrymen fell for the subterfuge—approaching to within 200-yards of the Confederate position—whereupon the Confederates, hearing Fitz Lee's signal, turned and attacked Kilpatrick's leading brigade, commanded by Brig. Gen. Henry E. Davies. The Federal horsemen were surprised and fled in confusion. Located in the rear, Bvt. Brig. Gen. George Armstrong Custer's brigade did not fall for the trap but defended the Broad Run position from Fitz Lee. While Custer's troopers were holding off Fitz Lee, Stuart led Hampton's division in pursuit of Davies along the Warrenton Turnpike. Brigadier General James B. Gordon led his North Carolina cavalry in a frontal attack on the Federal column, while brigadier generals Thomas Rosser and Pierce Young (not yet confirmed brigadier) attacked Federal cavalry on both sides of the Warrenton Turnpike. During Kilpatrick's rapid flight, he abandoned all of his division's transport, including Custer's headquarters' wagons and personal effects. The fleeing Federals overran Custer, but he retired in good order. Kilpatrick's division continued its flight until it reached safety behind Meade's I Corps. Ultimately, Stuart captured about 250 prisoners and a few wagons. Custer would not soon forget his humiliating defeat at the hands of Rosser's horsemen.

On October 19, Wickham's brigade moved to Auburn via Bristoe and Catlett's Stations. Owen learned from a courier that Stuart, commanding Hampton's division, had been forced back nearly to Warrenton before Federal forces. When Fitz Lee stuck the Union flank near Buckland, Wickham's brigade was positioned in front, with all of Wickham's sharpshooters dismounted on both sides of the road.

90. *OR* 29/1:451. Hampton was still recovering from his Gettysburg wound.

Breathed's artillery battery was brought up. After hearing Fitz Lee's gunfire as the signal, Stuart faced about and attacked the front of the Federal column, while Lee attacked on their flank. The Confederates routed the Union troopers, driving them back pell mell across the run near Buckland. Owen pressed forward, taking possession of the bridge and ford at Buckland, forcing those of the enemy who were cut off to leave the road to their right and flee across the run above the bridge and ford. The Federals fled in great disorder, with many being captured, killed, or drowned.[91]

Fitz Lee ordered Owen to continue to pursue the retreating Federal horsemen. Proceeding to catch up within 100 yards of them, Owen ordered the 3rd Virginia to charge, followed by the 2nd Virginia, and finally the 1st Virginia. Owen's troopers drove the enemy back upon their infantry reserve. Darkness ended the fight; and Owen pulled back, leaving a picket, and camped for the night at near Buckland. Owen reported 17 killed, 129 (four mortally) wounded, and eight missing. This pursuit of Federal cavalry became known as "the Buckland Races."[92]

Colonel Thomas Owen, 3rd Virginia Cavalry, led Wickham's brigade at Buckland. He was cited by Stuart in his official report for "conspicuous gallantry in command of the dismounted men, chasing on foot the enemy's cavalry over open ground. Owens had led Wickham's command due to Wickham's "absence by serious of serious injury received by the fall of his horse."[93]

Between October 10–21, Wickham's command lost 23 killed and 124 wounded.[94]

Fighting Along the Rappahannock and Rapidan Rivers

After the Bristoe campaign and the cavalry fight at Buckland, the Confederate and Union armies reoccupied their previous positions on the Rappahannock and Rapidan rivers. On the evening of October 20, Wickham's brigade, still under Owen, encamped on the Green farm near Beverly Ford, while establishing its pickers along the Rapidan. The troopers of the 4th Virginia had been without food for three days. Robert E. Lee summed up the Buckland fight: "the Cavalry covered themselves in glory."[95]

---

91. Ibid., 473.
92. Ibid., 473-74.
93. *OR* 29/1:452.
94. *OR* 29/1:454.
95. Stiles, *4th Virginia Cavalry*, 39.

The Federal army crossed the Rappahannock at Kelly's Ford on November 7, reoccupying its former position at Culpeper Court House. Robert E. Lee withdrew to the south bank of the Rapidan, preparing to go into winter quarters. Meanwhile, during a nighttime attack, the Federal III, V, and VI Corps—the latter two under Maj. Gen. John Sedgwick—overran Maj. Gen. Jubal Early's division at Rappahannock Bridge. The Confederates lost 1,630 killed, wounded, or captured; in comparison, Federal casualties totaled only 419.[96]

On November 26, Federal demonstrations occurred at Morton's and Raccoon fords. Wickham's brigade, still under Owen—in response—quickly rode to Raccoon Ford. At 9 a.m. the following day, Federal cavalry forged a crossing at Raccoon Ford but were immediately confronted by Wickham's 4th Virginia and driven back across the river. Skirmishing continued along the river all day. On the 28th, it was relatively quiet all day; a steady rain and bitterly cold wind discouraged any troop movement. General Meade concluded that the Confederate line was too strong to attack and retired during the night of December 1–2, ending the fall campaign. Lee was chagrined to find that he had no one left in his front to attack. The Mine Run campaign was General Meade's last attempt in 1863 to destroy Lee's Army of Northern Virginia before winter halted military operations.[97]

On a clear and cold December 1, 1863, Brig. Gen. Williams Wickham returned to duty from his serious leg wound that occurred on October 1.[98]

On December 10, Wickham, with part of the 1st, 2nd, and 4th Virginia Regiments, and Rooney Lee's brigade (led by Chambliss) rode toward Albermarle County.[99] On December 11, Wickham's brigade broke camp and headed for Charlottesville, where forage was more available. On December 14, Stuart ordered Fitz Lee, with Wickham's brigade, to intercept a Federal raiding party threatening Staunton. Riding through Port Republic on December 15, Wickham's brigade moved to Mount Crawford, turning south on the pike toward Staunton. Arriving at Staunton the next day and finding no Union forces, Wickham's brigade turned around and headed back to Mount Crawford.[100]

During the second week of December, Fitzhugh Lee and the brigades of Williams Wickham and John Chambliss, with batteries of

---

96. *OR* 29/1:624; Douglas Southall Freeman, *Lee's Lieutenants*. 3 vols. (New York, 1942), 3:267.
97. Ibid.
98. Swank, *Lieutenant Colonel William R. Carter, CSA*, 103.
99. Ibid., 104.
100. Stiles, *4th Virginia Cavalry*, 39–40.

horse artillery, marched south toward Albemarle County but were rerouted to the Shenandoah Valley to interdict a Union raiding force in western Virginia. When that operation was concluded, Fitz Lee scattered the regiments on both sides of the Blue Ridge Mountains. In time, Lee disbanded them, permitting the officers and men to go home until recalled.[101]

Still attempting to catch the raiders, Fitz Lee finally gave up the two-week chase on December 27. Wickham's brigade reached New Market. Captain Richard Watkins wrote to his wife of the difficulty crossing the rapid, swollen rivers, "The most hazardous part of the march consisted in crossing the rivers. Many of them were much swollen and very rapid. In crossing the Jackson near Covington a member of the 2nd Regiment was drowned and, but for the vigilance of General Wickham, I reckon many more would have been lost, but he stood on the bank and directed and continued to order and direct until the whole column passed."[102]

In the same letter, Watkins wrote of the severe cold:

> **Many of the regiment have been badly frostbitten on the late chase after Averill. But, fortunately, I escaped owing mainly to the fact that I walked a great deal. Whenever pinched by the cold, [I] would jump down and walk or run until the circulation was completely restored, then mount and ride again. Often [I] wished that you could see us crossing the mountains. At times, there was so much ice on the roads that the whole command would have to dismount and walk. Sometimes those in the extreme rear would begin to cheer and it would be caught up along the line and extend almost entirely across the mountain.[103]**

Telling his wife of his health, Watkins wrote, "But, darling, am happy to say that I was never in better health in my life and never had a better appetite. [I] can sit down by a log fire in the woods and eat nearly a half-pound of raw bacon (the fatest [sic] that can be found) and two or three hard crackers, then make up a shelter of fence rails with oil cloths over them, rake up a pile of leaves, roll myself and my

---

101. Wert, *Cavalryman of the Lost Cause*, 325; Nanzig, ed., *The Civil War Memoirs of a Virginia Cavalryman*, 127; Garnett, *Riding with Stuart*, 38.
102. Richard Watkins to his wife, Mary, December 30, 1863, VMHC.
103. Ibid.

blankets and tumble over and sleep as soundly and dream as sweetly of home and as if I were in the most comfortable house and on the best mattress."[104]

December had been hard on the army of Northern Virginia and on its cavalry. Shortages of food, clothing, equipment, and good mounts presented tough hardships on Wickham's brigade and Robert E. Lee's entire army.

---

104. Ibid.

Chapter Seven

1864: Wickham Resigns
His Commission and Takes His seat
in the Confederate Congress

"Old Wickham rode around waving his sabe and cursing like a trooper."
–Lt. Robert T. Hubard, Jr. of the 3rd Virginia Cavalry at Haw's Shop

1864 presented new opportunities for Williams C. Wickham. He and his brigade returned east to help Gen. Robert E. Lee's army face new Federal commander Lt. Gen. Ulysses S. Grant's opening spring campaign. The battles of the Wilderness, Trevilian Station, and Second Reams's Station--along with a cavalry reorganization loomed large in the events during this period. Wickham continued his service in an admirable manner, even though he must have known that the Confederacy's days were numbered.

With the 1864 spring campaign approaching, President Abraham Lincoln decided to transfer Ulysses S. Grant from the Western Theater to take command of the entire Union Army. Lincoln had Grant promoted to the rank of lieutenant general, the first United States military man since George Washington to hold that rank. Grant's strategic plan involved attacking the Army of Northern Virginia and Brig. Gen. Joseph E. Johnston's Army of Tennessee, as well as not capturing and occupying cities, rejecting the prevailing military thinking. Unsatisfied with the Federal cavalry's performance in the East, Grant transferred Maj. Gen. Philip H. Sheridan from Tennessee to take command of the Army of the Potomac's cavalry corps. Grant attached himself to the Army of the Potomac, leaving Maj. Gen. William T. Sherman with the task of defeating Johnson. Grant reduced the Army of the Potomac from five to three corps—the II, V, and VI—commanded by major generals Winfield S. Hancock, Gouverneur K. Warren, and John Sedgwick, respectively. The IX Corps, with Maj. Gen. Ambrose E. Burnside commanding, was not incorporated into the Army of the Potomac until May 24, 1864, although it served with the unit in the Wilderness and Spotsylvania campaigns. Grant's army in Virginia consisted of about 116,000 men, including the IX Corps.[1]

Meanwhile, General Lee did not reorganize his army in preparation for the spring campaign. The Army of Northern Virginia still consisted of three corps commanded by lieutenant generals James Longstreet, Richard Ewell, and Ambrose P. Hill. The war of attrition took its toll on Confederate manpower with the number of available recruits declining. Lee's army could only muster about 64,000 soldiers in its ranks.[2]

Wickham's brigade left Mount Jackson on New Year's Eve for Moorefield, crossing the North Mountains via the Orkney Springs Road. They then turned north toward Lost River. Meanwhile, Fitzhugh Lee, at Moorefield on New Year's Day, learned that enemy troops were entrenched at Petersburg. Lacking artillery and with his troopers' ammunition wet, Fitz Lee opted to attack New Creek Depot in lieu of Petersburg.[3]

Moving through Moorefield and Burlington, Fitz Lee's cavalry reached Ridgeville on January 4, and encamped. The next morning, Fitz had his division riding by 4 a.m., moving painstakingly through a hailstorm. Lee's troopers marched to within six miles of New Creek Depot before being forced to turn back. The mountain trails were impassible, due to the road conditions, and the fact that the smooth-shod horses could not gain traction. Lee's horsemen returned to Shenandoah by way of Romney and Brock's Gap. Despite failing to reach New Creek Depot, Fitz Lee's division returned with 27 wagons, 110 prisoners, 460 head of cattle, and more than 300 horses and mules.[4]

The Confederate Senate confirmed Williams Wickham's promotion to brigadier general on January 25, 1864, to rank from September 1, 1863.[5]

On Feb. 8, 1864, Williams wrote to Lucy: "Genl. (R. E.) Lee has issued the first of his orders that has failed to receive my admiration. It is in his handsomest style but is as bad as his choosing to have meat but twice a week."[6]

On February 28, seven Union cavalry regiments left Pony Mountain for a raid into Albermarle County. The Federal force forded

---

1. *OR* 36/1:198, 915.
2. Freeman, *Lee's Lieutenants*, 3:345.
3. Stiles, *4th Virginia Cavalry*, 42.
4. Ibid.
5. *Journal of the Congress of the Confederate States of America, 1861-1865*, Vol. 3:618. Washington, Government Printing Office, 1904.
6. Williams C. Wickham to Lucy Wickham, February 8, 1864, Wickham Family Papers, UVA.

Robertson's River and drove Wickham's pickets in during the morning hours. As the Confederates were yielding Madison Court House, Brig. Gen. George Custer moved to Charlottesville. Fitz Lee ordered Wickham's brigade to intercept Custer's raiders, hoping to trap him at Stanardsville. After reaching Charlottesville, Custer's horsemen retired in the same direction they had come. The raiders camped at Stanardsville, where Wickham had taken a position along the road after riding all day and most of the night. During the night, a freezing, biting sleet storm occurred, freezing many men to their saddles and horses to the road. When the Union column of invaders rode through Stanardsville, Wickham's brigade could do little to prevent their escape, being as frozen as they were. Custer's raiders exited quickly, with little fighting, and headed for its encampment back in Culpeper County.[7]

Wickham's brigade protected Robert E. Lee's army during the month of March as they picketed the Rappahannock and Rapidan Rivers. On March 2, Wickham's brigade rode through the Wilderness on a scout to locate the Federal cavalry. Wickham's headquarters was at Montpelier. On March 26, Wickham's brigade was relieved of picket duty on the Robertson-Rapidan River and headed for Fredericksburg. The brigade has been ordered to investigate a report of Union cavalry at Germanna Ford.[8]

Captain Richard Watkins wrote his wife, Mary, of the terrible weather and the good food he was having dining with Wickham:

> Since my arrival we have had every conceivable variety of bad weather and the snow is now falling thick & fast. I am in a comfortable tent, though, with a plenty of good wheat straw & heavy blankets and a good stove, to boot, and fare sumptuously (for camp) at the General's table. Twould [sic] amuse you to see how the General is fixed. He has a splendid cow & hen house with seventeen hens so we have very nice egg-bread, butter & milk, nice ham, peas, rice, etc. etc. Oh, what a wide difference between the fare of a General & a private.[9]

Watkins wrote of breakfast the next morning, "Captain, come to breakfast," says the General. Bless his dear old heart. My appetite is as keen as a razor. A few steps from the door of my tent takes me to the dining tent and I find myself seated by a little table around which are the General and his staff & upon it batter bread with butter and ham.

7. Stiles, *4th Virginia Cavalry*, 42-43.
8. Ibid., 44.
9. Richard Watkins to wife, Mary, April 4, 1864, VMHC.

We all sit with hats on, eat fast & keep up a lively chat. The breakfast is soon over and I find myself again at the desk."[10]

On March 9, 1864, Capt. John Esteen Cooke recalled, "Today General (Williams C.) Wickham spent several hours with us and Mrs. Stuart, Mrs. Berkeley, he, Capt. (Thomas M.) Garnett and dined. General R. E. Lee was here before dinner in his old blue cape ..."[11]

On March 30, Rooney Lee was finally exchanged from imprisonment and rejoined Stuart's cavalry. He was promoted to major general and given his own division, consisting of his old brigade (then under Brig. Gen. John R. Chambliss), the 9th. 10th, and 13th Virginia from Fitzhugh Lee's division, and James B. Gordon's brigade of the 1st, 2nd, and 5th North Carolina cavalry regiments from Hampton's division. Hampton retained Pierce Young's brigade of the Jeff Davis Legion, Cobb Legion, and two new units, the 7th Georgia and the 20th Georgia Battalion. Also, in Hampton's division was Rosser's Laurel Brigade of the 7th, 11th, and 12th Virginia Regiments and the 35th Virginia Battalion. Rosser's brigade, however, had been sent to the Shenandoah Valley and was not at Hampton's calling.[12]

Fitz Lee's division, stationed in the Shenandoah Valley, then consisted of Wickham's brigade of the 1st, 2nd, 3rd, and 4th Virginia regiments. Lunsford Lomax's brigade changed slightly, giving up the 1st Maryland Battalion to Bradley Johnson's new brigade. Months earlier Lomax had exchanged the 11th Virginia to Rosser for the 6th Virginia.[13]

On April 12, Richard Watkins wrote his wife of the previous evening's entertainment, "General Wickham was serenaded by a large glee club lately formed in the 1st Regiment and I don't remember ever having heard more beautiful singing. [I] was especially pleased with a song "Farewell to the Star-Spangled Banner"... We have a great deal of music nowadays; just at this moment, a few hundred yards off, a large brass band is playing "The Marsellaise." The most of it, though, is martial music and I get a little tired of it. [I] would like a change sometimes."[14]

On April 26, General Wickham led his brigade from Orange Court House, encamping at Parker's Tavern. On May 4, Grant crossed the Rapidan at Germanna Ford downriver from R. E. Lee with about 112,000 infantry, 15,000 cavalry, and 200-300 artillery pieces. Facing

---

10. Ibid., April 5, 1864.
11. *The Journal of Southern History*, Published by: Southern Historical Association, Vol. 7, No. 4 (Nov., 1941), 539.
12. Longacre, *Lee's Cavalrymen*, 273–74.
13. Ibid., 274.
14. Richard Watkins to Mary Watkins, April 12, 1864, VMHC.

them was Robert E. Lee's approximately 45,000 infantry effectives, 8,000 cavalry, and 200 artillery pieces. One May 5, Fitz Lee's division of Confederate cavalry marched up to Massaponax Church. The next day, Wickham's brigade of about 2,250 troopers rode up beyond Spotsylvania Court House, dismounting to form a battle line two-miles southeast east of Todd's Tavern on the Brock Road. Here, Wickham sent them forward in skirmish formation toward the videttes south of Todd's Tavern. Brigadier General David McMurtrie Gregg, commanding the 2nd Division of Federal Cavalry Corps was wounded, though not seriously. He had ordered Brig. Gen. Henry E. Davies, Jr. to mount his four regiments at 3 a.m. and to wait in a large field west of Todd's Tavern. Except for the 2nd Pennsylvania, General Gregg had retired Col. J. Irvin Gregg's remaining five regiments to the tavern before daylight, deploying them along a half-mile line, stretching from the tavern along Piney Branch Run to the Piney Church Road. Wickham's horsemen corralled the 2nd Pennsylvania to within one mile of the tavern. The Confederates, dismounted then lay prone in the woods on both sides of the road. They fired at the Union cavalrymen at a range of about 500 yards.[15]

Soon Companies E, F, G, and K of the 8th Pennsylvania Cavalry came to the aid of the 2nd Pennsylvania. The 4th Virginia, positioned on the right of the Confederate line just northeast of the road, took cover behind a rail fence on the north edge of the woods. An expansive, wide-open field separated the combatants, with desultory firing continuing the remainder of the afternoon.[16]

By early afternoon, the 16th Pennsylvania relieved the 1st Maine Cavalry near Piney Church Road. The long-distance skirmishing continued throughout the day until 4:30 p.m., when the Federals retired from the fight. Gregg's brigade went to Piney Branch Church, while the 1st Maine went on picket. Davies's brigade pulled back to Aldrich's, about four-and-a-half-miles northeast of Todd's Tavern. The 4th Virginia noted ten wounded for the day.[17]

On May 7, the 3rd Virginia Cavalry, commanded by Lieutenant Colonel Carter, was left on picket. At 3 a.m. the following morning, Lt. Robert T. Hubard, Jr. of the 3rd Virginia recalled:

15. Thomas P. Nanzig, ed., *The Civil War Memoirs of a Virginia Cavalryman: Lt. Robert T. Hubard, Jr.* (Tuscaloosa: University of Alabama Press, 2007), 133, 136; John Michael Priest, *Victory without Triumph: The Wilderness May 6th and 7th, 1864* (El Dorado Hills, CA: Savas Beatie Publishing, 2014), 95.
16. Ibid., 97.
17. John Michael Priest, *Victory without Triumph: The Wilderness May 6th and 7th, 1864*, 97-98.

> We heard the Yankee bugles sounding to horse. So, we prepared for immediate attack and sent couriers to inform the generals. They took but little notice, however of the messages. We had heard a movement on our right as of a marching column with trains etc., but this, when told (to) Brigadier General [Williams] Wickham and Major General Fitzhugh Lee, was likewise little heeded; they turned over and 'slumbered and slept.'[18]

Lieutenant Colonel Carter, after sending the 3rd's horses to the rear, formed four squadrons with him in line behind a barricade, intent on holding his position. At 4 a.m., Hubard recalled plainly hearing Federal commands in the nearby woods of "Battalion forward, guide center march and in a few moments more, we were firing as fast as we could load, at a very heavy line of blue jackets. It was one incessant, deafening rattle while the smoke arose so thick we could scarcely see."[19]

At last, Fitzhugh Lee and Williams Wickham, having awoken, sent a courier to Carter, instructing him to "hold on and the brigade would be up after a while." Carter, discovering that his right flank had been completely passed by a heavy Federal column, ordered his troopers to retreat, firing as they went. The retreat continued for about 300 yards, having lasted about an hour against odds of four-or-five to one. Finally, Wickham's brigade came up in support, forming a longer line along a ridge in dense woods. The troopers lay down, fighting incessantly for another three hours.[20]

Phil Sheridan moved east along the Brock Road to Spotsylvania Court House on May 7. The sole force impeding Sheridan was Fitzhugh Lee's division of cavalry, which was hard-pressed that day—dismounting, building barricades, fighting a slow retiring action toward the court house. After desperate fighting, Fitzhugh Lee's troopers fell back to Alsop's farm. Federal artillery supporting the Federal advance was just too strong for the Confederates to hold Todd's Tavern.[21]

By mid-afternoon the Federals had halted their advance a couple of miles short of the critical court house crossroad. The Confederates had been forced back but still held Spotsylvania Court House. Trooper Lt. John A. Holtzman of the 4th Virginia recalled, "We were attacked very

18. Nanzig, ed., *The Civil War Memoirs of a Virginia Cavalryman: Lt. Robert T. Hubard, Jr.*, 136.; Swank, *Lieutenant Colonel William R. Carter, CSA*, 136.
19. Ibid.
20. Ibid.
21. Stiles, *4th Virginia Cavalry*. 45.

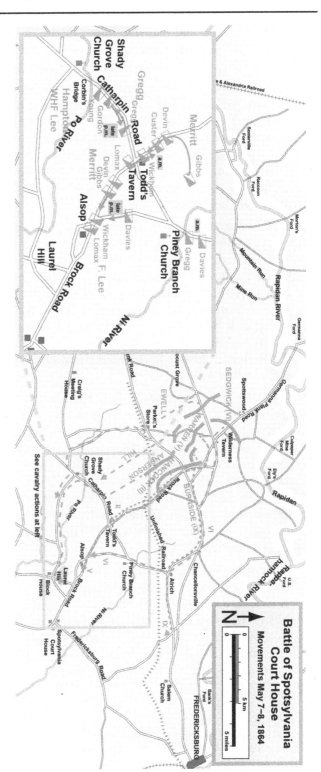

*Spotsylvania
Court House,
May 7-8, 1864*

(Hal Jespersen)

early this morning and had five hours of the most severe fighting we had ever had. Things were getting very serious for us, but soon Longstreet came to our rescue and it was a great relief."[22]

Meanwhile, Fitz Lee, at first light, discovered that his immediate front was unoccupied and marched west along the fog-covered Brock Road. Soon, Fitz Lee's horsemen ran into troopers of Alfred Torbert's division near Alsop's, dismounted, and began a slow, stubborn withdrawal toward the court house. Soon the Federal V Corps would join the fight against the Confederate horsemen. Fitz Lee's cavalry, using just axes, built barricades across the road and fought Union infantry from behind these ramparts.[23]

The Confederates were able to hold the Federal forces back for four hours, while falling back in good order from breastwork-to-breastwork with the division. By mid-morning, Maj. Gen. Richard Anderson's infantry had arrived, quickly filling in the rifle pits and saving Spotsylvania Court House from the Federals. Troopers William W. Scott of Company H of the 4th Virginia Cavalry recalled, "It was a very close call, but no one will deny that it was the stubborn tenacity of the cavalry that enabled the infantry to reach that strategic point first."[24] Robert E. Lee had prevented the federals from coming between himself and Richmond.

Just after dawn on May 9, Phil Sheridan had his cavalry force of more than 10,000 troopers marching south from Hamilton's Crossing along the Telegraph Road. Fitz Lee posted Wickham's troopers to guard the Gayle house's approach to Spotsylvania Court House. The Gayle house occupied high ground a short distance from north of the Ni River, and a half-mile northeast of the Court House. By 8 a.m., the 13-mile-long Federal train passed Massaponax Church. At 7:15 a.m., Major General Orlando Willcox's IX Corps division, led by 60th Ohio, approached the Gayle house. They quickly drove Wickham's troopers across the Ni River.[25]

Robert Johnston's brigade of Gordon's division, having occupied the reserve line behind Ewell in the morning, accompanied about 400 of his men in a recon toward Fredericksburg Road, where they joined Wickham and the horse artillery. Together, they tested Willcox's position on the Beverly's property lane, with the goal—that of stalling Willcox—until Ewell could bring up his infantry. Wickham and Johnston probed for weak points, finding one in the 60th Ohio. This

22. Ibid.
23. Ibid.
24. Ibid., 46.
25. Gordon Rhea, *The Battles for Spotsylvania Court House and the Road to Yellow Tavern, May 7–12, 1864* (Baton Rouge: LSU Press, 1997), 103; OR 36/2: 581.

Ohio regiment had been recruited just three weeks prior and had never been in battle. Confederates sprang from concealment in the woods at the fringe of the Beverly fields, scattering the Ohioans in confusion. Next the Rebel soldiers continued onto the high ground near the Beverly house. They opened a deadly enfilading fire on the 1st Michigan's sharpshooters. Some of Wickham's horsemen attacked the 79th New York's skirmish line, manned by Native Americans. Routed, the Ohioans broke and fled, forcing a Pennsylvania regiment to retreat. The 8th and 17th Michigan regiments, under Colonel John F. Hartranft, came to the rescue, aided by the 60th Ohio, the 1st Michigan, and the 51st Pennsylvania, forcing the Confederates pell mell back to the woods.[26]

At daylight, May 9, 1864, as infantry battled at Spotsylvania Court House, Maj. Gen. Phil Sheridan's cavalry— seven brigades, six batteries, and a wagon train, 10,000 men strong—saddled up and rode out from Spotsylvania in a column of fours that stretched for 13 miles. Brig. Gen. George Armstrong Custer's Michigan brigade led the huge procession, which headed east of Spotsylvania then south on the Telegraph Road. Telegraph road ran to the North Anna River, 25 miles south, and then to Richmond. Sheridan purposely moved at an easy pace, hoping to draw Stuart out for a fight.[27]

This bold move—to pass around the farthest of Stuart's outposts—was immediately detected by Confederate Brig. Gen. Williams Wickham's brigade. Wickham dispatched a courier to inform Stuart and then dashed off in pursuit. The Confederate cavalry reached the Union rear guard and engaged in a running battle. The Federals made a determined stand near Mitchell's Shop, temporarily fighting off the Rebels. By this time, Stuart mounted three brigades—about 4,500 men—and took up the chase.[28]

Sheridan turned his column toward Beaver Dam Station on the Virginia Central Railroad, indicating to Stuart that the march would proceed toward Richmond. Stuart knew that he had to interpose his cavalry between Sheridan and the capital. Stuart was also concerned about his family, who had established residence in Beaver Dam Station, 30-miles north of Richmond, and were now in imminent danger.[29]

Custer's 1st and 6th Michigan raced to the railroad station and seized two locomotives and three trains laden with several million dollars worth of supplies destined for the Confederate army. Custer

26. Ibid., 106.
27. Thom Hatch, *Historynet*, July 6, 2017; Rhea, *The Battles for Spotsylvania Court House and the Road to Yellow Tavern, May 7–12, 1864*, 97, 100.
28. Ibid.
29. Ibid.

reported that the boxcars were full of "bacon (200,000 pounds), flour, meal, sugar, molasses, liquor, and medical stores."[30]

Custer "distributed all the rations his men could carry, then burned the remainder. He also ordered the 100 railroad cars and depot put to the torch, disabled the locomotives by firing artillery shells through the boilers, tore up the tracks in the vicinity and cut ten miles of telegraph line. The Wolverines then departed to bivouac south of the South Anna River."[31]

Stuart decided to pursue with Lomax's Virginians and Marylanders—who in mid afternoon were relieved by infantry—and the North Carolina Brigade of Brigadier General James B. Gordon, recently detached from Hampton's command. These forces would be augmented by Wickham's Virginians, whom Stuart ordered to trail the Federal column, slowing it as much as possible.[32]

By 3:00 p.m. Stuart was heading south from Spotsylvania, accompanied by Fitz Lee, Lomax's troopers, a horse artillery unit, and a two-gun section of a second battery. Sheridan had such a head start that this force, even riding at top speed, would not catch him until the next morning. Having the much shorter route, Wickham's troops enjoyed what one of his troopers described as "the satisfaction of harassing the enemy to our heart's content." Late in the afternoon they made first contact at Jerrell's Mill on the Ta River, about 22 miles from Sheridan's starting point. In total, ten cavalry regiments, about 3,000 officers and troopers were chasing Sheridan's force of more than three times their number. It was nearly-dark when Stuart's force reached Telegraph Road.[33]

One trooper recalled the pursuit, "It was hot and the roads were dusty. To impede our pursuit, the fences on both sides of the roads were set on fire and march was through dust and smoke and sometimes between blazing fences, so that for miles at a time one could not see the set of fours in their front."[34]

Stuart was alerted to news that Sheridan's riders had left Telegraph Road, turning southwest through the villages of Mitchell's Shop and Chilesburg toward Beaver Dam Station. This news spurred Stuart on; for not only was this the last remaining store of food and medicine for Lee's army at Beaver Station, but Flora and the children were also there in Sheridan's path. Stuart raced after Sheridan's vanguard. At

30. Ibid.
31. Ibid.
32. *Historynet*, June 12, 2006.
33. Stiles, *4th Virginia Cavalry*, 47; Wert, *Cavalryman of the Lost Cause*, 347; Gallagher, ed., *Spotsylvania Campaign*, 129, 131.
34. Stiles, *4th Virginia Cavalry*, 47.

about 4 p.m., Wickham fell upon Sheridan's rear guard, ably-commanded by Major General Henry Davies, Jr. at Jerrell's Mill. A breathless Federal courier warned, "The rebels are closing in on us. The advance guard of their cavalry opened up on us back there in the woods. We gave them a volley and closed up to keep them from cutting us off, as they deployed well out on both sides of the road."[35]

Davies selected a defensive line about one-quarter mile south of the North Anna stream, deploying the 1st Massachusetts Cavalry across the road facing the Wickham's Confederates. The 1st New Jersey formed on the left, while a squadron of the 6th Ohio cavalry moved toward the expected Wickham attack. An Ohio trooper reported, "The enemy's advance came down on us in a furious charge which drove us back on our supports." A panic ensued, with pack mules scattering in all directions, while Davies hurried back to take control of the situation. The 1st Massachusetts saved the day for Davies, with one trooper remarking, "The rebels were checked just in time. It was a most disgraceful affair"[36]

After about half an hour of sparring, Davies moved on. For the next several hours, Wickham and Davies waged a running fight, while Davies protected the federal rear from Wickham's probing horsemen.

Wickham attacked Sheridan's rear guard at Jerrell's Mill, as the Federal cavalry was crossing the Ta River. Wickham's troopers, after sharp skirmish, were overpowered, withdrew, and followed at a distance. Marching south, Sheridan's rear guard made a stand at the small settlement of Mitchell's Shop as they approached Chilesburg. Davies, tired of Wickham's increasingly-bold attacks on his rear, formed the 1st Massachusetts Cavalry in the woods on the road's right side facing the bridge crossing the stream. The 1st Pennsylvania hid in the woods on the left. The 6th Ohio positioned itself in the roadway—as if to bait a trap for Wickham. The Confederate column, led by Wickham, proceeded alongside Captain George Matthews and the 3rd Virginia cavalry. The 6th Ohio retreated between the hidden troopers of the 1st Massachusetts and 1st Pennsylvania. Wickham's troopers attacked again but were stymied by 6th Ohio and the 1st New Jersey. Wickham, with only 1,000 troopers, dashed against the steadfast blue horsemen—one squadron after another— only to be rebuffed. Wickham ordered Capt. George H. Matthews of the 3rd Virginia to charge with his squadron, stating "I know Matthews will go through."

---

35. Rhea, *Battle for Spotsylvania Court House and the Road to Yellow Tavern*, 115; *Battles and Leaders*, IV: 188; *Sheridan's Memoirs*, I:374.
36. Rhea, *Battle for Spotsylvania Court House and the Road to Yellow Tavern*, 115.

Matthew's squadron of the 3rd Virginia pierced the enemy's lines but were overwhelmed. Mathews was mortally wounded. There were five killed, three wounded, and ten captured.[37]

Wickham's advance had isolated Captain Walter R. Robbins squadron of the 1st New Jersey Cavalry that had been scouting along a nearby road. Hearing the sound of musketry, Robbins led his squadron to the main road behind Wickham. He then charged Wickham's unsuspecting rear guard. Wickham, with Union cavalry in front of and behind him, declined to attack either—but ordered the artillery to fire at the Federals, who sought protection in a sunken part of the roadbed. There was some counter artillery fire from Union cannoneers, but little damage was done. Wickham was held in check by Davies, while the remainder of Sheridan's column continued south toward Richmond.[38]

Wickham, still determined to break through, ordered a detachment to circle around Davies, while the 3rd Virginia charged again down the roadway. Wickham's flanking troopers, working across country, came upon Davies's horses, which had been positioned in the rear, out of harm's way. Some of the Union horsemen, on foot, bolted for their horses as portions of the frontline gave way. From the front, some of the 3rd Virginia's troopers attempted to take some Union guns, which were positioned down the road. A hand-to-hand struggle ensued, but the Federal guns were saved. Sheridan's horsemen moved on, arriving at Chilesburg late in the afternoon and reaching Anderson's Ford before dark.[39]

Lee, Wickham, and Lomax held a meeting with Stuart, with one of them expressing the opinion that their much smaller force could not stop Sheridan. Stuart abruptly and angrily proclaimed, "No Sir, I'd rather die than let him go on." The meeting over, Stuart mounted up and led Wickham and Lomax south on an all-night march. As Sheridan reached Beaver Dam about 5 p.m., they began destroying the depot. As dusk approached, Wickham's brigade charged Sheridan's forces again, but darkness ended the affair. Sheridan encamped at Anderson's bridge, while Wickham's troopers remained saddled through the night.[40]

In one of the skirmishes that occurred that day, trooper Cpl. William Conway of Company C of the 4th Virginia wrote that Wickham had led the 4th in the charge, extolling them to "Give them

37. Ibid.; Burke Davis, *JEB Stuart, The Last Cavalier* (New York: Wing Books,1957), 386; McClellan, *Stuart's Cavalry*, 411; Rhea, *Battle of Spotsylvania Courthouse*, 116.
38. Rhea, *Battle of Spotsylvania Courthouse*, 116.
39. Ibid., 117.
40. Stiles, *4th Virginia Cavalry*, 47.

hell boys—damn 'em, give them hell." In the hand-to-hand ensuing combat, Conway was sabered and shot in the knee while Major William Wooldridge was wounded in the leg. Wooldridge eventually lost his leg to amputation.[41]

The 4th Virginia rounded a turn near Walter's Tavern on the Old Fredericksburg Road, coming face-to-face with Sheridan's rear guard. They were confronted by the 6th Ohio Cavalry on the opposite hill with skirmishers behind timbers on either side of the road. Splashing through a stream and charging up the hill, the troopers of the 4th Virginia dashed into the Federal ranks with sabers drawn. In the resulting melee, Lieutenant John F. Heunkle was killed, and his squad members were captured.[42]

At dawn on May 10, Wickham's brigade crossed Anderson's Ford, dismounted, and attacked Sheridan's rear guard three times near Beaver Dam. By 8 a.m. the Confederate troopers broke off the fight, and the Federals headed for Richmond.[43]

Phil Sheridan continued his march to Richmond by way of Trinity Church and Negro Foot, felling trees across the road to impede the pursuing Confederate cavalry. At Negro Foot, Stuart decided to parallel the Federals rather than pursue them, riding to Taylorville via Fork Churches. By 1 p.m., the gray riders reached Hanover Junction. That afternoon, Sheridan was reported to have been at Ground Squirrel Bridge, where he encamped.[44]

Wickham's brigade, exhausted by the oppressive heat and hard-riding the previous day, reached Taylorsville about 9 p.m. that evening. The rest of the Confederate force was trailing; and by the time Stuart arrived, he was alerted to news that the Federals had reached the South Anna River that very afternoon.[45]

By late morning of the 10th, Sheridan assembled his corps near Beaver Dam. As the Federal horsemen pulled out, some of Wickham's riders rode in, capturing some prisoners, including some unfortunate souls who had just been liberated by Custer the day before.

By this time, Stuart united Wickham, Lomax, and the mounted James B. Gordon's Tarheels below Beaver Dam. Anxious to stop Sheridan before he reached Richmond, Stuart formulated a plan—he would try to ambush the Federals near Richmond, where Confederate infantry would, hopefully, come to his support. Thus, Stuart divided

---

41. Ibid.
42. Ibid.
43. Ibid.
44. Ibid., 48.
45. Ibid.

his force: Gordon was tasked with following Sheridan and harassing his rear guard while Fitz Lee, with Wickham and Lomax, would hurry east to Hanover Junction and then descend upon Telegraph Road to intercept the main Federal body at the Mountain Road.[46]

Fitz Lee later described the situation: "Discovering Richmond to be the object of the enemy, and knowing the entire absence of troops in the works guarding the western side, General Stuart determined to move upon the chord of the arc the enemy were advancing upon, and by outmarching them interpose our little force in the enemy's front at some point contiguous to the city."[47]

At 2 a.m. on May 11, Stuart decided to ride to Ashland in order to intercept Sheridan on the Telegraph Road. Fitz Lee's division, led by Wickham's brigade, was in the saddle an hour later headed for Ashland Station. Reaching the Telegraph Road, Stuart led his troopers south to Yellow Tavern, just six miles from Richmond.[48]

In the first phase of the Battle of Yellow Tavern on May 11, 1864, Brig. Gen. Williams C. Wickham and his Confederate cavalry were posted just south of this location, below Old Francis Road. Wickham's men fired on Brig. Gen. George A. Custer's Union troopers as they charged Brig. Gen. Lunsford L. Lomax's line on the Federal left flank, preventing Custer's advance. Maj. Gen. Philip H. Sheridan, the Federal commander, then sent Col. George H. Chapman's regiment to attack Wickham's line. This freed Custer to continue up Telegraph Road, where one of his men mortally wounded Maj. Gen. J. E. B. Stuart later that day.[49]

On a clear and balmy May 11, Custer's Michigan brigade, many dismounted, charged Stuart at Yellow Tavern near the intersection of the Brook Turnpike and Telegraph Road, just six miles outside Richmond. Stuart was far outmanned; Sheridan's main force, consisting of Wilson's division and Custer's brigade, pressed Stuart in his front, and another brigade dashed at his left. Stuart had positioned Lunsford Lomax's troopers along the road with its left flank near Yellow Tavern. Wickham's troopers were to the right of Lomax, stretching his line north of the road junction some two-and-one-half miles, to a place called "Half Sink." Most of the artillery of guns was placed along the line of Lomax. All of the troopers were dismounted at this point. About 4 p.m., before Stuart could reach the embattled flank, Custer had broken through; and most of Stuart's line had

46. Jimmy Price, "Freedom by the Sword: May 2014" (sablearm.blogspot.com)
47. Ibid.
48. Stiles, *4th Virginia Cavalry*, 48; Rhea, *The Battles for Spotsylvania Court House and the Road to Yellow Tavern, May 7–12, 1864*, 191.
49. Ibid., 207-08.

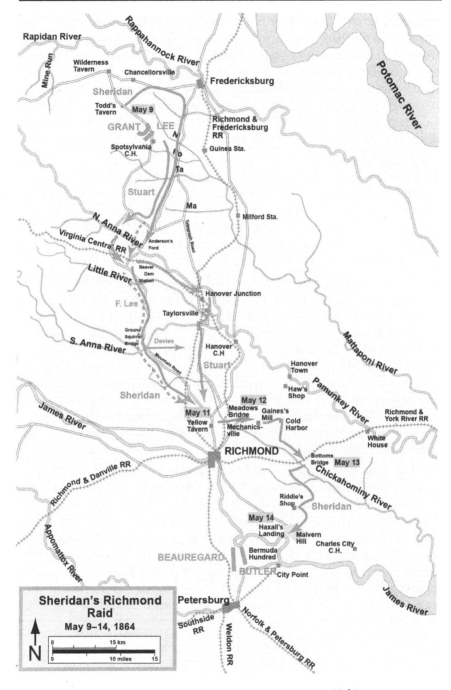

Hal Jespersen

collapsed. Stuart desperately tried to rally his men. Along with a few troopers who had stayed put, he fired into the charging Union troopers' flank and rear as they passed. The 12th Virginia valiantly tried to drive Sheridan's horsemen back; but a Union trooper, remaining dismounted, "turned" as he passed the General [Stuart] and discharging his pistol, inflicted the fatal wound." Stuart's final order to aide-de-camp, Lt. Theodore S. Garnet, was "Order Wickham to dismount his brigade and attack on the right."[50]

J.E.B. Stuart died the next day. The 5th Virginia's commander, Col. Henry Pate, who had displayed exemplary fighting on the field that day, was killed shortly before Stuart received his mortal wound. The next day another great loss to the Confederate cavalry occurred; one of Stuart's protégés, dependable Brig. Gen. James B. Gordon, commander of the North Carolina Cavalry Brigade, was mortally wounded at nearby Brook Church.[51]

With J. E. B. Stuart's death came a reorganization of the Army of Northern Virginia's cavalry. Hampton was the senior ranking division commander; he had proved his value on the battlefield in numerous engagements and was the natural choice to take Stuart's place; but Gen. Robert E. Lee hesitated in naming Hampton as chief of cavalry. Hampton and Fitz Lee were rivals, harboring hard feelings toward one another since Gettysburg. Instead of promoting Hampton to head of the cavalry corps, on May 14 Robert E. Lee announced that "until further orders, the three Divisions of cavalry serving with this Army will constitute separate commands and will report directly to and receive orders from these headquarters."[52]

On May 12 the bloody battle of Spotsylvania Court House began. Hampton's division positioned itself on Robert E. Lee's left, with his sharpshooters in trenches and his artillery posted to impede the Federals' right flank. On the 14th, Robert E. Lee ordered a reconnaissance north of Grant's repositioning lines to determine the Federal commander's intentions. At 5:00 p.m. Rosser's troopers splashed across the Po River, heading for Susan Alsop's farm at the junction of the Brock and Gordon roads. Rosser's horsemen turned east on the Gordon Road toward Archibald Armstromg's farm,

---

50. Clement Anselm Evans, ed., *Confederate Military History* (Atlanta, GA: Confederate Publishing Company, 1899), vol 3:687; John Esten Cooke, *Mohun; or, the Last days of Lee and his Paladins: Final memoirs of a staff Officer Serving in Virginia* (New York: F. J. Huntington & Company, 1869), 211; Davis, *JEB Stuart, The Last Cavalier*, 399.

51. *OR* 36/1:780, 791; Perhaps significantly, Rosser's letters to Betty do not mention Stuart's death. Later, Custer cited one of his privates for Stuart's killing.

52. *OR* 36/2:1001.

Robert E. Lee hesitated in naming Wade Hampton as the new chief of cavalry until August 1864. Fitzhugh Lee was under consideration due to obvious nepotism. Fitz Lee was a fun-loving man, who sometimes took to the bottle. His command performance did not match Wade Hampton's.

(Library of Congress)

Grant's former headquarters. About two miles east of Alsop's farm, Rosser's riders approached "Laurel Hill," the estate and home of 64-year-old Elizabeth Couse, a Union sympathizer from New Jersey.[53]

Major General G. K. Warren had converted Mrs. Couse's yard into a field hospital for the Federal's V Corps, with more than 600 wounded soldiers spread across the grounds. Mrs. Couse and her daughters were carrying meals to the wounded when Rosser's troopers rode up, causing Mrs. Couse's daughter Katherine to recall later, "[It] was a very unwelcome sight to me." Katherine wrote in a letter to a friend that Rosser's men had stolen 'everything they could lay hands on." They also took 80 wounded Confederate prisoners who could still walk. When Maj. Gen. Winfield Hancock got word of the raid, he sent the 12th New Jersey to the Couse estate, but Rosser had escaped in the direction of Fredericksburg by the time they arrived.[54]

After the battle of Spotsylvania, with Grant failing to position himself between Robert E. Lee and Richmond, Rosser's troopers made a reconnaissance as far as the Poor House—northeast of the Mule Shoe, on the road to Fredericksburg—driving off all Federal cavalry they encountered. A short distance south of Chancellorsville, in the pouring rain on May 15, Rosser surprised troopers of the 2nd Ohio, driving them east of the Plank Road, with his troopers then occupying the Plank Road and Catharpin Road intersection at the Alrich's house. Lieutenant Colonel Marshall L. Dempsey's 23rd United States Colored Troops formed a line on the Plank Road by the house, forcing Rosser to withdraw. Rosser had captured a few prisoners while discovering the Federal IX Corps in the area. Not wanting to risk a major engagement, he withdrew to behind Confederate lines, reporting what he had learned.[55]

While Robert E. Lee was battling Ulysses S. Grant at the North Anna River, General Wickham was involved in another fight at Wilson's Wharf. Brigadier General Edward A. Wild's brigade of colored troops, after fighting in North Carolina, landed in Virginia in May 1864. They began building the fort at Wilson's Wharf, one of a series of protective outposts guarding supply lines for Union Maj. Gen. Benjamin Butler's Bermuda Hundred Campaign. The wharf was at a strategic bend in the James River, overlooked by high bluffs, two miles from Sherwood Forest, the home of former U.S. President John Tyler. By this time, Wild's unit had a frightening reputation among Southerners. Wild's subsequent actions alarmed them all the more. His

53. Rhea, *To the North Anna River*, 88; OR 36/1:232, 36/2:753; Katherine Couse to a friend, May 4–22, 1864, UVA, Accession #10441.
54. OR 36/1:893–94.
55. McDonald, *Laurel Brigade*, 243.

soldiers freed and recruited slaves and, in one case, whipped a plantation owner who had a reputation for harshness to his slaves. The Richmond newspapers denounced these activities and put intense pressure on President Jefferson Davis to put a stop to Wild's depredations.[56]

Succumbing to the political pressure, Davis's military adviser, Maj. Gen. Braxton Bragg, ordered Fitzhugh Lee's cavalry division to "break up this nest and stop their uncivilized proceedings." While Robert E. Lee, was battling Ulysses S. Grant at the North Anna River, Fitz Lee took elements of three cavalry brigades, plus the 5th South Carolina Cavalry's 2,500 horsemen, and one cannon on a 40-mile march from Atlee's Station to reach Wilson's Wharf. Lee expected to fight an unorganized horde, but instead he found the defenders of Fort Pocahontas alert and ready for action.[57]

Wild commanded 1,100 men and two cannons. The Union force consisted of the 1st United States Colored Infantry Regiment (1st USCI) and four companies of the 10th USCI. Battery M, 3rd New York Artillery was the only all-white unit in the defenses. The gunboat USS Dawn lay in the James River to deliver fire support to the fort's defenders. The fort was crescent-shaped facing north, about 0.8 miles long, straddling the road to the wharf. It was anchored on both ends—to the west on a bluff and on the east by a branch of Kennon Creek—so it could not be flanked. It was fronted by a deep, broad ditch and abatis.[58]

On May 24, Confederate Major General Fitzhugh Lee's cavalry division's 2,500 troopers attacked; the battle was the first combat encounter of Robert E. Lee's Army of Northern Virginia with African-American troops.[59]

Around noon that day, Fitz Lee's troopers charged and drove in the Union pickets who were posted near the Charles City Road, about one-mile north of the fort. By 1:30 p.m. the fort was surrounded, and Lee sent two officers under a flag of truce with a message demanding the surrender of the garrison. He promised that the black soldiers would be taken to Richmond and treated as prisoners of war; but if they did not surrender, he would not be "answerable for the consequences." Wild and his men interpreted this to mean that some of the men would be returned to their former masters and others would

56. Rhea, Gordon C., *To the North Anna River: Grant and Lee, May 13–25, 1864* (Baton Rouge, LSU Press, 2000), 362.
57. Ibid., 363-64.
58. Ibid, 364.
59. Ibid., 362-67.

be tried by state authorities for inciting insurrection. Wild sent back a written reply that said "We will try it" and verbally told the two officers, "Take the fort if you can."[60]

Lee planned a two-pronged attack. Brig. Gen. Williams C. Wickham's brigade moved east of the fort, concealed in ravines of Kennon Creek. To distract the Federals from Wickham's attack, Col. John Dunovant of the 5th South Carolina demonstrated on the western end of the fort. Dunovant's men advanced as far as the ditch and abatis but were driven back by heavy fire. Wickham's men rushed forward across an open field and were met by interlocking fields of musket fire, canister rounds from two 10-pound Parrot guns, and naval gunfire from the *Dawn*.[61]

As Lee looked for a weak point in the fort's defenses, Union reinforcements arrived at about 4 p.m. on the steamer *George Washington*, carrying four companies of the 10th USCI. Lee ordered his men to withdraw to Charles City Court House, and the next morning they rode back to Atlee's Station.[62] About 200 Confederates were killed or wounded in the abortive attack. Federal losses were six killed and 40 wounded.[63]

The Union Army next crossed the Pamunkey River at Hanovertown at about 4 p.m. on Friday, May 27. Fitzhugh Lee concentrated his cavalry division with Wade Hampton's at Atlee's Station, six miles outside Richmond. The Federal cavalry was then near Haw's Shop and Aenon Church. Wickham's brigade arrived at Haw's Shop from the vicinity of Hanover Court House, and joined Fitz Lee's division on the Confederate right, while Hampton positioned his cavalry on the left. Fighting, mostly behind hastily-constructed breastworks of timber, commenced about 10 a.m., lasting seven hours, with heavy losses on both sides.[64]

The next morning, Rosser's and Brig. Gen. Williams C. Wickham's brigades led the assault, which turned into a heavy engagement. Private James Wood recorded, "Moved toward Sheridan's raiders. Engage him about 11 o'clock a.m. with sharpshooters. Have a stubborn and determined fight with him until about 3 p.m. when he was reinforced with infantry, and we are compelled to fall back, being flanked by them." At one point, where Confederate troopers had been badly routed, some had become badly disorganized; but some held their own. Two squadrons of the 3rd Virginia and the 2nd Virginia

60. Ibid., 364-65. The fort was to be named "Fort Pocahontas."
61. Ibid., 365.
62. Ibid., 366.
63. Ibid., 366.
64. Stiles, *4th Virginia Cavalry*, 50-51.

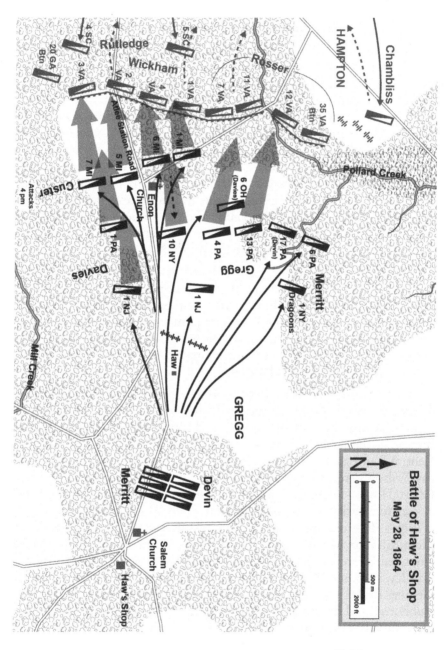

Hal Jespersen

held their ground. Two of the 3rd Virginia squadrons were overwhelmed and along with the 1st and 4th Regiments fell back to restore the line. Lt. Hubard recalled, "Old Wickham rode around waving his saber and cursing like a trooper."[65]

After the Haw's Shop fight on May 30, Wickham led his brigade to Atlee's Station and then on to Mechanicsville. Phil Sheridan began to move south toward Old Cold Harbor in the early hours of May 31. Fitz Lee was ordered to intercept Sheridan's cavalry. Fitz Lee reported at 3:15 p.m. that the Federal cavalry was moving into Old Cold Harbor. Too strong for Fitz Lee's division, he retreated as darkness fell. Fitz Lee's division picketed the right flank of R. E. Lee's army from New Cold Harbor to Dispatch Station. On June 2, Wickham's brigade was engaged then dismounted in the fortifications near Gaines Mill. Wickham's brigade was relieved in the afternoon and was ordered to Bottom's Bridge, accompanied by M. C. Butler's and Lunsford Lomax's brigades. These troopers were to guard the Chickahominy River from any Federal crossing to the south.[66]

During the morning of June 2, Fitz Lee's horsemen watched the river from New Bridge to Long Bridge, waiting for the appearance of the Union army; but it didn't occur. The next day was spent in peace and quiet. On Tuesday, June 7, Federal pontoons appeared as Sheridan began crossing the Pamunkey at Newcastle Ferry. Robert E. Lee immediately ordered Fitz Lee and Hampton to Hanover Junction to protect the railroad and Richmond.[67]

Grant, unsuccessful in frontal attacks on Robert E. Lee's army, decided he would launch a series of cavalry attacks on Lee's lines of communication and supply. Accordingly, on May 31, Grant ordered Brig. Gen. James H. Wilson's cavalry division to assault the Virginia Central Railroad and tear up as much of the line as possible. The next day Wilson's troopers attacked Rooney Lee's horsemen near Hanover Court House, forcing them back toward Ashland. Hampton ordered Rosser to attack the rear of Brig. Gen. John B. McIntosh's brigade of Wilson's division. Rosser's vigorous assault was successful. He drove McIntosh into Ashland and captured about 100 prisoners, including 50 wounded, as well as 200 horses and a cache of arms. The 12th Virginia Cavalry, commanded by Col. Thomas Massie, led the assault, with Lt. George Baylor's squadrons B and I in the lead. Wilson made a stubborn stand in Ashland, positioning his troopers behind houses and the railroad embankment. Hampton directed Rooney Lee to attack.[68]

65. Nanzig, ed., *The Civil War Memoirs of a Virginia Cavalryman*, 167.
66. Stiles, *4th Virginia Cavalry*, 51-52.
67. Ibid., 52.
68. *OR* 36/3:867; *Richmond Daily Dispatch*, June 3, 1864.

Rooney Lee sent the North Carolina Cavalry Brigade—which Brig. Gen. Pierce Young temporarily commanded and who had dismounted his troopers for the assault. The very first volley Wilson's horsemen fired severely wounded the gallant and capable Young.[69]

Deprived of Young's leadership, the assault failed to dislodge Wilson. Rooney Lee reformed his troopers for another attack, while Hampton took the 10th Virginia, along with part of Rooney Lee's 3rd North Carolina and a squadron of Rosser's 7th Virginia, and attacked Wilson's right flank. At one time during the fight, the Federals poured artillery into the charging 7th and 11th Virginia regiments, causing confusion in the ranks. In the melee, mounted Federals charged Rosser's flank with pistols in-hand, adding to the chaos. Rosser, unwavering, ordered a counterattack; but his troopers were stunned by the suddenness of the Federal assault. Rosser reported:

They failed to obey, but faltered and hesitated until the enemy were well-nigh closed upon me and everything was about to break, when Private Holmes [Conrad], who was at my side, rushed to his old regiment (the 11th Virginia) and seized its colors, and called to his old comrades to save their flag that had waved so triumphantly upon so many glorious fields and rushed with it into the ranks of the enemy. My men roused by this example of daring and chivalry, rushed upon the enemy with the saber, put him to flight, saved the gallant Conrad, their flag, [and] their honor.[70]

The tide of battle had turned by the action of one trooper, Pvt. Holmes Conrad of the 11th Virginia, who charged straight at the Federal column. With banner waving, Conrad penetrated the frontal files, turned left, and escaped unharmed. Men had followed Conrad into the breach and soon confronted the astonished Federals who had failed to shoot him. The inspired Confederates drove the Federals back upon their main body. Wilson withdrew his command after leaving many dead, wounded, or taken prisoner. Conrad's brave actions during the fight had earned him promotion to major. Rosser's losses totaled 20 killed or wounded.[71]

In another attempt to outflank General Lee's right, the Confederates butchered Grant at the June 1 to 3, 1864, battle of Cold Harbor. No matter what losses he was willing to endure, Grant realized that he could not penetrate Lee's army, so he came up with a

---

69. Ibid. Young had been nominated for promotion to brigadier, but was killed before Senate confirmation.
70. McDonald, *Laurel Brigade*, 245–47; *OR* 36/3:867; Thomas L. Rosser to Samuel Cooper, January 2, 1865, Holmes Conrad Papers, VMHC.
71. McDonald, *Laurel Brigade*, 247–48; *Philadelphia Weekly Times*, April 19, 1884; Keller, *Riding with Rosser*, 28–29.

new strategy to win the war. He decided to cross the James River and attack Richmond from the south. He began the movement on June 12, with his men facing the Confederate trenches at Petersburg by June 17. Petersburg held the key to Richmond. Grant planned to destroy the railroads supplying Petersburg and Richmond, as well as to ravage the countryside where Lee drew supplies and food for his army.[72]

In early June, General Wickham's home, "Hickory Hill," was again raided by Union cavalry. This time, they took "about 80 slaves, all of his horses, cattle, etc., his clothes, almost everything that he and his family had and destroyed his furniture, even breaking the locks off the doors."[73]

Trevilian Station

As part of his strategy, on June 7 Grant sent Maj. Gen. Philip Sheridan to the Shenandoah Valley with Brig. Gen. David M. Gregg's and Gen. Alfred T. A. Torbert's cavalry divisions—totaling about 9,300 troopers and 24 artillery pieces—to begin an infamous mission to burn and destroy. The first objective of the operation involved raiding and demolishing the railroads at Gordonsville and Charlottesville. Grant hoped Maj. Gen. David Hunter, who replaced Maj. Gen. Franz Siegel after his defeat at New Market, would advance on Lynchburg and Lexington, and then join Sheridan in Charlottesville. Hampton, with information from scouts and a servant who had escaped from Sheridan's camp, correctly concluded that the Federals' immediate objectives were the important railroad towns of Gordonsville and Charlottesville. Robert E. Lee ordered Hampton to follow with an additional cavalry division. Hampton ordered Fitz Lee to join him as soon as possible, and on June 8 Hampton proceeded to move between Gordonsville and Sheridan. Hampton, with about 6,400 horsemen and 15 guns in his command, managed to outmarch Sheridan and camped the night of June 10 at Green Spring Valley, three-miles from Trevilian Station on the Virginia Central Railroad. Fitz Lee camped that night at Louisa Court House, while Rosser bivouacked two-miles west of Trevilian.[74]

72. James Marshall-Cornwall, *Grant as Military Commander* (New York, 1995), 181–82.
73. Richard Watkins to Mary Watkins, June 6. 1864, VMHC.
74. *OR* 36/1:1095–97; *Philadelphia Weekly Times*, April 19, 1884. According to Rosser, the night before Sheridan began to march, a black slave, 19 or 20 years old, who one of Sheridan's officers employed as a servant, left camp, crossed to Confederate lines, and asked to see Rosser. When Rosser was a captain, the slave had been assigned to him as a valet. The slave, whose name is unknown, told Rosser and Hampton the details of Sheridan's plans, as he

Hampton learned during the night that Sheridan had crossed the North Anna River at Carpenter's Ford. He decided to attack at dawn. He ordered Fitz Lee's division to march up the Marquiz Road (present-day Virginia Route 22) from Louisa Court House to Clayton's Store, while Hampton, with his division, planned to assault Sheridan on the road leading from Trevilian Station to Clayton's Store. With this disposition, Hampton hoped to "cover Lee's left flank and my right flank, and drive the enemy back if he attempted to reach Gordonsville, by passing to my left, and to conceal my real design, which was to strike him at Clayton's Store after uniting the two divisions."[75]

At dawn on June 11, Hampton had his troopers in the saddle. He moved out with Matthew Calbraith Butler's and Pierce Young's brigades, while Rosser's command covered the Gordonsville Road on Hampton's left. Hampton attacked, pressing Union troopers of Torbert's division until 9:00 a.m., pushing them back up the Trevilian Station Road toward Clayton's Store. Here they positioned themselves behind breastworks. Meanwhile, Fitzhugh Lee's Division (including Wickham), which had bivouacked at Louisa Court House, encountered Custer's brigade on the Louisa Court House Road, a few miles east of Trevilian Station. After establishing contact with Custer, Fitz Lee fell back, opening a dangerous gap between himself and Hampton. Thus, Fitz Lee failed to fight through Custer and come up to join Hampton as planned.

On the morning of June 11, 1864, Custer's Michigan cavalrymen were picketing the historic Marquis Road, south of Buck Chile's, when, at around 5:00 a.m. Confederate horsemen of the 1st, 2nd, 3rd, and 4th Virginia, under Brig. Gen. Williams Wickham, surprised the Yankees, many of whom were eating breakfast. Wickham's brigade had left its camp east of Louisa Court House, heading north, followed by Brig. Gen. Lunsford Lomax's 5th, 6th, and 15th Virginia Regiments. Against no opposition, Wickham proceeded toward Clayton's Store, where he hoped to link up with Wade Hampton's division and attack the Phil Sheridan's Federals.[76]

---

knew them. Rosser later recalled that when he left the artillery service the slave had gone back to New Orleans with his master. When the Federals captured New Orleans a Union officer employed the slave. Since then, the slave had begun to look for an opportunity to escape to Confederate lines; Keller, *Riding with Rosser*, 37. Rosser's account is corroborated by Capt. Thomas Nelson Conrad's story in The Rebel Scout (Washington City, 1904), 109–111.

75. *OR* 36/1:1096.
76. Joseph W. McKinney, *Trevilian Station, June 11-12, 1864: Wade Hampton, Philip Sheridan and the Largest All- Cavalry Battle of the Civil War* (Jefferson, N.C.: McFarland and Company, 2016), 139.

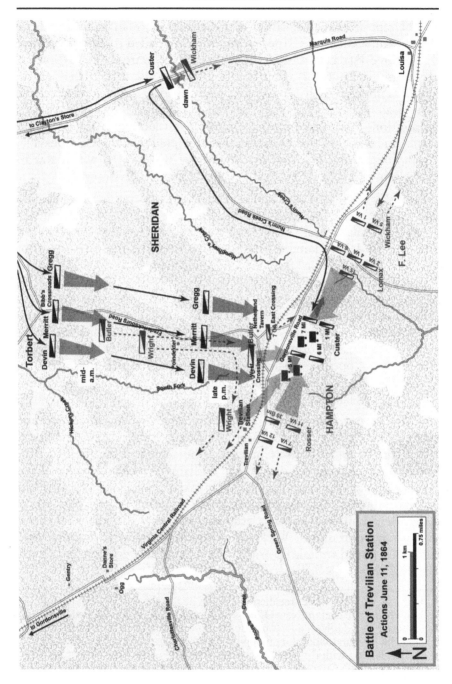

Trevilion Station, June 11-12, 1864

(Hal Jespersen)

Meanwhile, about halfway between Clayton's Store and Louisa Court House, Union Major Melvin Brewer, commanding Custer's 7th Michigan Regiment, were just beginning to breakfast. By daylight, Wickham had advanced three miles before making contact with Brewer's picket line. Wickham, without hesitation, attacked with one of his regiments against the picket line, forcing Brewer's troopers to abandon their breakfast to reinforce their picket line. Wickham's attack stalled when his troopers could not overcome the Union picket security screen and drive them rearward.[77]

Fitz Lee—probably worried that he had progressed beyond Wade Hampton's position, and that he might bring on a general engagement before Hampton was ready—did not send reinforcements to Wickham. Custer reacted quickly to Wickham's attack, sending the 1st Michigan, commanded by Lt. Col. Peter Stagg, to the aid of Brewer. Confederate and Union horsemen skirmished inconclusively along the Marquis Road for about an hour.

Wickham's riders drove the Federals up the Marquis Road, capturing several of Custer's men. Ultimately, the Wolverines repulsed Wickham's attack before being called away to another part of the field. However, the fierce firefight marked the beginning of the largest all-cavalry battle of the Civil War. The battle of Trevilian Station had begun. Without reinforcements from Fitz Lee, Custer was free to move as he wished. In obeyance of orders from Brig. Gen. Alfred Torbert, Custer commenced his movement on a narrow road off to the right and through the woods toward Trevilian Station.[78]

Coming into the open just east of the station, Custer ordered Col. Russell Alger to charge with his 5th Michigan and a battalion of four companies commanded by Major H. S. Hastings as the advance guard. Custer and his aides de camp rode directly behind Hastings's battalion. Alger and the main body of the 5th Michigan followed Custer and Capt. Alexander Pennington's four guns of Battery M, 2nd U.S. Artillery, followed by Alger. Major James H. Kidd's 6th Michigan followed Pennington. The 7th Michigan, after some confusion, moved in behind the 6th Michigan. The 1st Michigan brought up the rear, acting as the rear guard. Custer's wagons and ambulances were most probably between the 1st and 7th Michigan Regiments.[79]

Alger charged with his 5th Michigan of about 300 troopers, galloping up the Gordonsville Road, easily overrunning Wade Hampton's exposed baggage train and driving off Confederate cavalry.

---

77. Ibid. It is not known how large Wickham's attacking force was, but it did include the 3rd Virginia.
78. Ibid., 140.
79. Ibid.

The Confederate artillery battery of Capt. James F. Hart, supporting Brig. Gen. Matthew Butler, was nearly-overrun and captured by Alger's troopers. Hart, being ill, was back at camp; and his battery was commanded that day by Lt. E. Lindsay Halsey. Halsey was able to withdraw his guns to a nearby hill, where they were effectively used against Federal cavalry. Although Custer had ordered Alger to halt at the station to allow the main body of the brigade to close up, Alger—in the heat of battle—continued his attack about a mile beyond the station, where his horsemen captured about 800 horses from Butler's brigade, along with several of Hampton's caissons of Hampton's artillery.[80]

Hampton's staff officers—and perhaps Hampton himself—later regarded Fitz Lee's tardiness as proof of his unwillingness to support any superior other than J.E.B. Stuart.[81]

Meanwhile, at mid-morning, Brig. Gen. George A. Custer's brigade exploited the gap between Hampton and Fitzhugh Lee. Custer interposed his forces between the rail depot and Louisa Court House by way of a diagonal track that ran through the forest, placing them in the rear of Butler's and Col. Gilbert J. Wright's Georgia brigades. Custer had left one of his four regiments to deal with the tardy Fitz Lee, while he proceeded until he was in position to strike Hampton from the rear. The remainder of Torbert's troopers pressed Hampton in his front. Custer's 5th Michigan came upon lightly-guarded ambulances, caissons, wagons, and 1,500 horses of Hampton's division. Custer spotted Maj. James W. Thompson's battery of Butler's brigade—behind him on his right, near Netherland Tavern—and decided to take the unattended battery. Colonel Roger P. Chew of the Horse Artillery, recalled, "Butler was at this time hotly engaged in front. I went back rapidly and found Custer's men advancing from the rear to capture the guns."[82]

Fortunately for the Confederates, Custer had overlooked Thompson's two guns, which Thomson immediately repositioned on the Gordonsville Road. Meanwhile, Butler faced more firepower than he could handle and retreated toward Trevilian Station, withdrawing

80. Ibid, 142-43.
81. Longacre, *Lee's Cavalrymen*, 300; Wade Hampton to Edward L. Wells, January 18, 1900, Wells Manuscript, Charleston Library Society, Charleston, SC; Edward L. Wells, *Hampton and His Cavalry in 1864* (Richmond, VA. 1899), 198–99; Keller, *Riding with Rosser*, 38.
82. Longacre, *Lee's Cavalrymen*, 300–302; OR 36/1:784–85, 800–801, 806–808, 823–24, 849–51; Eric J. Wittenberg, *Glory Enough For All: Sheridan's Second Raid and The Battle of Trevilian Station* (Washington, D.C., 2002), 101; McDonald, *Laurel Brigade*, 252.

Capt. James F. Hart's guns. Chew repositioned the guns on the Gordonsville Road in a spot to damage Custer—provided Chew was to receive cavalry support.[83]

At this stage of affairs, Hampton quickly recalled Rosser, who was on the Gordonsville Road some distance off to the west, to oppose Custer. Hampton ordered his line consolidated around Netherland Tavern. He ordered Butler to send the 6th South Carolina and the Phillips Legion to reinforce the Confederate position near the train station. These troopers charged Custer's horsemen, driving them back from the railroad. Rosser returned rapidly, but Custer was now trying to escape with his captures by traveling off the Gordonsville Road—around Butler, Young, and the horse artillery—attempting to get through on their left. Fitz Lee was late in joining Hampton's line, and the Confederate cavalry chief sent a courier after him. Fitz Lee's unexplained tardiness was devastating for the Confederates at Trevilian Station; the delay allowed Custer to drive a wedge between Fitzhugh Lee's and Hampton's divisions. In recalling Rosser, Hampton had asked Lt. Wiley C. Howard, Company C of the Cobb Legion, to deliver an oral message to the general. Howard recollected: "[Hampton] giving me directions as to the location of Rosser's brigade, I put my Yankee steed on his metal and after a time came upon the brigade hotly engaged dismounted. It was powerful uncomfortable where I found Rosser, but I was bound to go to him unless bullets stopped me. When delivered Hampton's message, that gallant commander and superb fighter said, "Give the general my compliments and tell him we are giving 'em hell."[84]

Howard remembered:

> I need not say I rode swiftly away, for it was hot and uncomfortable and I hastened to rejoin our chief who had then been rejoined by staff officers and moved in another direction and nearer a portion of the line. When I saluted and delivered Rosser's message, Hampton snapped his eyes, smiled and said to the staff, General Rosser is a magnificent fighter and has done much to turn the tide in our favor today.[85]

---

83. Trout, *Galloping Thunder,* 497.

84. *OR* 36/1:1095; McDonald, *Laurel Brigade,* 253; Keller, *Riding With Rosser,* 38; Wiley C. Howard, "Sketch of the Cobb Legion Cavalry and Some Incidents and Scenes Remembered," Prepared and Read under appointment of Atlanta Camp 159, U. C. V., August 19, 1901, (Davis Library, UNC-Chapel Hill), 16.

85. Ibid.

General Thomas Rosser helped save the day at Trevilion Station on June 11, 1864. Sheridan claimed victory, but even northern newspapers told of Wade Hampton's victory.

(*Thomas L. Rosser Papers, Albert and Shirley Small Collections Library, UVA)*

From his new position Chew opened an effective fire on Custer's troopers, pushing them back toward Trevilian Station and delaying their escape by crippling the horses and stopping the captured wagons. After a considerable delay, again Custer tried to escape; but Rosser heard the firing and brought his brigade at a gallop down the Gordonsville Road. He then wheeled about and attacked the left of Custer's column, doubling it up on Fitz Lee's troopers who were coming up from the other side of the station. Rosser's horsemen attacked vigorously, pressing Custer back and recapturing many wagons and five caissons. Rosser made his well-timed assault in double columns, with the 11th Virginia on the front right of the Gordonsville Road and Col. Lige White's battalion on the front left. Fitz Lee, finally on the scene with Lomax's brigade, captured Custer's headquarters wagon, other wagons, horses, and prisoners. Butler's 6th South Carolina and the Phillips Legion of Wright's brigade attacked Custer from the north. Custer, driven from the field, suffered 11 killed, 51 wounded, and 299 captured before Maj. Gen. Wesley Merritt and Col. Thomas C. Devin arrived as support. He was fortunate to have escaped at all.[86]

Artilleryman George M. Neese later recalled, "The enemy had already pierced General Hampton's line ... when General Rosser, who had been hurriedly dispatched for, dashed on the field with gleaming saber at the head of his brigade of gallant trusty veterans, all rushing to the rescue with naked sabers or drawn pistols, with teeth set and knit brow, determined to do or die." After a tough fight, the blue line retreated. Neese concluded, "The timely arrival of General Rosser at the head of his brigade was all that saved our side from sustaining a disastrous defeat." In some soldiers like Rosser and Custer, the frenzy of battle produced an almost mesmerizing state of mind—a rage and audacity—whereby the soldier lost himself, becoming detached from any sense of danger and caught up in what Rosser called "fury's mad delirium." Major General George Meade's aide, Col. Theodore Lyman, observed that "most officers would go into any danger when it was their duty, but fighting for fun is rare ... [only] such men as ... Custer and some others [like Rosser], attacked whenever they got a chance, and of their own accord."[87]

---

86. OR 36/1:1095; *Philadelphia Weekly Times*, April 19, 1884; Trout, *Galloping Thunder*, 495–96; Rod Andrew, *Wade Hampton: Confederate Warrior to Southern Redeemer* (Chapel Hill, 2008), 210; J. H. Kidd, *Personal Recollections of a Cavalryman Riding with Custer's Michigan Cavalry Brigade* (Ionia, Michigan, 1908), 222.
87. George M. Neese, *Three Years in the Confederate Horse Artillery*, 285; Thomas L. Rosser, *Addresses of Gen'l T. L. Rosser at the Seventh Annual Reunion, Association of the Maryland Line, Baltimore, February 22, 1889 & Staunton, Virginia, June 3, 1889* (New York, 1889), 9; Glenn W. LaFantasie,

After the war, William H. Payne admiringly wrote Rosser:

> I always see you, figure you, ready to push into battle.
> Cheerful, daring full of expedience, knowing no
> difficulties, arbitrary and despotic too. Loving and
> admiring brave deeds and brave men so highly as to set
> all law and precedent aside to show your admiration.
> Restless, ambitious, but on the battlefield, with more of
> the "Guadio certaminis," Latin for the joys of battle than
> any man I ever knew.[88]

Confederate horsemen hotly pursued Custer toward Trevilian Station, 25 miles northeast of Charlottesville. After arriving, Custer formed his men, controlled the approaches, and positioned artillery. Forming his regiments, Rosser prepared to attack. Colonel Chew informed Rosser that he had observed Custer with only about 1,200 troopers. Rosser, who had eagerly envisioned capturing Custer, ordered White to charge; but just then Hampton rode up and countermanded the order. Custer remained at Trevilian Station while Sheridan's entire command advanced against Hampton's right flank. If Fitz Lee had been on time and fought aggressively, it is likely that Custer's Wolverines would have been nearly destroyed, along with many captured. Generals Butler and Rosser asked Hampton to seek a court-martial of Fitz Lee, but Hampton would hear nothing of it.[89]

That evening Sheridan attempted to dislodge Hampton from his new position unsuccessfully. After one of the Federals' failed assaults, Rosser—still believing that he could drive Custer from his position—ordered a charge and, at once, suffered a bad leg wound at the hands of a Federal sharpshooter. Reeling in the saddle, Rosser finally sought safety, ending any thoughts of assaulting Custer.[90]

Sergeant Charles McVicar, of Major Thompson's battery, watched as Rosser swayed in the saddle upon being wounded. Several of Thompson's battery rushed forward to help the wounded general off his horse and laid him down on the grass. A quick examination revealed that Rosser had been hit in the leg, breaking bones below the knee; and his boot was filling with blood. Rosser still tried to direct

---

Twilight at Little Round Top: July 2, 1863—The Tide Turns at Gettysburg
(New York, 2007), 125; Monaghan, *Custer*, 199; William H. Payne to
Thomas Rosser, March 2, 1866, Thomas L. Rosser Papers, UVA; Miller,
Decision at Tom's Brook, 50. "Guadio certaminis," translated from Latin,
means "the joy of the fight."
88. Ibid.
89. McDonald, *Laurel Brigade*, 253–54; Manly Wade Wellman, *Giant in Gray:
A Biography of Wade Hampton* (New York, 1949), 151.
90. McDonald, *Laurel Brigade*, 254.

the fighting even as a tourniquet was quickly applied to his leg. McVicar heard Rosser proclaim "that he could whip Sheridan with his gallant brigade, that God never placed better men on earth."[91]

Rosser's personal surgeon, Dr. Burton, treated the wounded warrior and had him removed to safety. All the while Rosser called for his senior regimental commander, Col. Richard H. Dulany of the 7th Virginia and issued instructions to him, saying, "Col., fight with the men mounted. Let the other cavalry fight as infantry!" Dulany admired Rosser and knew that his commander detested having to fight dismounted, even though the woody terrain sometimes necessitated it.[92]

The Confederate horsemen spent the remainder of June 11 repelling Sheridan's limited assaults. Night closed the action, and both sides entrenched to prepare for the next day's decisive struggle.[93]

At dawn on June 12, both sides faced each other; but nothing happened in the morning. Fitz Lee had attacked Custer on the other side of Trevilian Station the previous day and rejoined Hampton about noon. About 3:00 p.m. Sheridan began a series of vigorous assaults. His dismounted men, armed with Spencer repeating rifles or carbines, had a tremendous advantage compared to the Confederate troopers, who were armed with single-shot carbines or muskets. The fighting on June 12 was chiefly on-foot, and the woods provided good cover. Federal fire concentrated on Butler's brigade and on the artillery, which were able to fend off the attacks. Only 250 yards separated the opposing forces. The fighting continued until nightfall. Fitz Lee reinforced Butler's left with Wickham's brigade, taking Lomax's brigade across to the Gordonsville Road to attack the Union's right flank. Sheridan was unable to force Hampton from his position.[94]

The Confederates pressed heavily on Sheridan's front and attacked on his left. He had had enough. Under the cover of darkness Sheridan slipped away to rejoin Grant's army, abandoning his dead and wounded. Sheridan may have failed to defeat Hampton at Trevilian Station, but he was successful and brutal in his raids throughout the Shenandoah Valley, where he burned houses and barns, taking anything that might be of use to the Confederate army. Starving Lee's army was part of Grant's plan.[95]

---

91. Wittenberg, *Glory Enough for All*, 154; McVicar Diary, June 11, 1864, LVA.
92. Wittenberg, *Glory Enough for All*, 154; Rosser, Keller, *Riding with Rosser*, 38; *Philadelphia Weekly Times*, April 19, 1884.
93. *Philadelphia Weekly Times*, April 19, 1884.
94. McDonald, *Laurel Brigade*, 255–56.
95. Ibid., 256.

Sheridan claimed victory at Trevilian Station, but some of the Northern newspapers quickly realized that he was grossly exaggerating. Rosser was even harsher in his criticism of Sheridan's claims, stating, "Sheridan was fairly and completely beaten, and all of his apologies for his retreat, 'ammunition exhausted and presence of infantry' are unworthy of a great soldier. Why was he there without ammunition? Didn't he expect to have some fighting? ... These excuses are really too ridiculous to be discussed."[96]

Battle of Reams's Station—June 29, 1864

On July 2, 1864, General Wickham filed a report of the fight at Reams's Station:

> Upon reaching Carter's house I was ordered to dismount one of my regiments and send it in to the support of General Lomax, who had been ordered to make a flank attack whilst General Mahone attacked in front; to keep two regiments in hand ready for mounted action, and to put one in rear of our trains to guard them.

The Second Virginia cavalry was dismounted, and supported General Lomax in his attack. This attack was followed by a rout. So soon as the enemy began to fly my two mounted regiments (the Third and Fourth Virginia) were thrown forward in the pursuit, passing the park of the enemy's wagons and caissons that they had fired. I made a detail that saved nineteen of the wagons and one caisson. Crossing Rowanty Creek, where the enemy had left their ambulances and wounded, these regiments (the Third in front) soon came upon the rear guard of the enemy, and scattered it in every direction, capturing and bringing off three pieces of artillery, taking two mountain howitzers, and forcing the enemy to abandon all but one of his guns (which were afterwards taken possession of by General Mahone's men when they came up), capturing, so far as I can learn, all of the wagons and ambulances that they attempted to take with them, and capturing many prisoners, negroes and small arms; recapturing a considerable number [108] of our own infantry who had been captured in the morning. The pursuit was pressed on with but trivial opposition until we reached Stony Creek, where the enemy (having torn up the bridge) made a stand, but were soon dislodged by General Lomax, with his men dismounted, when the pursuit was again resumed and pressed far into the night.

---

96. Keller, *Riding with Rosser*, 39.

The next morning, on crossing Nottoway River, we found that the enemy had there abandoned their last gun, which I recovered from the river, into which they had thrown it, and it was brought back with us on our return.

The conduct of my men and officers was in the highest degree creditable to them.[97]

During the last week of July, Wickham's brigade fought Union horsemen in Charles City County, before it was ordered back to Dinwiddie. The 4th Virginia then reoccupied its previous campsite near Reams's Station, remaining there for a week. The weather was intensely hot; and the corn was suffering, wrote one 4th Virginia trooper, adding that the weather remained that way most of the time the 4th south of the James River.[98]

By August 10 Fitzhugh Lee's division, including Wickham's brigade, was ordered to the Shenandoah Valley to support Gen. Jubal Early. The next day, Fitz Lee's cavalry joined Maj. Gen. Joseph Kershaw's infantry division and Col. W. E. Cutshaw's artillery at Mitchell's Station.

After starting early on the next day, Fitz Lee's and Kershaw's soldiers reached Culpeper Court House about noon. As Kershaw set up camp on the banks of the Hazel River, Fitz Lee's troopers continued westward. By Saturday, August 13, Fitz Lee's cavalry encamped two miles north of Flint Hill. At sunrise the next morning, Lee's horsemen continued toward Front Royal, arriving at the town nestled in the western foot of the Blue Ridge Mountains in the afternoon. The next day, Lee's cavalrymen helped drive off a Union force entering the town.[99]

Action at Front Royal, August 17, 1864
Battle of Guard Hill
(or Crooked Run or Front Royal)

In August 1864, part of Confederate Lt. Gen. Richard H. Anderson's infantry corps threatened the left of Union Maj. Gen. Philip H. Sheridan's army. As Brig. Gen. Wesley Merritt's division approached on August 15 to protect the Federal flank, Anderson ordered Brig. Gen. William T. Wofford's infantry brigade and Brig.

97. "Battle of Ream's Station" Report of General W. C. Wickham (July 2, 1864), *Southern Historical Society Papers*, IX (1881), 108.
98. Stiles, *4th Virginia Cavalry*, 58.
99. Ibid.

Gen. Williams C. Wickham's cavalry brigade across the Shenandoah River to confront Merritt. Wickham was overwhelmed, however; the following day his troopers retreated toward Front Royal while Union Bvt. Brig. Gen. George A. Custer's brigade drove Wofford from Guard Hill. Sheridan then retired north to Charles Town, West Virginia.[100]

Around noon on a hot August 16, Fitz Lee received reports of four Union cavalry brigades moving toward Cedarville. Countering this threat, Lee sent Wickham's brigade and Brig. Gen. W. T. Wofford's infantry to Guard Hill. About 2 p.m., Wickham's cavalry attacked Maj. Gen. Wesley Merritt's cavalry on the western half of Guard Hill. Concurrently, Wofford moved his infantry to the right and formed his battle line. Initially, the Confederates were successful, as Wickham's troopers drove in Federal pickets and pushed Merritt's advance forces off the hill and north of Crooked Run. As the Federals fell back, Merritt's brigade was reinforced by Custer's Michigan Brigade. In a final attempt to break the Union hold on Winchester pike, Wickham led an assault up the road into Merritt's front. The 4th Virginia led the charge down the hill and across Crooked Run as Wofford's infantry moved against the Union left. With supporting artillery, Wickham rode headlong into the Federal's lines.[101]

Merritt then threw two regiments against Wickham's flank, pushing him back across Crooked Run. In coordination, Merritt's cavalry attacked Wofford's right, pushing the Confederate infantry back further. The now-combined Southern force returned to Guard Hill as the fight dwindled to an artillery duel at dusk. The Confederates suffered 300 casualties, most of them in Wofford's command. Wickham's losses were about a dozen casualties. Both sides encamped after dusk.[102]

The next morning, the Union forces left Guard Hill to Wickham and Wofford and marched to Winchester. Wickham moved up to attack Sheridan's rear whenever the opportunity presented itself, as Sheridan continued his Shenandoah Valley burning campaign. Riding through Cedarville and Nineveh, the Confederate cavalry pursued the Federal horsemen to the Opequon. Wickham, with two brigades, followed Union troops east to White Post, encamping near Frederick's Mill.[103]

Jubal Early's infantry closed up by darkness. After dark, Wickham was ordered to position his and Lomax's troopers at Berryville. They moved out that night as rain began to fall.[104]

---

100. Ibid.
101. Ibid., 58, 60.
102. Ibid., 60.
103. Ibid., 60.
104. Ibid.

Fitz Lee's troopers saddled up after sunrise on Thursday, August 18, and rode to Winchester. As Richard H. Anderson and Early occupied the town, Fitz Lee's horsemen picketed in front of the infantry. After securing Winchester, Early led his infantry down to Bunker Hill the following day. Wickham's brigade remained on the Opequon, skirmishing daily with Union scouting parties. On Friday, August 18, Wickham's troopers encountered an enemy force near Spout Spring. Fighting dismounted, Wickham's horsemen drove off the Federal force before crossing the Opequon.[105]

The following day, a minor skirmish occurred when a Union force of about 60 soldiers crossed the Opequon before encountering Wickham's riders. The 4th and 3rd Virginia regiments dismounted and moved up the Pike, as the 1st and 2nd Virginia regiments covered the flanks. The federal party quickly withdrew, ending the affair.[106]

It was about this time when brilliant and courageous artillery battery commander Capt. James Breathed, in poor spirits, submitted his resignation. Breathed stated that he "tired of his arm of the service" and felt that he could do better in another arm of the service— perhaps the cavalry. His commanders, from Wickham to Hampton, knowing of his invaluable artillery service, thought otherwise. Williams Wickham, now a brigadier general in command of a brigade of cavalry, disapproved of Breathed's resignation request. "Capt. Breathed is the best man for the management of a battery of horse artillery that I ever saw," he wrote. Fitz Lee agreed, as did Hampton and Robert E. Lee.[107]

For the next week, the Union and Confederate forces probed each others' positions but brought on no engagements. On August 25, Wickham and Lomax joined at Leetown, under Fitz Lee's command, marching to Williamsport via Martinsburg. Fitz Lee's troopers engaged Federal pickets along river bank at Williamsport, before moving on to Shepherdstown on August 27. Lee then fell back to Leetown and Smithfield, disappointing some of Wickham's troopers, who wanted to fight.[108]

Wickham recalled the fight at Guard Hill:

> **I received an order from Genl [Richard] Anderson to send a Brigade of Cavalry to seize and hold Guard Hill and was informed that [Brig.] Genl William T. Wofford would support me with a brigade of infantry. Taking my own**

---

105. Ibid.
106. Ibid.
107. Daniel P. Bridges, *Fighting with Jeb Stuart: Major James Breathed and the Confederate Horse Artillery* (Arlington, VA: Breathed Bridges Best, 2006), 183.
108. Stiles, *4th Virginia Cavalry*, 61.

Brigade and Capt. Johnson's battery, I moved to the river where I met Genl Wofford who proposed to cross [the river with] his command and surge across the hill. I furnished him half the regmts of cavalry to precede him. I then had pushed two regiments. The 1st and 2nd over both branches of the river and with little difficulty got possession of the Hill and dismounted the two regiments to hold their positions which was a strong one. At the same time noting the third regiment in hand for any mounted service that might be required and placing my artillery in position on the hill. Being annoyed by the enemy's sharpshooters in the flat below me, I sent the Third Regmt to drive them off which was very well done, but the regiment pushing their pursuit rather too far was driven back in disorder by a large force upon which it ran. Seeing what I understood to be the head of the column of infantry coming over the hill at the point agreed upon between Genl. Wofford and myself. I sent for the detachment of the 4th to have it to support the Third. Soon after I had gotten in position, I perceived that the brigade of Infantry with the exception of our regiment which I had taken for the head of the column had your unit on the flat by a sound to his right and was advancing across the field about a mile from me and was about to be attacked on their left flank by the enemies' cavalry. I at once ordered my mounted Regiment and a half to push forward at a gallop to their support, but the distance was so apart that the enemy struck the flank of the brigade before I could intervene to protect and reached the rear of those only in time to [??] by our infantry and to see that my little handful was confronted by one brigade and had another on each flank. Nothing was left to do but to retire the command as speedily as possible which was done by bringing one regiment back by the pike and the other by a gap in the hill lower down the stream and was affected with but little loss. My entire loss was 3 killed 8 wounded captured 18. Total 29.[109]

The 1864 Shenandoah Valley Campaign

In September 1864, after the Confederate defeat at the battle of Fisher's Hill, Wickham, at Milford, blocked attempts by Maj. Gen.

109. Report of Williams C. Wickham to Maj. Gen. Fitzhugh Lee, August 23, 1864 (Copy in Wickham Family Papers, UVA), August 23, 1864.

Philip Sheridan to encircle and destroy the Confederate forces of Maj. Gen. Jubal Anderson Early. Wickham then attacked the Federal cavalry at Waynesboro and forced them to Bridgewater.

On September 19, 1864, Matthew Calbraith Butler was officially promoted to major general in command of Hampton's former cavalry division. There were some hard feelings from Rosser and others, at not having received the coveted promotion. However, the attitude of most of his troopers at his return to duty encouraged him.

Virginia's Shenandoah Valley was a key theater in the Civil War. The opposing armies fiercely contested for the Valley throughout the war, as it provided a natural highway between north and south and was a richly-productive agricultural region, which fed the Confederate troops. More than 300 conflicts took place in the Valley, with Stonewall Jackson's 1862 campaign perhaps known as the most famous series of actions. The valley lay at the heart of the struggle, and as the war dragged on, the area assumed increasing significance as the "breadbasket" for the Southern cause. Union forces responded by laying waste to this region—burning its fields, farms, and towns in a devastating campaign of total warfare.

Major General Phil Sheridan was given command of the and dispatched to the Shenandoah Valley to deal with Jubal Early's Confederate threat. For much of the early fall of 1864, Sheridan and Early cautiously engaged in minor skirmishes while each side tested the other's strength. Early mistook this limited action to mean that Sheridan's force was not large and that "Little Phil" didn't want a major engagement. Early left his army spread out from Martinsburg to Winchester. Sheridan learned of Early's dispersed forces and immediately struck out for Winchester.[110]

Battle of Third Winchester
(Opequon or Opequon Creek)

Early quickly gathered his army back together at Winchester just in time to meet Sheridan's attack on September 19. The Union forces coming in from the east had to march on the narrow road through Berryville Canyon, which soon got clogged up with supply wagons and troops, delaying the attack. This delay allowed Early to strengthen his lines further. Maj. Gen. John B. Gordon's division arrived from the north and took up position on the Confederate left.[111]

110. Gary W. Gallagher, ed. *The Shenandoah Valley Campaign of 1864. Military Campaigns of the Civil War* (Chapel Hill: University of North Carolina Press, 2006), 324.
111. Ibid.

The Union VI Corps, commanded by Maj. Gen. Horatio G. Wright, advanced and began driving back the Confederate right flank; but the VI and XIX Corps, commanded by Maj. Gen. William H. Emory, were slowly moving apart from each other, and a gap appeared between them. Brigadier General David A. Russell's division was rushed forward to plug the gap. Russell was hit in the chest but continued moving his division forward. The brigade of Brig. Gen. Emory Upton reached the gap, but was too late—the Confederates had already launched a counterattack through the gap. Upton placed his men in line of battle and charged. Leading the charge was a young colonel named Ranald S. Mackenzie, commanding the 2nd Connecticut Heavy Artillery regiment, serving as infantry. Russell then received a second bullet and fell mortally-wounded. Upton assumed command of the division, and a lull came over the battlefield.[112]

Phil Sheridan, with about 35,000 effectives, then claimed victory and had proceeded to push his advance southward towards Staunton. Early retreated southward, with only about 10,000 troops remaining. He occupied a strong defensive position at Fisher's Hill, then extended his lines across this narrow section of the main valley between Massanutten Mountain on the east and North Mountain on the west. Early realized, however, that he could be flanked and attacked from the rear by a force that moved up the Page Valley and crossed Massanutten Mountain at New Market Gap. He, therefore, sent two brigades of Maj. Gen. Fitzhugh Lee's cavalry (commanded by Brig. Gen. Williams C. Wickham) to prevent such an occurrence. It was fortunate that he did, as Sheridan successfully flanked Early on the west side of the Confederate lines at Fisher's Hill—and again routed his army and sent it retreating southward for the second time in three days.[113]

At Milford, Wickham blocked an attempt by Maj. Gen. Philip Sheridan to encircle and destroy the Confederate forces of Early. Since both sides had fought dismounted at Milford, Wickham then attacked the Federal cavalry at Waynesboro and forced them to retreat to Bridgewater. Sheridan learned that Wickham's cavalry (Wickham commanded Fitz Lee's division due to Lee's having sustained a thigh wound at Winchester) was on the other side of Massanutten Ridge at Front Royal and dispatched Brig. Gen. James Wilson's cavalry division to drive them out. An engagement began near Crooked Run and the Front Royal Road that resulted in the Confederates being driven across the South Fork of the Shenandoah River. Wilson renewed his attacks on September 21, and part of his force succeeded in flanking the

---

112. Ibid.
113. Wert, *From Winchester to Cedar Creek*, 110.

Confederates by crossing the river at Kendrick's and Richard's Fords. A running battle then ensued as the Confederates retreated up the valley (southward) toward Luray. They made two stands and retreated from the first but held the second on the south bank of Gooney Run. An artillery duel then began that lasted well into the night. Later that evening, Wickham's troops withdrew and entrenched along the slopes immediately south of Milford, extending their lines from the river eastward to the steep slope in the vicinity of the present-day Shenandoah National Park boundary.[114]

The Southerners burned, or at least partially-burned, the little bridge over Milford Run in their front. During the night, Brig. Gen. Wesley Merritt's cavalry reinforced Wilson, bringing total Union strength to two divisions, the First and Third (each comprised of two brigades), with each division supported by three to five batteries of artillery. Brig. Gen. George Armstrong Custer commanded the 1st Brigade (consisting of one New York and four Michigan regiments) of Merritt's 1st Division. After midnight, the Federals discovered Wickham's new position at Milford. The Union cavalry and horse artillery then moved southward and set up their guns (some of which were placed at the present-day location of Skymont).[115]

On September 21, Wilson drove Wickham's horsemen across the North Fork of the Shenandoah River. Wilson did not pursue Wickham after dark, while under a dense fog. Wilson worried that the fog might cause units of his division to become separated from each other and be unable to communicate with each other. Wilson's failure to pursue and destroy Wickham's cavalry incensed Phil Sheridan. Sheridan immediately dispatched Alfred Torbert and Wesley Merritt's divisions to the scene. Then, at daybreak the next morning, Wilson attacked, ordering bugles blaring as they charged Wickham's cavalry, which was driven back across Gooney Run. Here, Wilson stalled about six miles south of Front Royal. Wickham learned that Wilson had been joined by Torbert and others, and he ordered a withdrawal under cover of night, marching south to Milford, about 12 miles from Luray. Torbert's forces camped north of Gooney Run.[116]

On September 22, Wickham posted Payne's brigade on the left (or west) between the roadway and the river. He then positioned his own

---

114. NPS Form 10-900 (Rev. 10-90) U. S. Department of The Interior Milford Battlefield National Park Service 093-5023_Milford_Battlefield_2004_Final_Nomination.pdf (virginia.gov), page 13.
115. Ibid., page 14.
116. Jay W. Simson, *Crisis of Command in the Army of the Potomac: Sheridan's Search for an Effective General* (Jefferson, N. C.: McFarland Publishing, 2004), 79.

brigade to the east, with the 4th Virginia Cavalry along the roadway and the other three regiments extending eastward to the steep slope at the foot of the Blue Ridge on the right. Wickham then placed Munford in command of both brigades before departing for a conference with Early at Fisher's Hill. He was, therefore not present during the actual fighting. Skirmishing began very early in the morning.[117]

Early in the battle, Torbert realized the strength of the Confederate position. The continuous skirmishing across Overall Run indicated Wickham's determination to hold against the attacks by the superior Union force. In Torbert's after-battle report, he described the strong Confederate position:

> Their left rested on the Shenandoah [River], which runs so close under the [Massanutten] mountain it was impossible to turn it, and their right rested against a high mountain [Blue Ridge]. The length of their line was very short, and the banks of the creek [Overall Run] so precipitous it was impossible for the men to get across in order to make a direct attack. In addition to their naturally strong position, they were posted behind loophole breastworks, which extended clear across the valley[118]

With all of the bridges across Gooney Run having been destroyed, a frontal attack by Torbert was precluded. Futhermore, the Luray Valley narrowed seemingly to prohibit a flanking movement. Torbert, not realizing that Wickham was already leaving the area, decided to try a flanking movement anyway. At midnight, he dispatched Custer's Michigan Cavalry brigade from Front Royal. Custer followed the South Fork of The Shenandoah River to McCoy's Ford.

Wickham is generally credited with having saved General Early's army by providing them a means of escape. Early noted such in his *A Memoir of the Last Year of the War for Independence*, published in 1866. However, William H. Payne wrote Jubal Early in 1867, criticizing Wickham in an effort to set the record straight:

> **Will you permit me to say, dear General, that the part which you have ascribed to his [Wickham's] Brigade is very different from the outside opinion at the time. Late in the day they came into action & were perched upon the hills above [the] Martinsburg Road, and there he remained, a spectator in the dress circle, watching the strife of the gladiators in the arena. It was the opinion of those who saw the whole [thing], that there was**

117. Stiles, *4th Virginia Cavalry*, 65.
118. *OR* 43/1:428.

opportunity after opportunity presented, in the flux & reflux of the Battle tide below, to have dashed in, aye to have swooped down, with terrible effect upon the exposed flanks of the Yankees. One regiment left upon his hill would have held back the force in his front as effectively as his whole command. Our daring, headlong rushing charge, with the impetus of the hill would have so routed the main body below as to have checked for some time the determination on the hill ... In this engagement, I lost nearly one-sixth of my men. The other Brigade did not have a single casualty.[119]

The Battle of Waynesboro

Waynesboro was important to the Union forces because the Manassas Gap Railway ran through it. Food and produce from the Valley could easily be shipped to Richmond. There was a railroad bridge over the South River and beyond Waynesboro; to the east was the Crozet Tunnel through the Blue Ridge Mountains.

On September 26, cavalry troops under the command of Brig. Gen. James Wilson were sent to Waynesboro to burn the bridge and to capture the tunnel. The Union forces camped outside of the town, On September 28, a Confederate cavalry force-led by General Wickham—and infantry—commanded by Willie Pegram—moved south from Port Republic to meet the Union forces before any damage could be done to the bridge. On September 28 to 29, the forces clashed. A Union soldier named George Bliss, was awarded a Medal of Honor for valor during the battle. It was noted that he charged the Confederate forces alone. Along with cavalry and infantry units, he was told that there might have been a small artillery duel, too. However, according to some reports, the Union forces sustained substantial losses, up to 40 dead and 80 prisoners. There was little damage inflicted to the bridge, and the Union forces never came close to the tunnel. The Union forces withdrew to Staunton but would return in March of 1865. There, the Second Battle of Waynesboro was fought on March 2, 1865. The First Battle of Waynesboro in September of 1864 stalled the advance of the Union forces.

Trooper Lt. Robert Hubard recalled that the Confederate troopers, greatly outnumbered by Torbert's huge force, were repulsed a second

---

119. William H. Payne to Jubal A. Early, February 16, 1867, Iron Horse Military Antiques, Auction, Item No. 6790469, 2022, Sold for $795, jeff@ironhorsemilitaryantiques.com. Wickham had been away conferring with Jubal Early at Fisher's Hill and arrived on scene while the battle was fought.

time. General Wickham gallopped among the troopers of the 4th Virginia calling out, "Halt, men halt! Where the [hell] are you going to? Rally around your General."[120]

At the Confederate debacle at Tom's Brook on October 9, 1864, General Wickham slapped his gloves against his thigh, rasping, "Damned popinjay, we're going to bust him (Custer) up! Boys, give out with the 'Bonnie Blue Flag' and drown those damn-Yankees in song."[121]

But Wickham felt certain that the South was going to lose the battle for the Shenandoah Valley, which they did on October 16 at the battle of Cedar Creek. He turned his attention to ways he thought that he could help in attaining peace with the Union and stop the relentless bloodshed. He resigned his commission on October 5, 1864, leaving his command to General Rosser. He then took his seat in the Second Confederate Congress in November, to which he had been elected while in the field in 1863. Recognizing that the days of the Confederacy were waning—and perhaps thinking that Lincoln might lose reelection—he wanted to help in seeking a peaceful end to the war. He supported the Hampton Roads Peace Conference in an attempt to bring an early end to the war. He served as a lawyer and jurist in Hanover before and after the war.

According to his service record, Wickham officially resigned Nov. 9, 1864. He submitted his letter of resignation to the Secretary of War on Sept. 30, 1864: "Being a member of the Congress of The Confederate States, and being unwilling longer to withhold my services from my constituents, I tender my resignation as Brigadier General of Cavalry and ask its acceptance."[122]

Wickham's position on the question of arming negroes to help defend the Confederacy was addressed in the Confederate Congressional swirling debate in late 1864 and early 1865. He wished that "the question of arming and making soldiers of negroes be now disposed of, now and forever." He wished it to be decided "whether negroes are to be placed upon an equality the side of our brave soldiers who had faced the storm of battle for four long years. It were[sic] idle to say that if negroes were put into the army they would not be [looked] upon an equality with our soldiers. They would be compelled to. They would have to camp and bivouac together." Wickham said that "our brave soldiers, who have fought so long and nobly, would

120. Nanzig, ed., *The Civil War Memoir of a Virginia Cavalryman*, 191.
121. D. A. Kinsley, *Custer: Favor the Bold, A Soldier's Story* (New York: Promontory Press,1967, 240.
122. Service Record for Brig. Gen. Williams C. Wickham, Fold3.com; 2nd Confederate Congress Vol. 7.

not stand to be thus placed side by side with negro soldiers. He was opposed to such a measure. The day that such a bill passes Congress sounds the death knell of this Confederacy. This very moment an order goes forth from the War Department authorizing the arming and organizing of negro soldiers there was an eternal end to this struggle."[123]

On November 9, 1864, Wickham introduced a bill "to amend an act to increase the efficiency of the Army by the employment of free negroes and slaves in certain capacities, approved February seventeenth, eighteen hundred and sixty-four; "which was read a first and second time" and referred to the Committee on Military Affairs.[124]

On December 2, he offered the following resolution; which was adopted:

> **Resolved, That the President be requested to inform this House whether at this time there are in the employment of the Confederate States slaves impressed exceeding one in five of the male slaves between the ages of eighteen and forty-five of one owner, and whether any slaves have been impressed and are now in service, on a basis of calculation including female slaves, between the ages of eighteen and forty-five, and if such impressments have been made by what authority it has been done, and whether the credit directed to be allowed in the impressment of slaves by the provisions of the act of February seventeenth, eighteen hundred and sixty-four, has been allowed.**[125]

On December 28, 1864, Wickham offered the following resolution, which was adopted: "Resolved, That the Committee on Claims inquire into the expediency of providing by law for the payment of damages inflicted on citizens of the Confederate States by reason of the destruction of their property, by fire or otherwise, growing out of the occupancy of such property by the troops of the Confederate States."[126]

On December 30, 1864, Wickham, from the Committee on Military Affairs, reported a bill "to increase the efficiency of the cavalry of the Confederate States," which was read a first and second

123. Mark Graber and Howard Gillman, *The Complete American Constitutionalism, Vol V Part 1 The Constitution of the Confederate States* (New York: Oxford University Press, 2018), 463.
124. Second Confederate Congress, Vol. 7.
125. Ibid.
126. Ibid.

time. The question being on postponing the bill and placing it on the Calendar. It was decided in the negative."[127]

On January 5, 1865, Wickham reported a bill "to provide payment for horses lost in service," and a bill "to authorize the promotion of officers, non-commissioned officers, and privates for distinguished valor and skill, or peculiar competency or merit"[128]

Wickham advocated for the "Hampton Roads Peace Conference," promoting peace at any honorable price, save surrender. The conference was doomed to failure from the start as Jefferson Davis had instructed the Confederate representatives to demand southern independence, which of course, was non-negotiable from Lincoln's point of view.

After the surrender of the Confederacy, Wickham was active in improving harmony between the states and reorganizing Virginia's economy, which had been ruined by the war. He became a Republican; and in 1872 as a member of the Electoral College of Virginia, he voted for General Ulysses S. Grant.

Only three weeks after Lee's surrender, Wickham, a former Whig, aligned himself with the Republican Party. He corresponded with wartime Unionists, urging cooperation in Reconstruction. Wickham now spoke openly of the Confederacy as a "rebellion against lawful authority, conceived by self-serving schemers and coercing a reluctant people."[129]

Throughout the years after the Civil War, while developing railroads, Wickham also maintained an active political life. He maintained his offices in Richmond and his residence in Hanover County. He became the Republican Party State Executive Committee Chairman. He was elected chairman of the Hanover County, Virginia Board of Supervisors in 1871 and as a Senator in the upper house of the Virginia General Assembly in 1883. In 1882 Wickham was elected president of Virginia Agricultural Society. He was an officer of the C&O Railroad and held all of these other positions at the time of his death on July 23, 1888, at his office in Richmond.

127. Ibid.
128. Ibid.
129. Jack P. Maddex Jr., *The Virginia Conservatives, 1867-1879: A Study in Reconstruction Politics* (Chapel Hill: UNC Press, 1970), 31.

Chapter Eight

Postwar Period

"at once and assiduously ... work to bring about the termination of the blood strife that was being waged."
—Wickham after he was elected to the
Confederate Congress in April of 1863

Wickham, among others, voiced sentiments for peace during the war. As one of the last of Virginia's secession convention delegates to yield to the majority, he eventually abandoned all hope for a Confederate victory. He was elected to the Confederate Congress in April of 1863 on a pledge to, in his words, "at once and assiduously ... work to bring about the termination of the blood strife that was being waged. Such sentiments became widespread in parts of Virginia toward the end of the war."[1]

In Virginia, after Francis Harrison Pierpont's Alexandria government moved to Richmond, unionists split into two groups: moderates, mostly former Whigs, and radicals. John Botts, recognized for his intelligence and integrity, was the main moderate spokesman. He was among a few wealthy former Whigs who became Republicans in 1865-66. Others included Williams C. Wickham, a railroad president, who after 1863 had backed the peace bloc in the Confederate Congress, and John F. Lewis, a livestock breeder from Rockingham County. Despite misgivings among allies, Governor Pierpont endorsed appeals for presidential pardons and the removal of voting restrictions imposed by the wartime Alexandria government.[2]

Williams Wickham applied for a presidential pardon in 1865.[3] It was granted by President Andrew Johnson on June 24, 1865.[4]

In March 1865, General Wickham had published a letter to the public, stating his position on matters of urgency. He favored the

1. James Alex Baggett, *The Scalawags: Southern Dissenters in the Civil War and Reconstruction* (Baton Rouge: LSU Press, 2003), 89.
2. Ibid., 130.
3. *Harper's Weekly*, July 1, 1865, page 403.
4. Fold3.com, Civil War Records of participants.

"Reconstruction Acts," as the only door for getting back into the Union. He opposed "repudiation" and favored a "judicious" system of public schools. He favored the election of judicial officers by some mode other than popular election and favored promoting harmony of white and black races, regarding "the black race as a very valuable portion of our population." He favored accepting general suffrage "without distinction" and advised the Radicals to bring their support as much of the white population as they can.[5]

In a letter to the public published in the *Richmond Whig*, General Wickham expressed his views of the postwar situation and the future of Virginia. He was critical of those politicians who had caused the suffering of millions of their fellow countrymen, driving the South into almost irretrievable ruin by appeals and prejudices. "My own opinion is that the great mass of people of this State have never lost their reverence or their attachment for the Government of the United States, and that they have only wanted freedom of speech and liberty of action to avow their reattachment to it."[6]

Wickham added, "the result of the contest has taught those who really wished for separation that the power of the Government was too great to enable them to succeed in their unhallowed design of overthrowing it. And, I think we may safely say that the abstraction which declared that we had a central government, with the name and not the powers of a government, has met with a deserved and violent death."[7]

Wickham believed that Virginia must move to re-establish itself with the national Government, taking whatever measures required. He lamented the portioning of Virginia, which resulted in the new state of West Virginia. He hoped that open lines of communication would restore the original boundaries and relationship. He was to be disappointed.[8]

General Wickham concluded his public letter stating that he did not believe that a vital blow had been dealt Virginia by the effects of the war. He believed that the people of Virginia "have shown an energy, which, had it been properly directed, would have advanced her material interests to a very high degree of prosperity—that energy will now be properly directed, and the whole population of the State with one accord, will bend themselves to the effort to bring the state forward to the highest state of mental, moral, and physical improvement."[9]

5. *Alexandria Gazette*, March 12, 1865.
6. *Richmond Whig*, April 28, 1865.
7. Ibid.
8. Ibid.
9. Ibid.

In the fall of 1866, Wickham wrote to the public via the *Richmond Whig*:

> I opposed in 1860 and 1861, with all my heart, disunion as the greatest ill that could befall us. When the war began, I was not going to desert my own people, wrong or right. I abandoned three separate public positions, either of one of which would have exempted me from military service, where I rose without solicitation, unaided by extraneous influence, and in spite of my known political opinions, from a captaincy to the rank of a general officer. I was elected [in 1863] to the Confederate Congress, and thus again became exempt from military service, but I would not leave to the care of another the noble brigade which looked to me as its leader in the campaign of 1864, and thus again I was a volunteer for hardship and danger, whilst many of those who malign me were sheltering their carcasses behind petty offices, under Congressional exemptions, or bomb proofs; and yet, notwithstanding this, I am denounced—covertly denounced—by those who wish for their own ends, to destroy my influence with our people, because, forsooth, I have remained steadfast in the political principles I have always entertained, and because I have dared to say that disunion, which first manifested its power in the disruption in the Democratic party of Charleston and the organization of the Breckinridge party, and culminated in the overthrow of the unbounded prosperity of Virginia and the South, was, in great part, the work of secession leaders, and that the people should not again trust its instigators with the management of their public affairs.[10]

Looking ahead, Wickham continued:

> I want no constitutional inhibitions, but I want the people to show these men who steered the ship out of the safe harbor upon ruinous breakers that they will hold them accountable for it; and if we are permitted quietly to manage our own affairs, I firmly believe that their good sense will cause them to do so, For myself, I accept fully and completely the results of the war. I am in favor of perfect and entire reconciliation–social and political. I regard the whole United States as my own country; I will look with as much pride as in the former days upon its growing grandeur; and above all, I shall devote my whole

---

10. *Richmond Dispatch*, September 29, 1866.

energy to the resuscitation of the shattered fortunes of Virginia as one of the best means of increasing that grandeur. I shall labor most earnestly to restore to all the states every legitimate, constitutional right of the States; in which restoration Massachusetts has the same future interests with Virginia; nor shall I allow all the clamor of these would-be Democratic leaders, to whom outcries I have long been accustomed, to deter me from following line of policy as in my opinion is best calculated to attain these ends.[11]

Only three weeks after Lee's surrender, Wickham, a former Whig, aligned himself with Electoral College of the Virginia Republican Party. He corresponded with wartime Unionists, urging cooperation in Reconstruction. Wickham now spoke openly of the Confederacy as a "rebellion against lawful authority, conceived by self-serving schemers and coercing a reluctant people."[12]

After the surrender of the Confederacy, Wickham was active in improving harmony between the states and reorganizing Virginia's economy, which had been ruined by the war. He became a Republican and, as a member of the Electoral College of Virginia, voted for General Ulysses S. Grant in 1872.

In November 1865, he was named president of the war-ravaged Virginia Central Railroad, which ran westerly from Richmond. Needing capital to expand and update, the Virginia Central was merged with the Covington and Ohio Railroad to become the Chesapeake and Ohio Railway (C&O)—with the goal of completing a railroad link to the Ohio River. Williams Wickham is credited with having attracted transcontinental railroad builder and financier Collis P. Huntington and also fresh financing from New York City to complete the task by 1873. Wickham remained active with the C&O through a receivership and financial reorganization for the remainder of his life.

Slavery–Instances of Colonization by Individual Slaveholders

By the will of Samuel Gist, his slaves were emancipated; and William F. Wickham and Carter B. Page, of Richmond, appointed trustees to acquire land in some of the free states providing homes for newly manumitted freedmen. Accordingly, these trustees purchased

11. Ibid.
12. Jack P. Maddex Jr., *The Virginia Conservatives, 1867-1879: A Study in Reconstruction Politics* (Chapel Hill: UNC Press, 1970), 32.

New York Financier Collis P. Huntington and Williams C. Wickham teamed up to run the Chesapeake and Ohio Railroad.

Portrait by Stephen W. Shaw

(Library of Congress)

two tracts of land in Brown County, Ohio—one containing one thousand, and the other twelve hundred acres at a cost of $4400.00. In 1819, the freedmen, comprised of one hundred thirteen from Hanover County and one hundred fifty from Goochland and Amherst Counties, were transported to Ohio and settled on the lands purchased, as dictated, by the trustees. The facts are meagre with respect to the reception accorded these freed slaves and the measure of success which attended the colonization. From the best information obtainable, it seems that they were treated not in a friendly manner and that, in time, the freed slaves lost most of the lands provided for them by their former owner.[13]

In 1862 and 1863, especially after the Emancipation Proclamation, slaves struggled to harness (and masters to contain) the volatile new possibilities of political life in the war zone. Some slaves continued to bide their time, lacking confidence in Union motives or anticipating reversals that could turn deadly.[14]

Of Virginia planter William Fanning Wickham's 268 family slaves, 56 went to the Yankees in 1863. In Virginia, as in the coastal areas of Atlantic states, many planters lost all of their slaves to the enemy.[15]

The path to citizenship for most blacks in Hanover County was not economic. Over $130,000 was paid in agricultural wages. Hanover was decidedly rural; and most people—black and white—earned their living off the land. Many black people ended up working on the plantations where they had been enslaved. This was true of most of the laborers at Hickory Hill. After the war, the Wickham family—its owners found itself with limited means but eager to move forward. The Wickhams needed to maintain their labor force, so they paid their former slaves following Emancipation. Until around 1870, they paid the men $7.00 and the women $2.50 per month and offered them their former slave quarters as housing. In order to ensure that the workers remained all year, the Wickhams paid only two-thirds of the wages for each quarter and then paid the remainder at the end of the year.[16]

In July 1888, Collis P. Huntington and General Wickham went on an inspection trip to the Kanawha & Ohio Railroad, hoping to acquire it for the Chesapeake & Ohio with its through connections to Toledo. They also went over the Richmond & Allegheny Road, which the

13. Beverley Bland Munford, *Virginia's Attitude Toward Slavery and Secession* (London, Bombay and Calcutta: Longmans, Green and Company, 1909), 66.
14. Ibid., 248.
15. William Fanning Wickham Diary, Vol 8 (1862-1864), William Fanning Wickham Papers, VMHC.
16. Jody Lynn Allen College of William & Mary - Arts & Sciences, "Roses in December: Black life in Hanover County, Virginia during the era of Disfranchisement," 2007, 86-87.

directors also desired to purchase. This proved to be their farewell trip together: General Wickham died in his office on July 21, a few days after their return. The many years they had worked together in the interests of the Virginia railroads had created a bond of mutual respect and esteem. Some years later, soon after Mr. Huntington's death, Henry Taylor Wickham, General Wickham's only son, in a letter to Mrs. Huntington referred to Mr. Huntington as "one who was the best friend my dear father ever had."[17]

Williams's son, Henry Taylor Wickham, perhaps angered by his witnessing of 56 slaves leaving Hickory Hill in June 1863 "for the Yankees," seemingly despised all blacks for it. He would be described by some black people as one of the meanest white men they had ever encountered. There is no clear way of knowing why Wickham was so hostile, especially to those in his employ, but it may have stemmed from what he viewed as the desertion of his "colored" people that day in 1863.[18]

During the 1868 Presidential campaign, Williams Wickham supported the Republican nominee, General Ulysses Grant, stating that "if Grant was elected, the Democratic Party would be broken down, and the country would have peace." He added, "he was quite willing to be called a carpetbagger as a Democrat, the latter party having organized all the troubles of the country."[19]

Replying in April to a letter from Fitzhugh Lee, Wickham wrote concerning postwar politics:

> Upon practical matters, I have been so long accustomed to the misrepresentations and abuse from those who differ with me that I never trouble myself to try to stop it save by steadily pursuing the course that I think best calculated to advance the welfare of the people and trust to time to produce a more just approximation of my views and conduct and there is no appeasing? The most-vile that I would even dignify with a denial. But to personal friend who I regard I never have any hesitation in endeavoring to justify myself—and I do not know that I can do it better than by asking you to read the words that I favour[sic] I wouldn't include: "negro domination" is too absurd a charge for me to answer to anyone.

17. Cerinda W. Evans, *Collis Potter Huntington* (Vol. 2), 544.
18. Jody Lynn Allen College of William & Mary - Arts & Sciences, "Roses in December: Black life in Hanover County," Virginia during the era of disfranchisement, 2007, 4.
19. *Alexandria Gazette*, August 26, 1868.

Henry Taylor Wickham had a long and illustrious career in the Legislature of Virginia.

(*Men of Mark in Virginia, Vol. 1*)

The political principles of the "Republican" (not the Radicals) Party are I think the same with those formerly held by the Old Whig Party and those principles I wish bined [sic] on a firm basis.

Again, I am most perfectly convinced that Congress means to bring the States into the Union under Republicans organization and that they will stop at nothing to gain that end, and every instinct of our people thus requires us to give respectability to the party for if these cannot be respectable men in the party you cannot have those in power. I think that the persistent resistance on the part of the whites to the Congress final plan will result in much wholesale disfranchisement that the whole power of the State government will be thrown in to the hands of the blacks and it is the purest "negro domination" that I couldn't ever accept the situation and thus place themselves in a position to control thus our State and County affairs.

You say you wish I had remained quiet, entertaining the opinions I hold–I confess that ever since I first engaged in politics, I have entertained the same wish for when I see every unselfish effort of mine to aid our people met by the vilest abuse and reprehend on their part, I think it would be far wiser for me to let them go to the [devil] their own way...

No one in the army or elsewhere had a better opportunity of judging of my character than you had and I believe you will hold me out in the public that in no single act of mine was self ever put in the balance against duty or welfare of my command or the interest of the service. I tell you now that I am as purely unselfish in my just actions as I ever was there. My judgement may be in error (I do not think it is) but my whole effort is to benefit our people.[20]

Hickory Hill

The frame portion of the house at Hickory Hill was partially destroyed by a fire in 1875; the family resided in the three-story brick addition which had been erected in 1857, while the damaged frame portion was rebuilt with a magnificent Flemish-bond brick structure over the original brick English basement. The house was built to

20. Williams C. Wickham to Fitzhugh Lee, April 16, 1868, Wickham Family Papers, UVA.

Shown standing are Williams and Lucy Wickham. Seated on the steps on the left is William Fanning Wickham. Sitting to the right of William Fanning Wickham may be Henry Taylor Wickham. Photo is circa 1875.

(Shannon Pritchard)

commercial standards of the day and, consequently, has remained unusually solid. All of the sills were made of sandstone; and all of the lentils, granite. The back veranda is made of a checkerboard-pattern of slate and marble, surrounded by massive granite beams. The rich walnut doors, ornamental plaster, mantels, and heart-pine flooring still remain and have been preserved to meet modern living needs—but in such a way as to be virtually unchanged. One of the mansion's architectural gems is the massive two-story great hall with double balconies.

Hickory Hill produced wheat (its major crop), corn, oats, and assorted fruits and vegetables. Unlike other Hanover County plantations, which sold theirs locally, Hickory Hill sold its produce in Richmond where it brought a higher price. It had its own stop, Wickham Station, just below the manor house on the former Virginia Central Railroad. Clay was mined on the property and baked into bricks alongside the railroad tracks, and all of the brick used in Hickory Hill's construction was made on the plantation. It is also thought that many of the bricks that rebuilt Richmond after the War Between the States came from Hickory Hill. This revenue greatly aided in maintaining the lifestyle the Wickham's had enjoyed prior to the War.

General Wickham remained at Hickory Hill until his death on July 23, 1888, at which time his son, Henry Taylor Wickham, became master of the plantation. The house changed little for over fifty years; but in 1915, five bathrooms were added to the mansion. At the same time, a coal-fired steam boiler heating system was installed. A gas shed and carbide gas generator were also added; and gas for lighting was piped to the mansion, the kitchen and office. The house was not disturbed again until it was wired for electricity in 1930.

The mansion, though fallen into disrepair, remained surrounded by the Plantation office, kitchen, smokehouse, Mammy's house, root cellar, carriage house, and the first-floor brick of the barn and stable. The property remained in the Wickham family for six generations, not coming on the market until approximately 2005, when it was sold. The mansion and some of the dependencies have been meticulously restored to their former glory. The property now consists of fifty acres including the mansion and outbuildings. A 546-acre viewshed was placed around the remaining estate that can never be developed, thus preserving the mansion, grounds, and setting for the foreseeable future.

In 1879, Wickham and James B. Soner traveled to Philadelphia to pay a visit to former President Ulysses S. Grant. Soner, one Virginia's leading lawyers and a member of the Republican National Committee, and Wickham, Vice-President of the Chesapeake and Ohio Railroad Company, were visiting Grant out of admiration for him. Both men would have supported Grant for a third term. Wickham speaking to Soner said, "It's impossible to find a man so well fitted for the place as Grant is." Asked by a reporter as to his opinion of Grant as a military commander, Wickham stated, "... he is one of the greatest of military commanders." The reporter asked, "What did the South think of Grant when you were fighting him?" Wickham answered, "... We had not been pitted against Grant very long, however, when we came to the conclusion that the armies of the North had a different commander than they had been accustomed to... There was less nonsense and a good deal more fighting." "How is he liked in the South?" the reporter interjected. "Personally, he is held in very high esteem," answered Wickham.[21]

During the 1873 Virginia Gubernatorial campaign, Wickham was asked if he would accept the nomination of the Republican Party. Wickham declined, declaring that acceptance would interfere with his busy railroad business too much. He said he would attend the convention as a delegate.[22]

Civil Rights Act of 1875

The Civil Rights Act of 1875, enacted March 1, 1875, banned racial discrimination in public accommodations—hotels, public conveyances, and places of public amusement. In 1883 the U.S. Supreme Court declared the law unconstitutional, ushering in generations of segregation until 1964. The Civil Rights Act of March 1, 1875, banned racial discrimination in public accommodations.[23]

On September 1, 1875, Wickham wrote President Grant, "The government is I doubt not interested in having Gilbert C. Walker defeated for Congress in this district--I think then it should exert some influence upon the selection of a candidate--Of the persons spoken of for the nomination I am satisfied that only Mr. John Ambler Smith can make a successful run. The others if nominated can not avail themselves of the dissatisfaction in the Conservative ranks with Walker. Under these circumstances it strikes me as proper that the Government should take steps to prevent any one holding office under it from going before the people in a manner which will lose us this district."[24]

William Mahone (1826-1895) was a railroad president before the Civil War, a general in the Confederate Army, and afterward one of the most controversial of all Virginia political leaders. As founder of the Readjuster Party, which tried to reduce the amount of the expensive antebellum state debt that the taxpayers had to pay, Mahone formed a coalition of Democrats, Republicans, and African Americans. The Readjusters captured control of the General Assembly in 1879 and in 1881 elected Mahone to a six-year term in the United States Senate.

21. *Richmond Dispatch*, December 23, 1879.
22. Ibid., July 22, 1873.
23. Alan Friedlander, Richard Allan Gerber, *Welcoming Ruin: The Civil Rights Act of 1875* (Boston: Brill Publishing, 2019), 285.
24. John Y. Simon, ed., *Ulysses Simpson Grant, The Papers of Ulysses S. Grant*: Vol. 25, 1874 (Carbondale and Edwardsville, IL: Southern Illinois University Press, 2003), 139.

Mahone lost the support of most Democrats because of the alliance he and the Republicans had made with the state's many black voters. By the end of the century both major political parties had rejected participation of African Americans in Virginia politics. The biracial alliance that Mahone created during the 1870s and 1880s was radically different from any other nineteenth-century Virginia political party before or after. Mahone was one of many white Virginians who attempted to succeed in politics by accepting the enfranchisement of African Americans after the Civil War. His short-term success demonstrated what was possible, but his long-term failure illustrated the limits of what was attainable.

In 1880 James Garfield shared president Rutherford Hayes's disdain for William Mahone, who wanted to run for the United States Senate. Stephen Dorsey, an unscrupulous carpetbag senator from Arkansas, who was secretary of the Republican National Committee and something of a loose cannon on the deck of the Garfield campaign for president, was more open-minded. Conceding Virginia as lost to Garfield, in late October Stephen Dorsey and some other members of the national committee sent to Virginia a pair of agents to convince its Republicans to vote the Readjuster ticket. Claiming to bear the imprimatur of the national committee, these emissaries joined with James D. Brady, collector of the customs at Petersburg, in distributing circulars that declared "that the best interest of the Republican party of Virginia, and of the whole South, demands the defeat of the Regular, Bourbon, or Funder electoral ticket ... and the only way to accomplish this ... is by Republicans supporting the Re-Adjuster electoral ticket."[25]

Alarmed, the Virginia Republican leadership secured a quick disavowal of Brady's letters from Garfield and the full national committee. Williams C. Wickham, state Republican chairman, fired off circulars of his own in which he warned the black rank and file of "traitorous Republicans" who conspired with Readjusters "to defraud you of your inestimable privilege of voting for the Republican candidate for President. Wickham's damage control proved effective.[26]

---

25. Thomas V. Cooper and Hector T. Fenton, *American Politics {Non-Partisan} From the Beginning to Date* (Philadelphia: Fireside Publishing Company, 1882), I, 263; Vincent P. De Santis, *Republicans Face the Southern Question: The New Departure Years, 1877-1897* (Baltimore: The Johns Hopkins Press, 1959), 142, 143-144; Stanley P. Hirshson, *Farewell to the Bloody Shirt: Northern Republicans and the Southern Negro, 1877-1893* (Bloomington: Indiana University Press, 1962), 95.

26. "Attention Republicans of Virginia" [broadside], October 29, 1880, Williams C. Wickham to S. M. Yost [broadside], October 30 (quote), A. H. Lindsay to Asa Rogers, November 1, WM Papers, Duke; John J. Wise to John S. Wise, November 1, 1880 (quote) in Moore, "Black Militancy in Readjuster Virginia," 175.

Among the important matters in which he was a conspicuous factor during his service in the State Senate, special mention should be made of the memorable contest waged at that time to break the dictatorial power of General Mahone and his associates in Virginia politics. With the large negro vote as a nucleus, they waged a battle against the Democratic party and undertook to dominate the State on lines of policy obnoxious to the great body of intelligent Virginians. At the election held in the fall of 1881, they elected the governor of the State and a majority of both branches of the legislature. They had a large majority in the House of Delegates, but in the Senate they secured a majority of only eight. Serious alarm was felt in the State at the policies undertaken by this coalition headed by General Mahone, who was a distinguished Confederate general and a man of exceptional ability. General Mahone was backed in his policies by President Chester Arthur and the national Republican party. It seemed that his purpose was to put Virginia permanently in the Republican party. In carrying out that plan on his part he undertook to pass a large number of measures through the legislature which alarmed many people of the State—especially in view of the fact that in his movement General Mahone was compelled to rely on the negro vote. Relying on them, of course, he had to concede much to that element.

To thwart these plans of General Mahone, an organization was perfected in the State Senate, comprised of Democrats, Re-adjuster Democrats, and Independent Republicans. Mr. Henry T. Wickham and his distinguished father, General Williams C. Wickham, not only influenced and brought into this organization the senator from Hanover, but also were potential factors in the contest in this crisis of the State's history. Without their co-operation the fight could not have been successfully made to prevent General Mahone from carrying out his plans, and in the general election of 1883 General Wickham consented to be the candidate for the Virginia State senate because he was the only man who could carry that senatorial district. In spite of a special effort made by the coalition to defeat him, he was triumphantly elected.

"The Straightout splinter group insisted on nominating Williams Wickham for governor, but Wickham, realizing the hopelessness of the situation, declined the honor."[27]

---

27. James Tice Moore, *Two Paths to the New South* (Lexington: University Press of Kentucky, 2015), 80; *New York Times*, July 25, August 4, 1881.

Chapter Nine

Wickham the Railroad Businessman

"with eyes flashing," Wickham told Senator James J. McDonald that, "if he dared to intimate there had been any fraud in any transaction with which he was connected he would place him where the hand of God could not reach him."

–Wickham after being appointed

Receiver of the Chesapeake and Ohio

By the end of the war's hostilities in the spring of 1865, the Virginia Central Railroad had suffered severe damage. The states of Virginia and (newly-formed) West Virginia partnered to rebuild and expand this rail link so vital to their economic recoveries. Williams Carter Wickham was hired as president of the Virginia Central Railroad Company that November when the company merged with the Covington and Ohio Railroad in 1868 to form the Chesapeake and Ohio Railroad. Wickham was retained as president of the new corporation. Monies required to fund expansions to the refurbished railroad were severely lacking during the nation's reconstruction period. Wickham secured solid backing when he was able to trumpet the merits of the C&O to a group of investors headed by railroad magnate Collis P. Huntington. Huntington assumed the presidency of his newest investment, and Wickham became his vice-president.[1]

Colonel Edmund Fontaine served as President of the Virginia Central Railroad during its entire span, 1850-1868, with the exception of the fiscal year, 1865-1866, when Williams C. Wickham defeated him because of unfounded tales of ill health. In all Colonel Fontaine was President of the Chesapeake and Ohio Railroad Company and its predecessor for 22 years—of the Louisa, 1845-1850; of the Virginia Central, 1850-1865 and 1866-1867; and for approximately three months in 1868.[2] Fontaine died in 1869.

---

1. "The Building of the C&O Railway," WVa-USA.com, 1999-2001, page 1.
2. Charles V. Bias, "A History of the Chesapeake and Ohio Railroad Company and its Predecessors, 1784-1977" (Ann Arbor, MI: University Microfilms International, 1979) 81-83.

Just weeks after the cessation of hostilities, Wickham joined the Republican Party, providing his reasons in an open letter which estranged many of his colleagues. The former general was elected president of the Virginia Central Railroad Company in November 1865, and when that line merged with the Covington & Ohio Railroad in 1868 to become the C&O, Wickham was retained as the new company's president. He served as vice-president of the company from 1869 to 1878, when the company went into foreclosure with Wickham as receiver. Under reorganization of the company, Wickham served as second vice-president. During this time, he maintained an active political life, being elected chairman of the Hanover County board of supervisors in 1871 and a state senator in 1883. He held all of these positions at the time of his death on July 23, 1888.[3]

After the surrender of the Confederacy, Wickham was active in improving harmony between the states and reorganizing Virginia's economy, which had been ruined by the war. He became a Republican and, as a member of the Electoral College of Virginia, voted for General Ulysses S. Grant in 1872.[4]

During the Civil War, the Confederates utilized the Virginia Central Railroad to transport troops and goods throughout Virginia, making it one of the most targeted rail lines by the Union Army. Suffering extensive damage and crippling finances, the railroad limped through the war until the final surrender. Like most enterprises located in the South following the Civil War, Confederate currency was worthless; and the company was facing certain bankruptcy. However, the railroad still managed to survive until November of 1865, when the stockholders and directors of the railroad elected former Confederate General Williams C. Wickham to succeed longtime leader Edmund Fontaine as president of the railroad. Fontaine had remained as president of the railroad for almost twenty years when he originally began as president of the Louisa Railroad in 1845 until his eventual termination in 1865. For his services to the railroad and the communities it served, Fontaine was granted free tickets for life along the railroad.[5]

As president of the struggling railroad, Williams C. Wickham knew he had to attract financial aid to continue expanding and purchasing new equipment—along with restoring the rest of the still-damaged line. His solution was to persuade millionaire industrialist Collis P. Huntington—one of the "Big Four" who helped complete the

---

3. *Staunton Virginia Spectator*, October 28, 1891.
4. Ibid.
5. Bias, "A History of the Chesapeake and Ohio Railroad Company and its Predecessors, 1784-1977," 81-83.

Transcontinental Railroad—to finance the growth of the line. Collis accepted; and so on August 31, 1868, with Huntington's financial backing, Wickham authorized the merger of the Covington & Ohio Railroad with the Virginia Central Railroad to form the now-famous Chesapeake & Ohio Railroad.[6]

Wickham was retained as the new company's president. In the new capacity, he was anxious to complete a railroad line to the Ohio Railroad, long a dream of Virginians. However, unlike what fellow Confederate officer and railroad leader William Mahone had done, he was unable to secure capital or financing in Virginia, or from Europeans. Turning to New York City, he was successful in attracting an investment group headed by Collis P. Huntington. Fresh from recent completion of the western portion of the U.S. transcontinental railroad as a member of the so-called "Big Four," Huntington joined the effort, became the C&O's new president. His contacts and reputation helped obtain $15 million of funding from New York financiers for the project, which eventually cost $23 million to complete. The final spike ceremony for the 428-mile (689 km) long line from Richmond to the Ohio River was held on January 29, 1873, at Hawk's Nest railroad bridge in the New River Valley, near the town of Ansted in Fayette County, West Virginia.[7]

After Huntington assumed the presidency, Wickham served as vice-president of the C&O from 1869 to 1878, when the company went into foreclosure, with Wickham as receiver. In 1878 the Chesapeake and Ohio Railroad was sold under foreclosure and reorganized as the Chesapeake and Ohio Railway Company, with Collis P. Huntington assuming the office of President of the reorganized road; Wickham was named second vice-president. Henry T. Wickham served for years as chief counsel. The railways allowed the development of coal deposits in West Virginia, but a deep-water port was required for coal export; The York River in the Richmond area was too shallow for coal transports. Huntington decided that the southeastern portion of Warwick County was the best place to reload coal from rail to maritime transport and in 1881 began moving along the railway line to Newport News; The coastal farming region became a fast-growing port.

Building a railroad to these places was the first part of Huntington's plans to develop Virginia. In 1886, he began building the Newport News Shipbuilding and Dry Dock Company to build and repair ships arriving at the coal terminal. In 1891, the shipyard built its first ship, the tugboat "Dorothy." By 1897, Newport News had built

6. "The Building of the C&O Railway," WVa-USA.com, 1999-2001, pages 1-2.
7. Ibid.

three large ships for the U. S. Navy: gunboats Nashville, Wilmington, and Helena. However, Newport News grew so fast that already in 1896, by decision of the General Assembly of Virginia, Newport News became an independent city (one of two in the state), bypassing the traditional intermediate stage of the "incorporated city." Shipbuilding became the basis of the city's, and, indeed, of the entire Virginia lower peninsula's economy.

During the ten years from 1878 to 1888, C&O's coal resources began to be developed and shipped eastward. Coal became a staple of the C&O's business at that time—and still was over 125 years later under successor CSX Transportation. Collis P. Huntington expanded to develop his other holdings in Newport News. In modern times, Newport News, which merged with the former Warwick County in 1958, has grown to become one of the major cities of Hampton Roads. He also built housing for the Shipyard workers, mostly duplexes located a few miles west in a hamlet called Hilton Village.

Williams C. Wickham, then second vice president of the C&O, was elected to serve the Newport News & Mississippi Valley Company in the same capacity. The company was empowered by its articles of incorporation "to build, acquire by purchase, lease, and operate railroads, steamboat and steamship lines, and to acquire, hold and dispose of stocks, bonds and securities issued by any corporation or by Government, State and local authorities." The Newport News & Mississippi Valley Company obtained a lease of the Chesapeake & Ohio Railway, to run for two hundred fifty years from July 1, 1886; a lease of the Elizabethtown, Lexington & Big Sandy for the same number of years, beginning Feb. 1, 1886, and of the Chesapeake, Ohio and Southwestern, for fifty years from the same date. Immediately after leasing these properties, Collis P. Huntington reported to the stockholders of the Newport News & Mississippi Valley Company, as follows:

> These leases provide that the lessee will keep the leased properties in good repair, operate, maintain, add to and better the same as the business of the roads may from time to time require, and apply the surplus after payment of the expenses so accrued to or toward the payment of the principal and interest of equipment trust bonds and other interest obligations of the lessor companies in the order of their priority, making such other advances from time to time as may be determined upon.
>
> The organization also contemplates securing a further unification of the interest in the leased properties by an exchange of the stock of this company for stock and

other junior securities of the lessor companies at such prices as might be agreed upon, equalizing as far as might be in such an exchange the varied values and interest of the junior securities of the lessor companies, and substituting for them a security whose value could be better understood and determined, and more readily realized by the holders. The advantages of this exchange have been so manifest that a sufficient number of the holders of said securities have availed themselves of the proposition to substantially insure the consummation of this desirable measure.

Owing to the gap between Lexington and Louisville, it became for the present desirable to divide the property for purposes of physical operation into two divisions, viz., the Eastern and Western.

The EL&BS RR. Co. is now engaged in the construction of a line of railroad along the south side of the Ohio River from Ashland, Ky., to Covington, Ky., a distance of about 143 miles, and its completion is expected by the close of this year. This road will reduce the distance to Cincinnati, Ohio, about fifty-five miles. Its grades do not exceed thirteen feet per mile, and it will, in conjunction with the double-track railroad bridge, which is now building across the Ohio River, between Covington, Ky., and Cincinnati, Ohio, secure important advantages in the control of traffic between the western cities and the Atlantic seaboard. With the completion of this bridge the most serious obstacle to the development of our western business will be removed, and we shall then be able to carry the products of the West to tide-water, and coal, coke and other products to the West, under more favorable conditions than at present.[8]

The initial six months of operation under the Newport News & Mississippi Valley Company, July 1 to Dec. 31, 1886, was, on the surface, fraught with promise. The earnings, after operational expenses, during that period, exceeded by $200,000 in round numbers the results of the preceding six months under the C&O management. But, out of the earnings for the full year, amounting to $1,130,465.70, that had to be met current and past due obligations in the amount of $1,334,969. This meant a deficit for the C&O of approximately

8. Charles V. Bias, "A History of the Chesapeake and Ohio Railroad Company and its Predecessors, 1784-1977" (Ann Arbor, MI: University Microfilms International, 1979) 81-83.

$200,000. To attract export tonnage to the line of C&O, for sea-borne movement from Newport News, arrangements had been made for leasing and operating a line of freight steamers, plying between Newport News and Liverpool. In the first year of this steamship operation, the C&O sustained a loss of $119,000. Deficits had been anticipated for the first several years of this operation, but it was expected that the traffic over the rails would absorb them until such time as this steamship service was developed and popularized. Rates on rail traffic, however, proved to be hardly compensatory of the services performed. That discovery caused the C&O much concern. Whereas, in 1878, it had received $2.59 per ton on freight carried, which was nothing to boast about, it realized, in 1887, only $1.45 per ton, a decline of nearly one-half in less than ten years. In the meantime, heavy fixed charges had been added as a result of the new construction completed and the improvements made to right-of-way. These causes, along with the inadequacy of the rates, were due to the embarrassments under which the company was now laboring. A readjustment of indebtedness was imperative. Holders of upwards of two-thirds of the Series "B" bonds had accepted a proposition made in 1886 to reduce the rate of interest to four percent, but a minority refused to accept it. On Oct. 28, 1887, General Williams C. Wickham was appointed receiver of the Chesapeake & Ohio property, for the second time, by the courts of Virginia and West Virginia. Soon after General Wickham's appointment as receiver, State Senator James J. McDonald called for an investigation by the Virginia legislature of the depreciation of the stock of the C&O belonging to the State. Sitting in the Assembly at the time was General Wickham. He popped out of his seat like a cork from a champagne bottle and demanded to know if there was any criticism implied as to his conduct of the affairs of the road.[9]

He was assured that none was intended, but, evidently, the assurance wasn't enough, for "with eyes flashing," he told McDonald that, "if he dared to intimate there had been any fraud in any transaction with which he was connected he would place him where the hand of God could not reach him."[10] At the instance of holders of a large number of securities, Drexel Morgan & Company examined the affairs of the company. Consistent with this policy in reorganizations, J. Pierpont Morgan required that all of the stock be turned over to him, to be held and voted by him for a period of five years. Mr. Morgan found that the C&O was not in such bad straits after all. It

9. Ted O'Meara, ed., *TRACKS Magazine* (CHESAPEAKE & OHIO RAILWAY), v. 38, no. 10, Oct. 10, 1953, 266-270.
10. Ibid.

was embarrassed, but not distressed. It could be put back on its financial legs without foreclosure. General Wickham passed away before termination of the receivership period, and the property was turned over to Melville E. Ingalls, as the prospective new president of the Chesapeake & Ohio, in March, 1888, by order of the court.[11]

The Chesapeake and Ohio Railroad (C&O) under Collis Potter Huntington and Williams C. Wickham completed the Peninsula Extension to the small town of Newport News in 1881. This allowed the C&O to transport West Virginia coal to Hampton Roads—the largest warm-water port on the East Coast—and directly compete with the Norfolk and Western Railway. Between the coal exports and Huntington's Newport News Shipbuilding Company, Newport News soon became a major shipping and industrial area.

Building the extensive railroad lines was grueling work. Once the lines were established, other problems arose. For example, in West Virginia in January 1879, coal miners threatened to walk off the job, bringing about stoppage of excavating coal. Williams Wickham, exasperated at the possible damage to the railroad industry, telegraphed West Virginia Governor Henry M. Matthews, "Have just received the following from our or agent in Connelton, 'About four or five hundred miners will leave here in a day or two for Hawk's Nest to stop that mine from work.' ... Such conduct as this pursued much longer will result in absolute ruin to the mineral interests of the line in your state. Cannot you devise some means to put a stop to it?"[12]

The expected crisis did not develop until a year later when several Coal Valley miners traveled to Hawk's Nest mines to threaten other miners. The state felt that action was needed. In an effort to halt the strike and prevent violence, Governor Matthews attempted to convince Sheriff C.H. McClung of Fayette County to intervene. McClung feared a backlash from voters and refused to become involved in the conflict. Instead, Matthews sent in a militia group from Charleston and Lewisburg on McClung's recommendation. A total of 25 miners were arrested by the militia and held by Sheriff McClung, each of whom was charged with unlawful interference. The success of the militia's efforts to halt the strike was felt by many of those involved. This strategy was repeated by officials for strikes in many subsequent years.[13]

11. Ibid.

12. Telegraph from Williams C. Wickham to H. M. Matthews, January 8, 1879, West Virginia Dept. of Arts, Culture & History, Charleston, WV. The Hawk's nest Coal Mine was a dangerous place to work. Workers' careers were short as "black lung" disease was relentless.

13. Endres, Victoria. "Hawks Nest Coal Strike." Clio: Your Guide to History. March 27, 2019. Accessed April 10, 2022. https://theclio.com/entry/77108

Chapter Ten

Wickham's Death

As in war, in peace Wickham was loved by the men he led.
One C&O employee recounted:
"No man was ever more beloved by the men under him than
General Wickham and many of them, trainmen
and stationmen alike, wept as though
they [lost a] member of their immediate family."

The 1880s

In June 1881, Wickham become Chairman of the Virginia Republican Convention which was to be held in August 1881. He replaced John F. Lewis, who was removed. At the Convention, Wickham wrote the public a letter, stating his views on Virginia politics. He "Declared boldly and emphatically that the triumph of the Re-adjusters will be the death of the Republican party in Virginia, and the beginning, perhaps, of a movement to 're-adjust' the debt of the United States as [General] Mahone as Governor of Virginia would adjust the debt of Virginia. As a Republican who believes in the sanctity of public contracts as a cardinal principle of the Republican party, and who is now left but with a choice of evils, General Wickham unhesitatingly announces his purpose to support the Conservative candidates; but declares his intention, upon the close of the canvass, to devote himself to the task of reorganizing the disbanded Republican party."[1]

Wickham becomes Virginia State Senator in 1883.

On August 11, 1883 Wickham wrote his supporters and Hanover citizens:

---

1. *Richmond Dispatch*, August 27, 1881; *Staunton Spectator*, June 28, 1881.

Fellow Citizens, I announce myself a candidate for the Senatorship of this district. I do so in response to the urgent appeals of many too partial friends throughout the district, and especially in response to the unanimous call made upon me by the Democratic Senatorial Convention which met at Bowling Green on the 8th inst., a call which, in view of the fact that I am, recognized as a consistent Republican. I appreciate as the highest personal compliment that could be bestowed upon me by those among whom I have always lived. I am a born son of Virginia, and whenever her interests are assailed, come the assailant in what garb or under what name he may, I will stand shoulder to shoulder with her true sons, without regard to political bias or option, and resist with all the power I possess all measures, all men, all parties that attack her welfare. I regard the party calling itself the Coalition or Coalition-Readjuster Party, led my men seeking, as I think, only to advance their own personal ends, as baleful to the best interests of the State, false in its pretensions, corrupting in its practices, and utterly hostile to every honest principle of government. Holding these opinions of this party, I am in full accord with the Democratic Party of this State in their effort to defeat it. Most cordially will I strike hands with them to the end that Virginia may be redeemed from misrule; and most earnestly do I call upon the Republicans of the district to aid me in the effort. In more than a score of years that have elapsed since I was in a political canvass many of my old friends (and no man had truer) have passed away, but they have left sons worthy of their sirs, whose acquaintances I shall seek to make, not only at public gatherings, but to their homes, as was my want with their fathers. To my friends throughout the district, I look for earnest, active work throughout the canvass, and at the polls. They have never failed in the past: I know they will not do so now. Should I be elected, I promise to devote all the capacity I possess to advance the welfare of the people of this State.[2]

In 1886, Wickham expressed his opinion of where to place the impending statue of Robert E. Lee. He stated: "I beg to leave to say to you that it strikes me that the city square on Libby Hill, placing the monument and statue in full view of the line of Main Street, and at the same time of the river and the railroads that come into the city

2. *New York Times*, August 13, 1883.

In 1883 Williams C. Wickham returned to serve in the state senate of Virginia.

(Hanover County Historical Society)

crossing the James River, is in my judgment unquestionably the best location in the city of Richmond for the monument."[3]

Williams Wickham's son,
William F. Wickham, dies.

On March 19, 1900, Williams Wickham's son, W. F. Wickham, accidentally shot himself at his home in Powhatan County. Apparently, he was handling a pistol in his room, when somehow it was discharged; the bullet entered the side of his head and lodged in his jaw. The wound was serious, and doctors decided not to probe for the bullet, as Wickham was so weak from loss of blood. At that time, the wound was not considered to be mortal, and a recovery was anticipated. However, just ten days later, Wickham died. A prominent, unidentified citizen of Powhatan County reported that Wickham had been in ill health for several months prior to the shooting. His family and friends considered him to be despondent, raising the specter of a possible suicide. Others, including Wickham's private secretary, Mr. George Talley, disagreed, stating that Wickham "was never in better spirits ... One of his children was two years old at that time [the day before the shooting], and the birthday was being appropriately celebrated. We went hunting Friday evening, and the colonel was apparently very happy."[4]

Colonel Wickham had been prominent in the politics of his party in the State and had, apparently, an exceedingly bright and promising future. His untimely end in the bloom and vigor of young manhood was the cause of widespread sorrow wherever he was known. He spent the early part of his life in Hanover County at the place of his birth, Hickory Hill. For several years he was prominent in military circles and the colonel of the Fourth Virginia Cavalry, which he resigned after four years' service. He had practiced law in Richmond and adjoining counties for a number of years, and was the partner of his cousin, Judge T. Ashby Wickham, of Henrico County. He was a younger brother of Senator Henry T. Wickham.

Williams Wickham's later years

From 1871 to his death, Williams Wickham was chairman of the board of supervisors of Hanover County. At the same time, he was remarkably successful in business as president of the Virginia Central

---

3. *Richmond Dispatch*, March 28, 1886.
4. *Alexandria Gazette*, March 20, 1900, *New York Times*, March 31, 1900;
   Richmond Times, March 20, 1900.

Williams and Lucy Wickham, along with a grandson at Hickory Hill.

(Valentine Museum)

Railroad and later the Chesapeake and Ohio. Wickham became the president of the Virginia Central Railroad and later held the same post with the Chesapeake & Ohio Railroad. He was offered the post of Secretary of the Navy by President Rutherford B. Hayes in 1880, but he declined the post. The next year, he turned down the Republican nomination for Virginia governor. He served the final five years of his life in the state senate.

General Williams Carter Wickham, 69 years old, died suddenly on July 24, 1888, of heart failure while working at his office in the Chesapeake and Ohio Railroad Building at the corner of Eighth and Main Streets in Richmond. At 11 a.m., he seemed to be well, actively discharging his duties as usual; but he soon complained of feeling unwell and began suffering from nausea and cramps. His son, Henry T. Wickham, and others suggested sending for physicians, but Wickham declined. As he failed to improve, his son sent for Wickham's friend, Dr. McCaw; but he could not be located. Dr. Lewis Wheat was called for and arrived about 12:30 p.m. Dr. Wheat found Wickham "vomiting and purging," gave him some stimulant, which seemed to have a soothing effect. Wickham lay down on a settee in the office and about 1 p.m., appeared to be asleep. By 1:20 p.m., Henry Wickham told Dr. Wheat that his father looked very strange. Upon observation, Dr, Wheat told everyone, "He is dying."[5]

All efforts were made to resuscitate General Wickham—but to no avail. He was dead from heart failure. By this time, Drs. McCaw and Ross had arrived. The Coroner, Taylor was summoned, but he deemed it unnecessary to take any additional steps. Shortly after 2 p.m., the body of General Wickham was taken to undertaker L.T. Christian for embalming. At 6 p.m., the body was taken to the Chesapeake and Ohio depot, and sent forward to Wickham's Station, only one-half mile from his home, Hickory Hill. As in war, Wickham was equally loved by the men he led in peacetime. One C&O employee recounted, "No man was ever more beloved by the men under him than General Wickham and many of them, trainmen and stationmen alike, wept as though they lost a member of their immediate family."[6]

One newspaper lamented Wickham's death, stated, "Nobody will ever know how many a poor man and poor woman has been restored to home and friends by his permission for free transportation over the road of which he was no longer an officer. Nobody will ever know how many of the needy went to his door never to be turned away empty-handed. Kind to the unfortunate, loyal to his friends, and with a deep and abiding interest in the prosperity of his state, he performed many acts in public and private that make him worthy to be mourned by no smaller number who profited by his sound judgment and generous heart."[7]

---

5. *Richmond Dispatch*, July 24, 1888.
6. Ibid.
7. *The Norfolk Landmark (Norfolk, VA)*, July 26, 1888.

Wickham had married the daughter of John Taylor of Caroline County, an eminent writer in his day on agriculture and political economy. Mrs. Wickham and three children—Henry T., a prominent lawyer, William F., and Mrs. Annie Renshaw—survived him.[8]

Williams Wickham's final resting place and memorial

General Wickham is buried in a brick-enclosed small cemetery on the Hickory Hill plantation within view of the house.

The life of Williams Carter Wickham is commemorated with a fine seven-foot-tall bronze statue given by the General's men and employees of the C&O Railroad. Created by Edward Virginius Valentine and located in Monroe Park in Richmond, the effigy depicts Wickham wearing a Confederate uniform and holding a case for his field glasses in his right hand—and a pair of gloves behind his back in his left. (Originally, he had a sword, which vandals later removed.) On its granite base measuring approximately seven feet-tall are the same four words inscribed on his tombstone: "Soldier, Statesman, Patriot, Friend."[9]

Dedicated on October 29, 1891, General Fitzhugh Lee gave the speech for the unveiling.

An inscription on the front of the base reads:

WICKHAM

"SOLDIER STATESMAN

PATRIOT, FRIEND"

PRESENTED TO THE CITY OF RICHMOND BY COMRADES

IN THE CONFEDERATE ARMY

AND EMPLOYEES OF THE CHESAPEAKE AND OHIO RAILWAY COMPANY

The statue at Monroe Park, commissioned by his Confederate comrades and employees of the Chesapeake and Ohio Railroad, was

8. *Staunton Spectator*, July 25, 1888.
9. *Richmond Dispatch*, October 25, 1891.

*A bronze statue was erected in Monument Park in October 1891.
The money raised was from soldiers, friends, railroad associates
and workers.*

(Public Domain)

unveiled in October of 1891 by nine-year-old W. C. Wickham
Renshaw, Wickham's grandson, at a grand ceremony, during which
General Thomas Rosser was the Chief Marshall of the procession.
Both General Fitzhugh Lee and Governor McKinney gave orations.[10]

On October 29, 1891, the statue of Brigadier General Williams C.
Wickham, an Army of Northern Virginia cavalryman, was unveiled in
Richmond's Monroe Park. The statue was the project primarily of the
employees of the Chesapeake and Ohio railway—of which Wickham
who died in 1888) had been president—and also by the survivors of his
old cavalry brigade. *The Norfolk Landmark* described the statue:

> The pose of Wickham in the statue is suggestive in every
> particular of that solidity, massiveness and determination
> that characterized General Wickham—suggestive of the
> typical heavy trooper ready for combat, mounted or on
> foot. From crown of head to sole of firmly-planted foot

---

10. Ibid. The statue was torn down and then removed in June 2020 during the
uproar over Confederate statues.

individuality is illustrated. The modeling of the face and head is vigorous, the portraiture striking and faithful both as to expression and lines, and all the general details of the drapery, sword-belt, straps, saber, insignia of rank, etc. are carefully worked out.[11]

Wickham family slaves were interred in a slave cemetery, comprising 4.25 acres of the Hickory Hill plantation property and located west of the plantation itself. At least 149 burials took place there.

According to Hewlett family lore, Confederate General Williams Carter Wickham of Hanover fathered six children at Hickory Hill with an unmarried enslaved black woman named Bibanna, and later, four children with his white wife, Lucy Penn Taylor Wickham. General Wickham is the great-great-grandfather of both educator and current Caucasian resident of Brookline, Massachusetts, Wallis Raemer—and purportedly her cousin is popular African-American folk singer, storyteller, and social activist Reggie Harris.[12]

Reggie Harris, age 69, is an African-American and purported descendant of Williams C. Wickham and a Wickham family slave named Bibanna.[13] He recalled that the Wickham statue was "a painful

11. Ibid., October 31, 1891.
12. "A Message of Hope," 11/10/2020, St. Catherine's School, Richmond, VA.; Don Lemon, *This Is the Fire: What I Say to My Friends about Racism*, 100-101; Williams C. Wickham, born in 1820, married Lucy Penn Taylor in January 1848. The first child of Bibanna was born in 1832, when Williams Wickham was only 13 years old. Thus, I do not believe Williams is the father of the first child, or in my opinion any of the six children mentioned. In order to have fathered six slave children before marrying Lucy, he would have had to have begun his sexual liaisons with Bibanna when he was about 18 years old. Bibanna, born circa 1810, was 10 years older than Williams Wickham. The sexual liaisons would have to have occurred between about 1838 and 1846. In addition, Williams Wickham attended prep schools in northern Virginia in 1835 and 1836. He would, of course, visit home on holidays and other occasions. Then, from 1837 to 1841, Williams attended the University of Virginia, again probably visiting home from time to time. To date, no dna testing has been done.
13. *Newport News Daily Press,* June 29, 2020. Don Lemon, *This Is the Fire: What I Say to My Friends about Racism* (Boston: Little Brown and Company, 2021), 100-101. Kays Elaine Bush-Gray, Compiler and editor, *The Hewlett Family, Revised Third Edition*, The Hewlett Family Reunion Committee, Richmond, Va., 1999. The connection to Williams C. Wickham appears to be passed down verbally from generation to generation via Hewlett family members. If a Wickham was involved, it would have been Williams's father, William Fanning Wickham, owner of the plantation and the slaves. Another more likely possibility is that Reggie Harris and others are descendants of an overseer with the actual or assumed surname Hewlett and slave Bibanna [Hewlett].

reminder of the abuse his family suffered and of America's refusal to acknowledge its past."[14]

Williams Carter Wickham left a considerable estate upon his death. The estimated value was between $250,000 and $300,000.[15] Lucy inherited Hickory Hill and the remainder of Williams's wealth. Lucy wrote at least seven wills over a span of the next twenty-five years. She wrote new wills, not for any whims or passing fancies, but because the family circumstances changed. Her intent in her 1888 will was to divide her estate evenly among her three surviving children. Over time, circumstances changed, and Lucy's last will chose two grandsons, Williams C. W. Renshaw and Williams C. Wickham (the sons of daughter Anne and son Henry respectively) to receive the plantation after Anne and Henry held it in trust for 15 years.[16] Lucy died December 16, 1913, at age 83 and is buried at the Hickory Hill Cemetery.

Williams Carter Wickham was a member of one of Virginia's leading families and an important figure in Virginia politics, the Civil War, and in managing the postwar C&O railroad. He was against secession, claiming it was an illegal act. Still, he went with his state to defend Virginia, while commanding the 4th Virginia Cavalry and then a brigade. He was brave, quick to temper, and resolute in his desire to end the war as soon as possible—even in a negotiated, honorable defeat, if necessary, to end the bloodshed. He became a Republican after the war, angering many. His popularity, however, never dimmed. He was instrumental in the development and operation of the railroad systems in postwar Virginia, West Virginia, and Ohio. Besides leaving a treasure trove of letters and writings for historians to utilize, Williams Carter Wickham, "SOLDIER, STATESMAN, PATRIOT, FRIEND" has left an indelible mark on American history.

14. *Newport News Daily Press*, June 29, 2020. Don Lemon, *This Is the Fire: What I Say to My Friends about Racism* (Boston: Little Brown and Company, 2021), 100-101.
15. *The Norfolk Daily Landmark*, August 18,1888.
16. Wills of Lucy P. Wickham, May 24, 1900, March 20, 1903, October 28, 1904, and July 27, 1908, all in Wickham Family Papers, Virginia Museum of History and Culture; Jane Turner Censer, *The Reconstruction of White Southern Womanhood* (Baton Rouge, LSU Press, 2003), 17-18.

BIBLIOGRAPHY

Primary Sources

Manuscripts and Collections

Charleston Library Society,
          Charleston, South Carolina
Wade Hampton to Edward L. Wells, January 18, 1900, Wells Manuscript.

The College of William and Mary, Williamsburg, Virginia.
Mark Alexander Papers, Mss. 86sA12, Special Collections, Earl Gregg Swem
    Library.

Duke University, Durham, North Carolina.
Jacob Click Papers.
Munford-Ellis Family Papers.
Presley Carter Person Papers.
W. A. Curtis, "Reminiscences of the War"

Emory University, Atlanta Georgia.
J.E.B. Stuart Letters, Special Collections Department, Robert W. Woodruff
    Library.

Library of Congress, Washington.
Willard Family Papers. #1029. MSS5836, Jeb Stuart Correspondence, 1861-1862.
Jedediah Hotchkiss Papers.
Louis T. Wigfall Family Papers.
Aurestus S. Perham Papers.

Library of Virginia, Richmond, Virginia.
Common Law Order Book 5, Campbell County, Virginia.
Chancery Records of Campbell County, Virginia.

Proceedings of the General Court Martial in the case of Lieut. Col. H. Clay Pate, 5th Virginia Cavalry, Confederate Imprints, 1861-1865, No. 2535, Reel 82, Film 3556.

Diary of James W. Wood, Accession 25506.

Diary of Charles William McVicar.

March 20, 1861 speech by Williams C. Wickham to Virginia Secession. Convention, University of Richmond, Boatwright Memorial Library, Digital Initiatives, Digital Scholarship Lab, The Library of Virginia, University Communications, Web Service, https://secession.richmond.edu/documents/images/index.php/proceedings.vol 2.0126.jpg.

National Archives, Washington, D.C.

Compiled Service Records of Confederate Soldiers Who Served in Organizations From the State of Virginia, Record Group M324.

Compiled Service Records of Confederate Generals and Staff Officers, and Non regimental Enlisted Men, Record Group 94, M331.

Confederate States Army Inspection Reports.

Letters Received by the Confederate Adjutant and Inspector General, 1861-1865, Record Group 94.

Southern Historical Collection, Wilson Library, University of North Carolina, Chapel Hill, North Carolina

Southern Historical Society Papers.

Smith College, Northampton, Massachusetts.

Garrison Family Papers, Sophia Smith Collection.

University of North Carolina at Chapel Hill

Wiley C. Howard. "Sketch of the Cobb Legion Cavalry and Some Incidents and Scenes Remembered."

University of Virginia, Manuscripts and Special Collections, Alderman Library, Charlottesville, Virginia.

Wickham Family Papers.

The Papers of Robert E. Lee.

McVicar Diary.

Katherine Couse Papers.

United States Military History Institute, Carlisle, PA.

Frank M. Myers Papers.
August V. Kautz Papers.

Virginia Military Institute

Diary of I. Norval Baker, 18th Virginia Cavalry, VMI Archives.

Virginia Museum of History and Culture, Richmond, Virginia

Wickham Family Papers.
J.E.B. Stuart Letters.
Henry B. McClellan Papers.
William Kennedy Papers, 1853-1870.
Conrad Holmes Papers.
William Clark Corson Papers.
Robert E. Lee Family Papers.
"Autobiography of St. George Tucker Brooke"

Virginia Polytechnic Institute and State University, Blacksburg, Virginia.

Williams C. Wickham Letterbook.

West Virginia Department of Arts, Culture & History, Charleston, WV

H. M. Matthews Papers.

Newspapers

Alexandria (VA) Gazette.
Charleston (SC) Daily Courier.
Charleston Mercury.
Charlotte Democrat.
(Charlottesville, VA) Daily Progress.
Harper's Weekly.
The Norfolk Landmark (Norfolk, VA).
Philadelphia Weekly Times.
Richmond (VA) Dispatch.
Richmond (VA) Enquirer.
Richmond Whig.

Published Sources.

Special Orders No.276, Paragraph XVI, Adjutant & Inspector General's Office, Richmond, Virginia.

"Battle of Ream's Station," Report of General W. C. Wickham (July 2, 1864), *Southern Historical Society Papers*, IX (1881). 2nd Confederate Congress vol. 7.

Andrew, Rod. *Wade Hampton: Confederate Warrior to Southern Redeemer.* Chapel Hill: University of North Carolina Press, 2008.

Allen, Jody Lynn, College of William & Mary —Arts & Sciences, "Roses in December: Black Roses in December: Black Life in Hanover County, Virginia during the era of disfranchisement," 2007.

Akers, Monte. *Year of Desperate Struggle: Jeb Stuart and His Cavalry, from Gettysburg to Yellow Tavern, 1863-1864.* Philadelphia: Casemate Publishers, 2115.

Ayers, Edward L. *The Promise of the New South: Life After Reconstruction.* New York: Oxford University Press, 1982.

_____ and John C. Willis, eds. *The Edge of the New South: Life In Nineteenth Century Virginia.* Charlottesville: University Press of Virginia, 1991.

Baggett, James Alex *The Scalawags: Southern Dissenters in the Civil War and Reconstruction.* Baton Rouge: LSU Press, 2003.

Baylor, George Baylor, *From Bull Run to Bull Run: or Four Years in the Army of Northern Virginia.* Richmond: B. F. Johnson Publishing Company, 1900.

Beale, G. W. *A Lieutenant in Lee's Army.* Boston: The Gorham Press, 1918.

Beale, Richard L.T. *History of the Ninth Virginia Cavalry, in the War Between the States.* Cornell University Library: BiblioLife, 2009 Reprint.

Benedict, George G. *Vermont in the Civil War, A History of the Part Taken By The Vermont Soldiers in the War for the Union,1861-65.* Burlington, Vermont: The Free Press Association, 1888.

Bias, Charles V "A History of the Chesapeake and Ohio Railroad Company and Its Predecessors, 1784-1977." Ann Arbor, MI: University Microfilms International, 1979.

Blackford, William W. *War Years with Jeb Stuart.* New York: Charles Scribner's Sons,1946.

Susan Leigh Blackford and Charles Minor Blackford, compilers., *Letters from Lee's Army.* Lincoln, NE: University of Nebraska Press, 1998.

Borcke, Heros von. *Memoirs of the Confederate War of Independence.* Philadelphia: J. B. Lippincott & Company, 1867.

_____ *Memoirs of the Confederate War of Independence.* Volume II. Dayton, Ohio: Morningside Books, 1985 Reprint.

Bouyea, Brien, sports@saratogian.com, @thepinksheet on Twitter, Thoroughbred bloodlines, http://www.bloodlines.net/TB/Bios/Boston.htm; http://www.tbheritage.com/Portraits/Boston.html.

Bridges, David P. *Fighting with JEB Stuart: Major James Breathed and the Confederate Horse Artillery.* Arlington, VA: Breathed, Bridges, Best, Inc., 2006.

Buel, Clarence Clough (Author); Johnson, Robert Underwood, ed. *Battles and Leaders*, vols. 1, 2, 4. New York: Yoseloff, Later Edition, January 1, 1956.

Burton, Brian K. *Extraordinary Circumstances: The Seven Days Battles.* Bloomington, Indiana: Indiana University Press, 2001.

Bushong, Millard K and Dean M. Bushong. *Fightin' Tom Rosser.* Shippensburg, Pennsylvania: Beidel Printing House, Inc., 1983.

Bush-Gray,Kays Elaine, Compiler and editor, *The Hewlett Family, Revised Third Edition*, The Hewlett Family Reunion Committee, Richmond, Va., 1999.

Calkins, Chris M., "The Battle of Weldon Railroad (or Globe Tavern), August 18-19 & 21, 1864." *Blue and Gray Magazine.* (Winter 2007.

Carman, Ezra Ayers and Joseph Pierro, *The Maryland Campaign of September 1862: Ezra A. Carman's Definitive Study of the Union and Confederate Armies at Antietam.* New York: Taylor and Francis Group, 2008.

Casdorph, Paul D. *Prince John Magruder: His Life and Campaigns.* New York, New York: John Wiley and Sons, 1996.

Donald C. Caughey and Jimmy J. Jones. *The 6th United States Cavalry in the Civil War: A History and Roster.* Jefferson, NC: McFarland & Company, 2013.

Censer, Jane Turner. *The Reconstruction of White Southern Womanhood, 1865-1895.* Baton Rouge: LSU Press, 2003.

Cisco, Walter Brian. *Wade Hampton: Confederate Warrior, Conservative Statesman.* Washington, D.C.: Potomac Books, 2004.

Crist, Lynda Lassell Ed. Jefferson Davis, *The Papers of Jefferson Davis: January–September 1863*, vol 9. (Baton Rouge, LSU Press, 1998.

Clark, Walter. ed. *Histories of the Several Regiments and Battalions in the Great War, 1861-1865.* 5 Vols. Raleigh, North Carolina: E. M. Uzell, Printer and Binder, 1901.

Commager, Henry Steele. *The Blue and The Gray.* Two Vols. New York: The Fairfax Press, 1991.

Cohen, Benjamin R. Notes from the Ground, Science & Agricultural Improvement in the Early American Republic, Dissertation submitted to the Faculty of Virginia Polytechnic Institute and State University in partial fulfillment of the requirements for the degree of Doctor of Philosophy in Science and Technology Studies, February 25, 2005, Blacksburg, Virginia, 188-192.

Cooke, John Esten. *Wearing of the Gray: Personal Portraits. Scenes and Adventures of the War.* New York: E. B. Treat & Co., 1867.

_____ *Mohun; or, the Last days of Lee and his Paladins: Final memoirs of a staff Officer Serving in Virginia.* New York: F. J. Huntington & Company, 1869.

Corbell, La Salle (Mrs. George E. Pickett). *Pickett and His Men.* Atlanta: Foote and Davies, 1899.

Cornwall, James Marshall. *Grant as Military Commander.* New York: Barnes and Noble, 1995.

Cozzens, Peter and Robert I. Girardi, eds., John Pope, *The Military Memoirs of General John Pope.* Chapel Hill: The University of North Carolina Press, 1998.

Cozzens, Peter. *General John Pope: A Life for the Nation*. Chicago: University of Illinois Press, 2000.

Crist, Lynda Lasswell, Mary Seaton Dix, and Kenneth H. Williams, eds. *The Papers of Jefferson Davis: January-September 1863*. Baton Rouge: LSU Press, 1997.

Crowley, Robert, ed. *With My Face to the Enemy: Perspectives on the Civil War*. New York: Berkley Books, 2001.

Cunningham, S. A. *Confederate Veteran*. Serial, 40 Vols. Nashville, Tennessee: 1893-1932.

Cullen, Joseph P. Cullen. *The Peninsula Campaign,1862*. Crown Publishers, Inc., 1973.

Current, Richard N, (Editor in Chief). *Encyclopedia of the Confederacy*. New York: Simon and Schuster, 1993.

Daughtry, Mary Bandy. *Gray Cavalier: The Life and Wars of General W. H. F. "Rooney" Lee*. Cambridge, Massachusetts: Da Capo Press, 2002.

Davis, Burke. *The Last Cavalier: J.E.B. Stuart*. New York: Fairfax Press, 1988.

Davis, William C. *Confederate Generals*. Volume 1. Harrisburg, Pa: National Historical Society.

_____ *The Civil War: Strange & Fascinating Facts*. New York: Fairfax Press, 1982.

Dawes, Rufus Robinson, *Memoir of Rufus Dawes, in Service with the Sixth Wisconsin Volunteers*. Marietta, Ohio: E.R. Alderman & Sons, 1890.

Dawson, Francis Warrington. *Reminiscences of Confederate Service, 1861-1865*. Baton Rouge: LSU Press, 1980.

De Santis, Vincent P. *Republicans Face the Southern Question: The New Departure Years, 1877-1897*. Baltimore: The Johns Hopkins Press, 1959.

Dowdey, Clifford and Louis H. Manarin, eds., *The Wartime Papers of Robert E. Lee*. Originally Published - Boston: Little, Brown, 1961, Republished - New York: Da Capo, 1991.

Downey, Fairfax. *The Clash of Cavalry: The Battle of Brandy Station*. New York: David McKay Company, Inc., 1959. Reprinted in 1987 by Olde Soldier Books, Inc., Gaithersburg, Maryland.

Driver, Robert J. *5th Virginia Cavalry*. Virginia Regimental Series. Lynchburg, Virginia: H. E. Howard, Inc., 1997.

Dubbs, Carolyn Kettenburg. *Defend This Old Town, Williamsburg During the Civil War*. Baton Rouge: LSU Press, 2002.

Early, Jubal A. *Narrative of the War Between the States*. New York: Da Capo Press, 1989.

Early, Ruth Hairston. *Campbell Chronicles and Family Sketches: Embracing the History of Campbell County, Virginia, 1782-1926*. Baltimore: Regional Publishing Company, 1978.

Ellis, Thomas T. *Leaves from the Diary of an Army Surgeon*. New York: John Bradburn Publishing, 1863.

Endres, Victoria. "Hawk's Nest Coal Strike." Clio: Your Guide to History, March 27, 2019.

Evans, Cerinda W. *Collis Potter Huntington*, vol. 2. Newport News, VA: The Mariners' Museum Publication, Issue 24, 1954.

Evans, General Clement A., ed. *Confederate Military History*. 12 vols. New York: Thomas Yoseloff, 1992.

Faust, Patricia L. *Historical Times Illustrated Encyclopedia of the Civil War*. New York: Harper Perennial, 1991.

Foner, Eric. *Reconstruction: America's Unfinished Revolution, 1863-1877*. New York: Harper & Row, 1993.

Frank, Lisa Tendrich, ed. *An Encyclopedia of American Women at War: From the Home Front to the Battlefields*. Santa Barbara, CA: ABC-CLIO. LLC, 2013.

William W. Freehling and Craig M. Simpson, eds., *Showdown in Virginia: The 1861 Convention and the Fate of the Union*. Charlottesville: UVA Press, 2010.

Freeman, Douglas Southall. *Lee's Lieutenants*. 3 vols. New York: Scribner's Sons, 1942.

_____ ed. *Lee's Dispatches: Unpublished Letters of General Robert E. Lee to Jefferson Davis and the War Department of The Confederate States of America, 1862-1865*. New York: G. P. Putnam's Sons, 1957.

Frye, Dennis E. *12th Virginia Cavalry*. Lynchburg, Virginia: H. E. Howard, 1988.

Furgurson, Ernest B. *Freedom Rising: Washington in the Civil War*. New York: Vintage Books, a Division of Random House, 2005.

Gallagher, Gary W., ed. *Struggle for the Shenandoah: Essays on the 1864 Valley Campaign*. Kent, Ohio: Kent State University Press, 1991.

_____ *The Shenandoah Valley Campaign of 1864*. Chapel Hill, North Carolina: UNC Press, 2006.

_____ *The Wilderness Campaign*. Chapel Hill, North Carolina: UNC Press, 1997.

Garnett, Theodore Stanford. *Riding With Stuart: Reminiscences of an Aide-de-Camp*, Robert J. Trout, ed., Shippensburg, Pennsylvania: White Mane Publishing Company, 1994.

Gilmor, Harry. *Four Years in the Saddle*. New York: Harper & Brothers, 1866.

Glatthaar, Joseph T. *General Lee's Army: From Victory to Collapse*. New York: Free Press, Simon and Shuster, 2008.

Golden, Alan Lawrence. "The Secession Crisis in Virginia," Dissertation, Ohio State University, 1990.

Gordon, John Brown. *Reminiscences of the Civil War*. New York: Charles Scribner's Sons, 1904.

Mark Graber and Howard Gillman. *The Complete American Constitutionalism, Vol 5 Part 1 The Constitution of the Confederate States*. New York: Oxford University Press, 2018.

Greene, A. Wilson. *The Second Battle of Manassas*. National Park Service Civil War Series. Eastern National, 2006.

Grimsley, Daniel Amon. *Battles in Culpeper County, Virginia, 1861-1865: And other Articles*. Culpeper, Virginia: Raleigh Travers Green, 1900. vol. 21.

Haden, B. J. *Reminiscences of J. E. B. Stuart's Cavalry*. Palmyra, Virginia: Progress Publishing Company, 1993.

Hall, Clark B. "The Battle of Brandy Station." *Civil War Times Illustrated.* (May/June 1990).

_____ "Stevensburg Phase, Battle of Brandy Station," https://www.battlefields.org/learn/articles/fight-hansbrough-ridge-june-9-1863

Hanson, Joseph Mills. *Cavalry Journal*, vol. XLIII:182, 1934.

_____ *Dictionary of American Biography*, Dumas Malone, ed. 20 vols. New York: Scribner & Sons, 1935.

Harrell, Roger H. *The 2nd North Carolina Cavalry.* Jefferson, North Carolina: McFarland and Company Publishers, 2004.

Hartley, Chris J. *Stuart's Tarheels: James B. Gordon and His North Carolina Cavalry.* Baltimore: Butternut and Blue, 1996.

Hatch, Tom. *Clashes of Cavalry.* Mechanicsburg, PA: Stackpole Books, 2001.

Heatwole, John L. *The Burning: Sheridan in the Shenandoah Valley.* Charlottesville, Virginia: Rockbridge Publishing, 1998.

Heitman, Francis B. *Historical Register and Dictionary of the United States Army* vol.1. Washington, D. C.: Washington, Government Printing Office, 1903.

Henderson, William D. *The Road To Bristoe Station.* Lynchburg, VA: H. E. Howard, Inc., 1987.

Hennessy, John J., *The First Battle of Manassas* (Lynchburg, VA: H. E. Howard, 1989.

_____ *Return to Bull Run: The Campaign and Battle of Second Manassas.* Norman, Oklahoma: University of Oklahoma Press, 1993.

Herbert, Walter H. *Fighting Joe Hooker.* Lincoln, NE: University of Nebraska Press, 1999.

Hildebrand, Joh R., ed., *A Mennonite Journal, 1862–1865, A Father's Account of The Civil War in the Shenandoah Valley.* Shippensburg, Pa.: White Mane Publishing Co., 1996.

_____ "True Friends of the Confederacy," Virginia Tech, ejournal, *Smithfield Review*, 41, https://scholar.lib.vt.edu/ejournals/smithfieldreview/v21/sr_v21_hildebrand.pdf.

Oscar Hinrichs and Robert K. Krick, *Stonewall's Prussian Mapmaker: The Journals of Captain Oscar Hinrichs.* Chapel Hill: UNC Press, 2014.

Hirshson, Stanley P *Farewell to the Bloody Shirt: Northern Republicans and the Southern Negro, 1877-1893.* Bloomington: Indiana University Press, 1962.

Hopkins, Luther W. *From Bull Run to Appomattox: A Boy's View.* Baltimore: Fleet-McGinley Company, 1908.

Horn, John. *The Petersburg Campaign; The Destruction of the Weldon Railroad; Deep Bottom, Globe Tavern and Reams Station; August 1425, 1864.* Lynchburg, VA: H. E. Howard, Inc., 1991.

Hubart, Lt. Robert T., Jr., Thomas P. Nanzig, ed. *The Civil War Memoirs of a Virginia Cavalryman.* Tuscaloosa: The University of Alabama Press, 2007.

Hubbell, Jay B., ed. "The War Diary of John Esten Cooke." *The Journal of Southern History*, vol. 7, No. 4.

Humphreys, Andrew A. *The Virginia Campaign of 1864 and 1865: The Army of The Potomac and the Army of the James*. Reprint. New York: Da Capo Press, 1995.

Hunter, Alexander. *Johnny Reb and Billy Yank*. New York: The Neale Publishing Company, 1905.

JUEL. Jefferson's University—Early Life Project, 1819-1870 (JUEL), juel.iath.virginia.edu.

Johnson, John Lipscomb, ed., *The University Memorial; Biographical Sketches of Alumni Who Fell in the Confederate War; Pate biography by Robert S. Morgan*, Baltimore: Turnbull Brothers, 1871.

Jones, J. William. *Personal Reminiscences, Anecdotes, and Letters of Gen. Robert E. Lee*. New York: D. Appleton and Company, 1875.

Jones, William, et al, eds. *Southern Historical Society Papers*. volumes 1-52. Richmond, Virginia: Southern Historical Society, 1876-1959.

Jones, Wilmer L. *Generals in Blue and Gray: Davis's Generals*. Westport, CT: Praeger Publishers, 2004.

The Journal of Southern History, Published by: Southern Historical Association, vol. 7, No. 4 (Nov., 1941).

Journal of the Congress of the Confederate States of America, 1861-1865, Vol. 3:618. Washington, Government Printing Office, 1904.

Keller, Roger S. *Riding with Rosser*. Burd Street Press, 1997.

Kennedy, Frances H., ed. *The Civil War Battlefield Guide*, Second Edition. New York: Houghton-Mifflin Company, 1998.

William Kennedy. *Dixie's Other Daughters: African-American Women in Virginia, 1861-1868*, Volume 1.

Kidd, J. H. *Personal Recollections of a Cavalryman Riding with Custer's Michigan Cavalry Brigade*. Ionia, Michigan, 1908.

Krick, Robert K. *Lee's Colonels: A Biographical Register of the Field Officers of The Army of Northern Virginia*. Dayton, Ohio: Morningside Press, 1992.

_____ *The American Civil War: The War in the East 1863-1865*. Great Britain: Osprey Publishing, 2001.

_____ *The Smoothbore Volley That Doomed the Confederacy*. Baton Rouge, Louisiana: LSU Press, 2002.

LaFantasie, Glenn W. *Twilight at Little Round Top: July 2, 1863--The Tide Turns At Gettysburg*. New York: Wiley, 2007.

Lamb, John. "The Confederate Cavalry," *Southern Historical Society Papers (SHSP)*.

Lemon, Don. *This Is the Fire: What I Say to My Friends about Racism*. Boston: Little Brown and Company, 2021.

Lepa, Jack H. *The Shenandoah Valley Campaign of 1864*. Jefferson, North Carolina: McFarland, 2003.

Longacre, Edward G. *The Cavalry at Gettysburg*. Lincoln: The University of Nebraska Press, 1993.

_____ *Mounted Raids of the Civil War*. Lincoln, Nebraska and London: University of Nebraska Press, 1994.

_____ *Lincoln's Cavalrymen: A History of the Mounted Forces of the Army of the Potomac.* Mechanicsville, Pa: Stackpole Books, 2000.

_____ *Lee's Cavalrymen*, Mechanicsburg, Pennsylvania: Stackpole Books, 2002.

_____ *Fitz Lee: A Military Biography of Major General Fitzhugh Lee, C.S.A.* Cambridge, Massachusetts: Da Capo Press, 2005.

Longstreet, Helen D. *Lee and Longstreet At High Tide: Gettysburg in the Light of the Official Records.* Gainesville, Georgia: Published by Helen D. Longstreet, 1904.

Maddex Jr., Jack P. *The Virginia Conservatives, 1867-1879: A Study in Reconstruction Politics.* Chapel Hill: UNC Press, 1970.

Manarin, Louis H., *North Carolina Troops, 1861-1865, A Roster.* Raleigh, North Carolina: State Division of Archives and History, 1989.

Marshall-Cornwall, James. *Grant as Military Commander.* New York, 1995.

Martin, David G. *The Peninsula Campaign.* Conshohocken, PA: Combined Books, 1992.

Massie, Eugene C. *Proceedings of the ... Annual Meeting of the Virginia State Bar Association, Report of the Twelfth Annual Meeting of the Virginia State Bar Association Held at Hotel Chamberlin, Fort Monroe, Virginia, July 17-19, 1900,* pp. 82-84. John T. West, Printer, 1900.

Maxwell, Jerry H. *The Perfect Lion: The Life and Death of Confederate Artillerist John Pelham.* Tuscaloosa, Alabama: University of Alabama Press, 2011.

McClellan, Major Henry Brainerd. *I Rode With Jeb Stuart: The Life and Campaigns of Major General J.E.B. Stuart.* Bloomington, Indiana: Indiana University Press, 1981.

McCurry, Stephanie. *Confederate Reckoning: Power and Politics in the Civil War,* South Cambridge, Ma: Harvard University Press, 2010.

McDonald, William N. *A History of the Laurel Brigade.* Baltimore and London: The Johns Hopkins University Press, 2002.

McKinney, Joseph W. *Trevilian Station, June 11-12, 1864: Wade Hampton, Philip Sheridan and the Largest All- Cavalry Battle of the Civil War.* Jefferson, N.C.: McFarland and Company, 2016.

McKim, Randolph Harrison. *A Soldier's Recollections.* Norwood, Massachusetts: The Plimpton Press, 1921.

McMullen, Glenn L. ed., *The Civil War Letters of Dr. Harvey Black.* Baltimore: Butternut and Blue, 1995.

Michel, Gregg L. "From Slavery to Freedom: Hickory Hill, 1850-80," in *The Edge of the South: Life in 19th-Century Virginia,* eds. Edward L. Ayers and John C. Willis. Charlottesville: University of Virginia Press, 1991.

Miller, William J. *Decision at Tom's Brook: George Custer, Thomas Rosser and the Joy of the Fight.* El dorado Hills, CA: Savas Beatie, 2016.

Mitchell, Adele H., ed. *The Letters of Major General James E. B. Stuart,* Stuart-Mosby Historical Society, 1990.

_____ *The Letters of John S. Mosby,* Stuart-Mosby Historical Society, 1986.

Moon, George Edward. *Wagon Tracks*. Bloomington, IN: Trafford Publishing, 2014.

Moore, Frank, ed. *The Rebellion Record: A Diary of American Events*. New York: D. Van Nostrand, 1865.

Morris, Charles. "Memories of Hanover County," Virginia Genealogical Society, vol. 23, No. 1 (1985).

Munford, "Reminiscences," *Cavalry Journal*, 280.

_____ "Reminiscences," *Cavalry Journal*, vol. 4 (Sept. 1891), 279.

Myers, Frank M. *The Comanches: A History of White's Battalion, Virginia Cavalry*. Marietta, Georgia: Continental Book Company, 1956.

Nanzig, Thomas P., ed. Lt. Robert T. Hubart, Jr., *The Civil War Memoirs of a Virginia Cavalryman*. Tuscaloosa, Alabama: The University of Alabama Press, 2007.

_____ *3rd Virginia Cavalry*. Lynchburg, Virginia: H. E. Howard, Inc., 1989.

Neese, George M. *Three Years in the Confederate Horse Artillery*. New York: The Neale Publishing Company, 1911.

Nesbitt, Mark. *Saber and Scapegoat: J.E.B. Stuart and the Gettysburg Controversy*. Mechanicsburg, PA, 1994.

Nichols, James L. *General Fitzhugh Lee: A Biography*. Virginia Battles and Leadership Series. Lynchburg, Virginia: H. E. Howard, Inc., 1989.

Nofi, Albert A. *The Civil War Treasury*. Boston: Da Capo Press,1992.

Noyalas, Jonathan A. *The Battle of Cedar Creek: Victory from the Jaws of Defeat*. Charleston, S. C.: History Press, 2009.

Owen, William Miller. *In Camp and Battle with the Washington Artillery of New Orleans*. Baton Rouge: Louisiana State University Press, 1999.

NPS Form 10-900 United States Department of the Interior National Park Service OMB No. 1024-0018 National Register of Historic Places Registration Form DHR 042-5792. This form is for use in nominating or requesting determinations for individual properties and districts. Name of Property Historic name: Hickory Hill.

O'Meara, Ted, ed., *TRACKS Magazine* (CHESAPEAKE & OHIO RAILWAY), v. 38, no. 10, Oct. 10, 1953.

Ovies, Adolfo. *The Boy Generals: George Custer, Wesley Merritt, and the Cavalry of the Army of the Potomac*. El Dorato Hills, CA: Savis Beatie, 2021.

Palmer, Oscar C. "Father Rode with Sheridan; Reminiscences of Oscar C. Palmer As A Cavalryman in Company B, 8th N. Y. Volunteer Cavalry." Petersburg, Virginia: Petersburg National Battlefield, n.d.

Parker, William L. *General James Dearing, CSA*. Lynchburg, VA: H. E. Howard, 1990.

Patton, John S. *Jefferson, Cabell, and The University of Virginia*. New York: The Neale Publishing Company, 1906.

Pavlovsky, Arnold M. *Riding in Circles J.E.B. Stuart and the Confederate Cavalry 1861-1862*. Southampton, New Jersey: Arnold M. Pavlovsky, 2010.

Peck, Rufus. *Reminiscences of a Confederate Soldier of Co. C of the 2nd Virginia Cavalry.* Fincastle, VA, 1913.

Pendleton, William Nelson. *Memoirs of William Nelson Pendleton, D.D.* Philadelphia, J. B. Lippincott, 1893.

Pfanz, Donald C. *The Petersburg Campaign: Abraham Lincoln at City Point, March 20 - April 9, 1865.* Lynchburg, VA: H. E. Howard, Inc., 1989.

_____ *Richard E. Ewell: A Soldier's Life.* Chapel Hill: UNC Press, 1998.

Phillips, Larissa. *Women Civil War Spies of the Confederacy.* New York: Rosen Publishing Group, Inc., 2004.

Piatt, Donn. *General George H. Thomas: A Critical Biography.* Cincinnati: Ohio: Robert Clarke & Company, 1893.

Pickett, La Salle Corbell (Mrs. George E.). *Pickett and His Men.* Atlanta: Foote and Davies, 1899.

Poland, Charles Preston, Jr. *The Glories of War: Small Battles and Early Heroes of 1861.* Bloomington, Indiana: Author House, 2006.

Power, J. Tracy. *Lee's Miserables: Life in the Army of Northern Virginia from the Wilderness to Appomattox.* Chapel Hill: UNC Press, 1998.

Priest, John Michael. *Victory without Triumph: The Wilderness May 5th and 7th, 1864.* El Dorado Hills, CA: Savas Publishing, 2014.

_____ *Nowhere to Run: The Wildernesss, May 4th and 5th, 1864.* Shippensburg, PA: White Main Publishing Company, 1995.

Rafuse, Ethan S. Rafuse. *McClellan's War: The Failure of Moderation in the Struggle for the Union.* Bloomington and Indianapolis, Indiana: Indiana University Press 2005.

Ramage, James A. *Gray Ghost.* Lexington, Kentucky: University of Kentucky Press, 1999.

Rawle, William Brook, William E. Miller, James W. McCorkell, Andrew J. Speese, and John C. Hunterson (Regimental History Committee). *History of the Third Pennsylvania Cavalry (Sixtieth Regiment Pennsylvania Volunteers) in the American Civil War, 1861-1865.* Philadelphia: Franklin Publishing Company, 1905.

Rawley, James A. *Turning Points of the Civil War.* Lincoln: University of Nebraska Press, 1966.

Rea, D. B. "Cavalry Incidents of the Maryland Campaign." *The Maine Bugle.* *Campaign II.* Rockland, Maine, April, 1895.

Rhea, Gordon C. *To The North Anna River: Grant and Lee, May 13-24, 1864.* Baton Rouge, Louisiana: LSU Press, 2000.

_____ *The Battle of the Wilderness, May 5-6.* Baton Rouge, Louisiana: LSU Press, 2004.

_____ *The Battles for Spotsylvania Court House and the Road to Yellow Tavern, May 7-12, 1864.* Baton Rouge: LSU Press, 1997.

Rhodes, Robert Hunt. *All For The Union: Diary of Elisha Hunt Rhodes.* New York: Orion Books, 1991.

Robertson, James I., Jr., *Stonewall Jackson: The Man, The Soldier, The Legend.* New York: Simon and Schuster McMillan, 1997.

Rosser, General Thomas L. *Addresses of Gen'l T. L. Rosser at the Seventh Annual Reunion, Association of the Maryland Line, Baltimore, February 22, 1889 & Staunton, Virginia, June 3, 1889*. New York: L. A. Williams Printing Company, 1889.

_____Reminiscences, Rosser Papers, Special Collections Library, UVA, Charlottesville, VA.

_____ Autobiographical Sketch, Rosser Papers, Special Collections Library, UVA, Charlottesville, VA.

Savage, Douglas. *The Last Years of Robert E. Lee: From Gettysburg to Lexington*. New York: Rowman and Littlefield, 2016.

Scarborough, William Kauffman. *Masters of the Big House: Elite Slaveholders of the Mid-Nineteenth-Century South*. Baton Rouge: LSU Press, 2003.

Sears, Stephen W. *To The Gates of Richmond: The Peninsula Campaign*. New York: Ticknor & Fields, 1992.

_____ *The Civil War Papers of George B. McClellan: Selected Correspondence 1860-1865*. New York, New York: Da Capo Press, 1992.

_____ *Gettysburg*. New York: Houghton Mifflin Company, 2003.

Sergent, Mary Elizabeth. "Classmates Divided." *American Heritage Magazine*, February, 1958, vol. 9, Issue 2.

_____ *They Lie Forgotten: The United States Military Academy, 1856-1861*. Middletown, New York: The Prior King Press, 1986.

Sheridan, Phil. *Personal Memoirs*. 2 Vols. New York: Charles L. Webster and Company, 1888.

Simon, John Y., ed. *The Papers of Ulysses S. Grant*. Carbondale and Edwardsville: Southern Illinois University Press, 1967.

_____ John Y. Simon, Michael E. Stevens, eds., *New Perspectives on the Civil War: Myths and Realities of the National Conflict*. New York: Roman and Littlefield, 1998.

Simpson, Brooks D. *The Civil War in the East: Struggle, Stalemate, and Victory*. Santa Barbara, CA: Praeger Publishing, 2011.

Snellgrove, Benjamin E. "The Confederate General," National Historical Society, 1991, part 6.

Starr, Stephen Z. *The Union Cavalry in the Civil War*. 3 Vols. Baton Rouge, La: LSU Press, 1979-1985.

Stedman, Charles M. "Battle at Ream's Station," R. A, Brock, ed. Richmond, Virginia: *Southern Historical Society Papers*, 1891. vol. 19.

Steer, Edward. *The Wilderness Campaign*. New York: Bonanza Books, 1960.

Stiles, Robert. *Four Years Under Marse Robert*. New York: The Neale Publishing Company, 1904.

Suderow, Bryce A. "Confederate Strengths & Losses from March 25- April 9, 1865," May, 1987; revised September 29, 1991, Washington, D.C.

Swank, Walbrook D. ed. *Battle of Trevilian Station: The Civil War's Greatest And Bloodiest All Cavalry Battle, with Eyewitness Memoirs.* Civil War Heritage, vol. 4. Shippensburg, Pennsylvania: White Mane Publishing Company, 2007.

_____ ed., *Lieutenant Colonel William R. Carter, CSA.* Shippensburg, PA: Burd Street Press, 1998), 91.

The War of the Rebellion: A Compilation of the Official Records of the Union and Confederate Armies. 70 Volumes. 128 Parts and Atlas. Washington, D.C.: Government Printing Office, 1880-1901.

Thomas, Emory M. *Bold Dragoon: Life of J.E.B. Stuart.* New York: Vintage Books, 1988.

_____ *Robert E. Lee: A Biography.* London: W. W. Norton and Company, 1995.

Thomason, John William. *Jeb Stuart.* New York: Charles Scribner's Sons, 1929.

Thomsen, Brian M., ed. *The Civil War Memoirs of Ulysses S. Grant.* New York: Tom Doherty Associates, 2002.

Tobie, Edward P. *History of the First Maine Cavalry, 1861-1865.* Boston: Press of Emery & Hughes, 1887.

Torrence, Clayton, ed., *Winston of Virginia and Allied Families.* Richmond: Whittet & Shepperson, 1927.

Toalson, Jeff, ed., *Send Me a Pair of Old Boots & Kiss My Little Girls: The Civil War Letters of Richard and Mary Watkins, 1861-1865.* New York: iUniverse Books, 2009.

Trout, Robert J. *Galloping Thunder: The Story of the Stuart Horse Artillery Battalion.* Mechanicsville, Pennsylvania: Stackpole Books, 2002.

_____ *With Pen and Saber: The Letters and Diaries of J.E.B. Stuart's Staff Officers.* Mechanicsburg, PA: Stackpole Books, 1995.

_____ *They Followed the Plume: The Story of J.E.B. Stuart and His Staff* (Mechanicsburg, PA: Stackpole Books, 1993), 280.

Trudeau, Noah Andre. *The Last Citadel: Petersburg, Virginia, June 1864-April 1865.* New York: Little, Brown & Company, 1991.

Tucker, Glenn. *Lee and Longstreet At Gettysburg.* New York: The Bobbs-Merrill Company, 1868.

Tucker, Spencer C. ed., *American Civil War: The Definitive Encyclopedia and Document Collection.* Santa Barbara, CA: ABC-CLIO, LLC, 2013.

Tyler, Lyon G. Editor-in-Chief. *Men of Mark in Virginia: A Collection of Biographies of The Leading Men of the State.* Volume I. Washington, D. C.: Men of Mark Publishing Company, 1906.

Tyler-McGraw, Marie. *At the Falls: Richmond, Virginia and Its People.* Chapel Hill: UNC Press, 1994.

United States Congressional Record: Proceedings and Debates of the 76th Congress, Third Session, Appendix, Vol 86, Part 17, August 6, 1940-September 27, 1940, 5892.

Venter, Bruce M. "Hancock the (Not So) Superb: The Second Battle of Reams' Station, August 25, 1864." *Blue and Gray Magazine.* (Winter 2007).

Vogtsberger, Margaret Ann. *The Dulany's of Welbourne.* Berryville, Virginia: Rockbridge Publishing, 1195.

Heros Von Borcke, *Memoirs of the Confederate War for Independence,* vol. 2.

Walker, C. Irvine Walker. *The Life of Lieutenant General Richard Heron Anderson of the Confederate States Army.* Charleston, South Carolina: Art Publishing Company,1917.

Warner, Ezra J. *Generals in Blue: Lives of the Union Commanders.* Baton Rouge: LSU Press, 1995.

Ezra J. Warner and Wilfred Buck Yearns. *The Biographical Register of the Confederate Congress.* Baton Rouge: LSU Press, 1975.

Watkins, Raymond W. *The Hicksford Raid.* The Greensville Historical Society, April 1978.

Walsh, George. *Those Damn Horse Soldiers: True Tales of the Civil War Cavalry.* New York: Tom Dohterty Associates, 2006.

Welsh, Jack Walsh, M. D. *Confederate Generals Medical Histories.* Kent, Ohio: Kent State University Press, 1995.

Wellman, Manly Wade. *Giant in Gray: A Biography of Wade Hampton.* New York: Charles Scribner's Sons, Inc., 1949.

Wells, Charles. *The Memoirs of Colonel John S. Mosby.* Boston: Little, Brown, and Company, 1917.

Wells, Edward L. *Hampton and His Cavalry in '64.* Richmond, Va.: B. F. Johnston Publishing Company, 1899.

Wert, Jeffrey D. *General James Longstreet: The Confederacy's Most Controversial Soldier.* New York: Simon & Schuster, 1993.

_____ *From Winchester to Cedar Creek: The Shenandoah Campaign of 1864.* New York: Simon & Schuster, 1997.

_____ *Cavalryman of the Lost Cause: A Biography of J.E.B. Stuart.* New York: Simon & Schuster, 2008.

_____ *The Sword of Lincoln: The Army of the Potomac.* New York: Simon and Schuster, 2005.

Whitehead, Edgar. "Campaigns of Mumford's 2nd Virginia Cavalry," UVA.

Wilson, James Harrison. *Under The Old Flag.* New York: D. Appleton and Company, 1912.

Wilson, William Lyne. *A Borderline Confederate.* Pittsburg: University of Pittsburgh Press, 1962. Edited by Festus P. Summers.

Wise, Jennings Cropper, *The Long Arm of Lee: Bull Run to Fredricksburg.* Lynchburg: J. P. Bell Company, 1915.

Wise, John. *End of An Era.* New York: Houghton, Mifflin and Company, 1902.

Wittenberg, Eric J. *The Union Cavalry Comes of Age: Hartwood Church to Brandy Station, 1863.* Washington, D.C.: Potomac Books, 2003.

_____ *Glory Enough For All: Sheridan's Second Raid and The Battle of Trevilian Station.* Washington, D. C.: Brassey's, Inc., 2002.

_____ *Six Awful Days of Fighting: Cavalry Operations on the Way to Cold Harbor.* Burlington, N.C.: Fox Run Publishing, 2020.

_____ *The Battle of Brandy Station: North America's Largest Cavalry Battle.*
Charleston, SC: The History Press, 2010.

_____ , J. David Petruzzi, and Michael F. Nugent, *One Continuous Fight: The Retreat from Gettysburg and the Pursuit of Lee's Army of Northern Virginia, July 4-14, 1863.* New York, Savas Beatie, 2008.

Wright, Catherine M., ed. *Robert W. Parker, Lee's Last Casualty: The Life and Letters of Sgt. Robert W. Parker, Second Virginia Cavalry.* Knoxville, TN: University of Tennessee Press, 2012.

Index

About the Author

Sheridan R. Barringer retired from NASA where he worked as a mechanical engineer and project manager at Langley Research Center for 37 years. He graduated from Virginia Tech in mechanical engineering in 1965. He is the author of *Fighting for General Lee: General Rufus Barringer and The North Carolina Cavalry Brigade* about his ancestor for which he won the Douglas Southall Freeman Best Southern History Book Award and the North Carolina Society of Historians History Book Award in 2016. He is also the author of *Custer's Gray Rival* about the life of Confederate Major General Thomas L. Rosser and *Unhonored Service: The Life of Lee's Senior Cavalry Commander, Colonel Thomas Taylor Munford, CSA.* He continues work on other cavalry figures from the Army of Northern Virginia. He and his wife Pam have two grown children and reside in Virginia.